T3-BUL-829

A Marriage of Convenience
Business and Social Work in Toronto, 1918–1957

No history of social work can overlook the diversified nature of the profession. To this day, social workers vary greatly in how they approach their work and in their primary goals. But social work histories have, until very recently, failed to acknowledge the gendered nature of the profession. In this study Gale Wills explores questions of corporate control of, and resistance to, the welfare state, the role of the Community Chest as an agent of that control, and the gendered nature of social planning.

Specifically, Wills analyses the conflicts between the social reform organizations in Toronto and the financial federations that provided their funds. These include the Child Welfare Council (1918–37), the Toronto Welfare Council (1937–57), the Federation for Community Service (1918–44), and the Community Chest (1944–57) – predecessors of the present-day Social Planning Council and United Way of Metropolitan Toronto.

All of these early organizations were at the centre of collective action by the emerging profession of social work and of the philanthropic community. As collective organizations, they brought together a cross-section of social workers and businessmen, which drew attention to differences within the profession as well as between social work and business. The gendered nature of the relationships that evolved is rooted in the fact that the ranks of social work are overwhelmingly female, and the funding bodies and hierarchy of the profession are male.

The eclipse of women in power politics, according to Wills, arose from a basic conflict of priorities within the welfare system. Women leaders concerned themselves with social reform, challenging the concerns for efficiency and enhancement of the system's legitimacy. Following the Second World War, in a climate increasingly favourable to corporate values, men took up public positions in the community, primarily in planning and fund allocation. Women became confined to the domestic sphere of case work.

Through exploring the historical factors leading to the birth of an autonomous Social Planning Council in Toronto, and the conflicts that arose in and around its formation, Gale Wills has made an significant contribution to social history and gender politics.

GALE WILLS is an assistant professor in the School of Social Work, Carleton University.

A Marriage of Convenience

Business and Social Work in Toronto, 1918–1957

GALE WILLS

UNIVERSITY OF TORONTO PRESS
Toronto   Buffalo   London

BRESCIA COLLEGE
LIBRARY
66769

© University of Toronto Press Incorporated 1995
Toronto Buffalo London
Printed in Canada

ISBN 0-8020-2870-5 (cloth)
ISBN 0-8020-7369-7 (paper)

Printed on acid-free paper

Canadian Cataloguing in Publication Data

Wills, Gale
A marriage of convenience : business and social
work in Toronto, 1918–1957

Includes bibliographical references and index.
ISBN 0-8020-2870-5 (bound) ISBN 0-8020-7369-7 (pbk.)

1. Social work administration – Ontario – Toronto –
History. 2. Charities – Ontario – Toronto – History. I. Title.

HV110.T6W5 1995   361.9713'541   C95-930332-4

University of Toronto Press acknowledges the financial assistance to its publishing
program of the Canada Council and the Ontario Arts Council.
This book has been published with the help of a grant from
the Social Science Federation of Canada, using funds
provided by the Social Sciences and Humanities Research
Council of Canada.

To

Gladys Gale Wills

Contents

viii   Contents

Preface

When I began the work that eventually led to this book, the last thing on my mind was a history of social work. I entered university from a position as director of social planning and allocations with one of Canada's medium-size local United Way organizations to pursue a career as a scholar and teacher. I had left in the midst of a protracted and sometimes acrimonious debate over whether social planning councils should be part of, or separate from, the United Way. My position, which combined the two functions of social planning and allocations, was generally regarded as a pioneer effort, and the United Way for which I worked championed the integration of planning, allocating, and fund-raising in the voluntary social service sector under the umbrella of a single united organization. I had also been executive director of an independent social planning council and found myself sitting on the fence, acknowledging the strengths and weaknesses of arguments on both sides.

My decision to explore this issue began a journey of discovery that, for me, has not ended. Like most of my colleagues, I had no experience of close association between the profession of social work and the United Way, and so the involvement of social workers in the early financial federations came as a surprise. I also did not anticipate the strong role women played in the councils of social agencies and other planning and reform organizations that preceded the social planning councils. These discoveries led me to explore both the historical record and recent scholarship in areas new to me. Perhaps my greatest astonishment came from the discovery that many of the issues and dilemmas that I had encountered as a social planner had remarkably similar historical antecedents reaching back to the nineteenth century.

I have both business and social work in my background, in formal education as well as experience. I also came to this project as a woman who worked comfortably in the technical and political world of social planning. Discovering new areas of feminist scholarship has led me to connect my experience in ways that I find enriching and unsettling at the same time. The contradictions between business and social work that are examined in this book exist also within me, and it is not a comfortable position. I still sit on the fence over what are some of the most serious and difficult issues in Canadian society, issues that require, at some point, the reconciliation of capital and human welfare. It will be clear to readers of this book that I lean to the side of social work and a belief in the primacy of values of social justice and cooperative democracy. But I cannot imagine a society in which efficiency and economy are ignored. I expect the thoughtful reader may be similarly ambivalent, but my hope is that a better understanding of these issues will help us clear the fence.

There are many people whose support and assistance have made this book possible. My colleagues at Carleton University School of Social Work have all helped by shouldering without complaint the added workload that fell to them when I was given time to write. Gillian Walker, in particular, gave me support and encouragement, read early drafts of my manuscript, and helped me make the difficult transition from thesis to book. Allan Irving at the University of Toronto read and commented on a draft of the new chapter on social work history written for this book. I am also grateful for the work of the anonymous reviewers whose comments, questions, and detailed suggestions were exceedingly helpful as I reworked the manuscript.

I owe much to those who helped me find my way through the research from which this work is drawn. My thesis supervisor, Donald Bellamy, and the other members of my committee, Albert Rose, Allan Irving, and James Lemon, each not only gave time and helpful suggestions, but also gave me the confidence to keep moving ahead when progress seemed elusive. I want to acknowledge the encouragement that this all-male committee gave me to include a feminist analysis within my dissertation. Without their initial prodding, I am not sure I would have had the courage to take this aspect of my analysis to the limits that I have. The result is, of course, entirely my responsibility.

Access to archival sources depends on help from the professionals who know the collections. Victor Russell and the staff at the City of Toronto Archives were more than helpful as I worked my way into the largest collection in that archive. Their assistance, as well as that of Barbara Craig at

the Ontario Archives, was also essential in my being granted access to
records closed at the time my research began. I would also like to thank
the staff of the Family Service Association of Metropolitan Toronto who
kindly helped me locate the early records of the Neighbourhood Workers
Association.

My research was supported by fellowships and scholarships from the
University of Toronto, the Ontario Government, and the Department of
National Health and Welfare. Support from the Social Science and
Humanities Research Council of Canada in the form of a doctoral fellow-
ship as well as assistance for the publication of this book was particularly
helpful in making it all possible.

A Marriage of Convenience

Business and Social Work
in Toronto, 1918–1957

CHAPTER ONE

Introduction

Social work, as a profession, originated in the 'progressive era' of the late nineteenth and early twentieth centuries. It was part of the widespread appearance of a professional and technical class that sought to bring order and efficiency to the social chaos of urban centres in the industrialized Western world.[1] In North America, growing poverty and crime and the arrival of the greatest proportional influx of immigrants in history seemed to threaten the foundations of social life, particularly in the cities. Vigorous social and urban reform movements, of which social work was a part, were an expression of widespread concern over the profound changes that were taking place.

The first social workers were middle-class women and men who banded together in support of one or more of the multitude of causes that were perceived to be solutions to what was frequently termed 'the social problem.' They were characteristically from the dominant class – English, Protestant, and economically secure – but they were neither unified nor single-minded. The progressive era was a volatile stew of new and sometimes radical ideas, and these early social reformers had too many differing causes and drew on too many differing values to be seen as a uniform group. Nevertheless, social reformers did share a belief in the importance of applied science and expertise, which led them to engage in a common search for the legitimacy and trappings of professionalism. In so doing, they sought to bind together what was essentially a disparate set of beliefs and practices into a single profession.

No history of social work can overlook the diversified nature of the profession. To this day, social workers vary greatly in how and where they approach their work and in their primary goals. Some are concerned with helping individuals, some with organizing communities, and some with both. Although in the minority, there are many social workers who are concerned primarily with reconstructing the relations that exist between individuals and society as a whole. Their emphasis is on structural change at the broadest possible level of community. Unfortunately, most histories, and indeed most people outside the profession, see only that aspect of social work that deals with the private troubles of individuals and families. I know well the surprise in people's eyes when I explain that although I am a social worker, I do not 'do counselling.'

The emphasis in this book is on the history of community and reform practices within social work. In part this is a reflection of the nature of my inquiry and because I have asked questions that come out of my own experience as a community-oriented social worker. But in doing so, I have tried to help remedy the imbalance in historical accounts of social work and flesh out the parameters of understanding. What has been written to date, usually as background for something else, concentrates on the conservative approaches to social work, such as the moral reform approach of the Charity Organization Society or the early child savers.[2] Historians have also tended to concentrated on casework methods of social work practice. These are an important and central part of the history of the profession, but there was much more to social work than moral reform and social casework. There is also a history of resistance to mainstream values and, in at least a minority group within the profession, a desire to bring about fundamental change in the 'social order.' Community work was as much a part of social work as casework, and early practitioners involved themselves deliberately in politics and unpopular causes.

Social work histories have also, until very recently, failed to acknowledge the gendered nature of the profession. It is overwhelmingly a woman's profession and its 'clients' are overwhelmingly female. Even those approaches to social work that seek change in the social order ultimately have greater impact on the lives of women than on men simply because it is women who most frequently bear the brunt of oppression. Furthermore, the levers of power, both within the profession and in the communities that are the target of intervention, are controlled by men – with the result that women in social work have often been marginalized along with their female clients.

When I began my work of discovering the experience of early social workers in Toronto, I did not expect to find that women were in the forefront of reform and social action. Perhaps I should not have been surprised, but my experience as a social planner had brought me into little contact with other women in this particular field. Before the Second World War, community work within the profession was dominated by women. Ideals of cooperation and democracy, and of community and collective, are integral to women's ways of organizing,[3] and pre-war community practices of both men and women reflected these values and ideals.

It also became clear, as my study unfolded, that there was a relationship between the marginalization of the reform aspects of social work and the status of women within the profession. As social work struggled with the social and economic crises of the Great Depression, community work and casework became isolated from each other. Men in the profession took up the public practices in the community and women were confined to the domestic sphere of casework. Now clearly under the control of men, social reform practices within social work shifted away from any activity considered overtly political to an emphasis on scientific expertise and rational planning.

It was not coincidental that the disappearance of women from the community aspect of social work subsequently became entrenched in the postwar period, a time when a male-dominated corporate hegemony engulfed North America. The fifties were an important watershed in the growth of social work in Canada. It was then, in the context of the cold war and an extremely repressive political and social order, that social work retreated into a narrow professionalism from which it is still struggling to emerge.

The understanding of social work in history that I present in this book is grounded in a study of the early organizations in Toronto that were created to raise funds for charity and to coordinate social agencies. Toronto was a rapidly growing industrial city at the beginning of the twentieth century and, as such, had its share of poverty and social problems. Efforts on the part of the city's elites to prevent poverty, disease, and crime and to organize and control local charities were in many respects typical of the urban social reform movements of the time. The city quickly became one of the centres of social work in Canada. Professional training was provided by Canada's first school of social work at the University of Toronto and its graduates formed an important part of the leadership within the Canadian profession.[4] Thus, while we cannot generalize from the events in Toronto, they are important for understanding the development of social work and social welfare in Canada.

The first organization to fund and coordinate charity in Toronto was the Federation for Community Service. It was created in 1918 by an alliance of social workers and their supporters in the business community who came together in the common cause of breathing efficiency and standards of professional practice into local charities. But it was a marriage of convenience and conflict emerged very quickly. Part of the problem was the underlying dichotomy between the service and professional interests of the social workers and the economic interests of the businessmen. Equally important were the gendered differences that existed within the profession, as well as between a profession largely practised by women and the male world of business. Men in social work acted as gatekeepers between the profession's patrons, most of whom were men, and the rank and file, almost all of whom were women. The reform and activist practices of these women evoked resistance from their male colleagues as well as from the businessmen who controlled the funds. As in many marriages, the economic dependency of women on the male side of the profession dictated the endurance of a partnership that had little else to hold it together.

Roy Lubove has pointed out in his history of the American profession that social work, unlike most professions, was 'almost exclusively a corporate activity.'[5] This was equally true in Canada, where social workers derived their role and status as well as their livelihood from the agencies that employed them. From this perspective, the history of the profession is inextricably tied to the history of efforts to fund and control charitable organizations. Beginning in the middle of the nineteenth century, such efforts were usually either attempts on the part of businessmen and philanthropists to reduce the numbers of demands for money, or attempts on the part of charity workers to prevent 'pauperism' and idleness among the poor. The first truly collaborative efforts were 'financial federations' that brought businessmen and charity workers together in joint fund-raising ventures and in an effort to raise standards of management practice in charity organizations. The idea took firm hold during the First World War when various patriotic causes used the mechanism of a 'Community Chest' to raise money for the war effort.

Financial federations have been singled out by Lubove and others as a conservative influence on social work and social reform.[6] But the assumption should not be made that social workers were always willing partners in this. Clearly some were, but others, many of whom were women, resisted. Concern for their goals of social reform, the desire for professional standards of practice, and their fears that economic goals would become paramount prompted considerable opposition within the profession to the growing power of the financial federations. Social workers sought autonomy for the agencies that were the base of their practice as well as a role within the financial federation that would ensure their voice was heard. The favoured approach in Toronto and elsewhere was the establishment of an agency-controlled 'council of social agencies.'

The struggle for control over the provision of social services that the conflict between these two kinds of organizations represents is a central phenomenon in the history of social welfare. One of the major contradictions in the history of social work is the profound ambivalence with which the profession regarded the evolution of the financial federations that were the source of funds and also the institutional means for promoting professional standards of service. On the one hand, the financial federations provided an opportunity for an important alliance with the monied and powerful interests in the community. At the same time, however, there was the risk that the values of efficiency and economy would take precedence over the needs both of the profession and of the people they sought to help. Social workers needed the funds and the legitimacy that the economic interests in the urban community could provide. But they did not bargain for the power over their work that was tied to the money. Neither did they recognize the gendered nature of the conflicts and the implications for women and social reform.

In Toronto the struggle was prolonged, perhaps because of the conservative nature of the community and the strength of the economic elite that dominated not only the city, but gradually the national economy of a fledgling Canadian state. Except for a brief six-year interlude, Toronto social workers tried unsuccessfully to establish a council of social agencies separate from the Federation for Community Service. When they finally succeeded, almost fifty years after the Federation was first established, it was a dubious victory. The Social Planning Council that was created in 1957 was immediately co-opted by one of the most powerful business lobbies in Canadian social welfare history.

Social workers used the councils of social agencies and the financial federations to further their own goals. When their goals clashed with those of others whose interests were different and sometimes totally contrary to their own, conflict ensued. Given the disparities of power, the economic and financial interests invariably prevailed. Given the relationship between power and gender, the interests of men both in the business community and in the profession were paramount. The experience of the various attempts to organize, fund, and coordinate social agencies in Toronto reveals how social work evolved into a professional practice dominated by men and by the values of the economic and political mainstream. It also reveals how the financial federations, forerunners of the modern United Way, became instruments in the hands of business for containment of a welfare state.

I begin in the next chapter by examining the values and philosophies that shaped the development of social work as a profession in English Canada.[7] Christian moral reform was the initial influence, reflecting the dominant values of colonial society and justifying the public work of women in particular. One of the most important influences on Canadian social work was the social gospel, which began in the Protestant churches but eventually provided an avenue of secular practice for social workers outside the church. While Christian motives for social work never disappeared completely, professional social work became, above all, a secularization of moral reform and a reaction against the evangelical purpose imposed by organized religion. The social gospel was accompanied by a secular faith in 'scientific sociology,' which provided an ostensibly amoral and neutral method for solving social problems. Around the turn of the century the often-used term 'scientific philanthropy' captured this contradictory set of values.

Social work also had strong roots in the utilitarian philosophies of the nineteenth century. The utilitarians placed science, rationality, and expertise at the centre of a moral order. They argued for state intervention in matters considered to be outside the economy in order to achieve 'the greatest good for the greatest number.' The movement in Great Britain known as Fabian socialism drew heavily on utilitarian values. In particular, Fabians believed in a humanitarian state driven by the power of knowledge derived from science and research. In Canada, as in Britain, Fabian ideas strongly influenced the profession's belief in scientific social work as well as its advocacy for a welfare state.

Chapter 2 also discusses the gendered nature of social work. Fabianism, scientism, and ideas of a welfare state are part of a modernism that led to the rational, hierarchical, and perceived amoral stance with which some social workers approached social reform. Feminist scholars have long pointed out that this view of the world does not speak to the experience and values of many women. Women in social work did not reject the utilitarian and patriarchal values of a welfare state, but they also brought into their work a legacy of ideals and a view of how the world ought to be ordered that differed from these values. The gendered nature of these values and their simultaneous existence within the profession accounts for much of the internal contradiction that existed then and exists now.

Chapter 3 provides the first substantive look at the organization of charity in Toronto. Early attempts on the part of businessmen to control and restrict charity through a municipally appointed Social Service Commission was part of an international 'endorsement movement' sponsored by the powerful boards of trade. The commission's coercive intentions were stoutly resisted by a coalition of sympathetic businessmen and social work and health professionals. They were led by the Bureau of Municipal Research, whose key strategy was to replace the Social Service Commission with the Federation for Community Service. The Toronto group drew on the model for a financial federation espoused by the New York Bureau, which was a leading proponent of scientific management in civic affairs and was controlled by men who had roots in the charity organizations of that city. But the cooperation between business and social work with which the Federation began very soon faltered and social workers began agitating for a council of social agencies. Their efforts failed when growing professionalism, coupled with the religious intolerance that prevailed in Toronto at the time, led to the withdrawal of the Roman Catholic charities, and the shelving of plans for an agency-controlled council.

In the absence of a council of social agencies, serious thought was given to expanding the Child Welfare Council, which was the leading organization in Toronto for social workers concerned with children's services and social reform. The Child Welfare Council was largely a women's organization and, although it allied itself with the Local Council of Women, was part of the Federation for Community Service. In many respects it was the first recognizable social planning organization in Toronto. Chapter 4 deals with the triumphs and demise of the Child Welfare Council. The women who led it believed in 'direct action' in the face of injustice and poverty. Their willingness to engage in politics raised the ire of their male colleagues, whose approach to social change was one of 'slow interpretation.' The Child Welfare Council's bid to expand into a comprehensive council of social agencies was defeated in an agency referendum held in 1937. In its place the social work community created the Toronto Welfare Council, a planning organization in which women were prevented from assuming control.

The Toronto Welfare Council took an approach to social change that reflected the growing importance of scientific sociology and the Fabian doctrine of a 'social minimum.' The reliance of the new Council on scientific methods was evident in the importance attached to its Cost of Living Study. This landmark study, first published in 1939, was intended as a neutral information tool for community action to improve the level of both relief and minimum wages. The idea that there was a social minimum below which no person should fall was the philosophical underpinning of both the Council's study and the social work profession's general effort to promote a welfare state.

While the Toronto Welfare Council began its existence as an independent organization, pragmatic considerations soon forced it to rejoin the financial federation, expanded during the Second World War to become a more comprehensive Community Chest. The reunion of the planning and fund-raising functions placed the fledgling Council in a very vulnerable position at a time when corporate hostility to social work was growing. Chapter 5 follows the struggle of the Toronto Welfare Council to assert the importance of research and an interventionist state. It also shows how the Community Chest succeeded in suppressing the Council's social action agenda, setting the stage for escalating conflict and eventual divorce in the decade following the war.

Chapter 6 is a story of corporate hegemony. Toronto's business elite used the Community Chest not only to contain and constrain the activities of the Welfare Council and the social agencies; they also targeted the Chest itself for reform, creating a United Community Fund designed to give 'big business' an instrument for wresting control from 'social workers and small businessmen' and for preventing further encroachment on free enterprise by a welfare state.

The establishment of a separate Social Planning Council at the time of the founding of the United Community Fund in 1957 was intended to free the social planners from the all-consuming tasks of assisting the Fund with allocations decisions. The design of the new Council included support for a growing network of citizen-controlled suburban councils and an agenda that included advocacy and social reform. But the Council too was deliberately placed under corporate control; one of Canada's most powerful businessmen assumed the Chair, and the Council's board was stacked with highly placed insurance executives hostile to a welfare state in which social insurance would play a major part.

The postwar corporate ethos carried with it an adherence to the liberal values of American society. Canadian social workers had always been strongly influenced by their American colleagues, but there were some differences.[8] In the fifties, these differences were virtually obliterated and the profession moved to adopt the standards and practices of social work in the United States. This included the separation of casework and community work, breaking the symbiosis that had been a strong part of the social work culture in Toronto. The rise of social planning during postwar reconstruction helped entrench community work as a male domain.

Women in social work were relegated to the private aspects of casework and co-opted or coerced into abandoning a previously public and political practice.

It was tempting to go beyond the time frame of this study, which was the founding of the Social Planning Council of Metropolitan Toronto. It would be worthwhile to explore the volatile politics between business and social work and within the profession during the sixties and seventies and beyond. My own experience leads me to assume that the patterns of conflict between fund-raisers and planners and between planners and social activists continued. In recent years, the United Way has repeatedly threatened to withdraw funding from the Toronto Social Planning Council in what appears to be a recurrence of the conflicts of the past.

However, the context for community work and social work generally has become increasingly complicated. The variety of issues – economic, social and cultural – has multiplied. The globalization of capital, the intensification of issues of gender and race, and the increasing tension between various factions within social work practice present new and different challenges for historical analysis. The United Way has replaced the United Community Fund and has become far more sophisticated in its philosophy and approach to both fund-raising and social planning. It also bears much of the pressure on the private social service sector, pressure that has increased dramatically with the fiscal crisis of the state and the recent retrenchment in state welfare programs. Furthermore, the role of social workers has almost disappeared from the United Way and from many social planning organizations. In short, the recent history of funding and planning social services deserves separate and careful scrutiny. Nevertheless, it seems likely that the ideological and gendered issues that characterized the first fifty years of 'organized philanthropy' have continued and would figure prominently in whatever findings such a study might provide.

CHAPTER TWO

The Roots of Social Work in English Canada

When social work emerged as a recognizable profession in the period following the First World War, it was in fact the consolidation of a number of disparate approaches to charitable work and social reform that coexisted in the pre-war period. The years between 1880 and 1920 are noted for the progressive reform movements that dominated urban industrial North America. Progressive reformers drew on a volatile mix of ideologies and dissent in their effort to reorder and control a society that was undergoing rapid and profound change. Such things as the introduction of the railroad, the invention of steel, and the expansion of Eastern Canada's industrial base were accompanied by rapid urbanization and the largest proportional influx of immigrants in Canada's history. Inevitably it created a 'social problem' that was one of the major objects of concern.

The progressive era was also noted for a preoccupation with, some would say a worship of, technology. The new technologies of this age not only emanated from the physical and engineering sciences, they also appeared as organizational technologies and the techniques of applied science. Bureaucratization and professionalization were the hallmarks of these new forms of technology and social work and social welfare were part and parcel of both. Progressive social reform, then, was the beginning of a long search for organization and expertise in the field of charity.[1]

While progressive reform served the dominant interests in late nineteenth-century society, there also existed vibrant streams of dissent and resistance to mainstream political, religious, and economic interests. Radical worker movements, the first wave of feminism, and religious ferment all challenged the existing order (or disorder as it was viewed by the progressives). Social work, as a creature of its time, absorbed these various and contradictory value sets, all of which operated within the profession simultaneously. Social workers collectively reflected both mainstream and radical ideals. Some were more important at one time than another, and chronologically the profession seems to have moved from a phase of moral reform to one of secular social reform and eventually applied social science. But through all these differences, social workers articulated a basic commitment to social change. Indeed, this is considered the very essence of social work.

In a general way, social change work may be seen as attempts to reorganize or transform the structures – political, economic, institutional, and/ or social – that mould people's lives. It is the antithesis of conservatism, which seeks to maintain and reproduce existing relations. But societal structures are themselves the visible face of ideologies, including but not exclusive to those ideologies of gender, class, and race. Thus both the means and the ends of working to change social structures, as well as the resistance to those changes, vary in important and contradictory ways.

It is therefore necessary for understanding past and present practices of social work to examine the diversity of ideologies and value premises that underpin what social workers do. It is wrong to insist that the entire profession reflects the dominant ideologies of a society; also wrong is the presumption made by many both inside and outside the profession that social work is a collection of left-wing individuals, or worse, simply a group of humanitarian bleeding hearts masquerading under the banner of professionalism. Social work is dedicated to changing the material conditions and well-being of individuals and groups of people who are 'disadvantaged.'[2] It is on the whole not seeking conservative ends, but in its avoidance of examining its political and ideological roots it frequently engages in contradictory practices that ultimately serve to maintain the existing order.

Thus many in the profession do tend to reflect in their practice the dominant ideals and ideologies of the society in which they work. Liberalism, which predominates in North America, is an important influence. Indeed, professionalism itself is an aspect of liberal ideology, and acquiring and holding professional qualifications presents a difficult contradiction for those who seek a radical practice. At the same time, community-based social work by its very nature, attracts people seeking ways to influence change that is oppositional and sometimes transformative. Both the liberal and oppositional approaches are represented among the social workers studied here. A small minority were radical. They disagreed among themselves as well as with others. All struggled in their own way to make the society of which they were a part better for people with whom they worked on a daily basis.

Much has been written about the early roots of social work in the Charity Organization Societies (COS) and settlement houses of the late nineteenth century. Both the COS and the settlements were essentially urban in locale and focus, and both engaged middle-class and usually Protestant reformers in projects designed to rescue and uplift the poorer classes and to prevent the spread of crime, disease, and dependency. Both were easily transferred from their origins in Great Britain to the urban centres of North America, and had a major impact on the development of social work in the United States and Canada.[3]

The COS originated in London, England, in the late 1860s. Its founders were upper-class women and men, dismayed by the multitude of charities that had appeared in the urban chaos of the time, without apparently stemming the growth of poverty. In creating the COS, they sought a systematic means of controlling and regulating both the charities and the poor.

The COS was notorious for its rigid moralistic stand, which rested on a firm belief that poverty was the hallmark of a sinful life and its relief a matter of Christian uplift. The giving of alms was believed to be the primary cause of pauperism, not a cure for poverty. COS supporters were convinced that material relief would only serve to lure individuals away from habits of thrift and hard work into a life dependent on handouts from the public purse. Thus, they reasoned, the primary task was to find ways of restoring individual responsibility in those seeking assistance, before they 'fell onto' public relief.

The COS sought to fulfil its task chiefly by sending 'friendly visitors' into the homes of the poor. With the arrogance of their class came the belief that by bringing rich and poor together, the poor would learn habits of thrift and hard work and see their benefactors as friends and teachers. Oblivious to the relationship between the conditions of labour and poverty, these early reformers honestly believed that poverty could be cured simply by helping the poor to help themselves.[4]

This desire to bring rich and poor together was also an end in itself, and not simply a by-product of the COS's central purpose. The bourgeoisie, of which the COS was a part, feared the visible breakdown of the organic community of an earlier time where classes mixed together and the poor of a community were known. Now the poor lived in city slums invisible to those who lived in middle- and upper-class neighbourhoods, and the potential for class-based conflict was both real and frightening. The practice of bringing middle- and working-class people together was an attempt to restore the communal relations between the classes, a modern revision of the feudal *noblesse oblige* that held together a social contract between rich and poor.

The belief that material relief caused pauperism also prompted a desire to control its provision. It seemed that the many new charities that sprang up not only duplicated what each other was doing, they were seen to be indiscriminate in their offering of aid, and in their largesse, believed to be creating more of that poverty they had set out to eliminate. The solution to both the problem of indiscriminate relief and the need to re-create a sense of community lay in the COS scheme of organizing charity work on the basis of neighbourhood. By bringing the charities together in district groups, their work could be coordinated, duplication could be avoided, and knowledge of the poor could be shared.

Thus the COS had three interconnected goals: restoring individuals to a life of self-sufficiency and moral rectitude, renewing bonds of obligation and understanding between the classes, and organizing and controlling charity work in the interest of both efficiency and communal relations. As it developed, the profession of social work reflected in varying ways all three of these purposes, but perhaps the most direct was the first, and the accompanying practice of sending friendly visitors to work with poor families. The daunting problems discovered by these early visitors, and the requirement that they study and record the causes of poverty that they found among the poor, led to the desire for training to improve their 'scientific' methods. Eventually, the training led to the standardization of techniques of working with individuals and families known as social casework.

The social casework approach that evolved primarily out of the COS experience became one of the major elements of social work practice. But it was never completely divorced from the context of urban reform from which it came. Mary Richmond, whose book *Social Diagnosis* became the first standard casework text, saw 'mass betterment and individual betterment [as] interdependent,' and 'social reform and social case work of necessity progressing together.'[5] Social casework concerned itself with individuals and families. Social reform was work in the community to change the social forces that caused the misery and poverty of the people with whom the social worker was involved. Although it concentrated on individual problems and was essentially conservative in nature, the social casework approach did not neglect the community change aspect of social work.

The settlements shared many of the same sentiments as the COS, particularly the desire to bring the classes together in bonds of neighbourliness. But they also differed in some important respects. First of all, the Settlement houses brought bourgeois youth, both men and women, to live in the poor neighbourhoods of the city. The first and perhaps most influential settlement house was Toynbee Hall, founded in 1884 in the east end of London, England. Begun as a project primarily for students at Oxford, Toynbee Hall was widely copied, beginning a practice common to settlement work of placing university students in the midst of lower-class life so that they might learn as well as teach.

Like the COS, the settlement house movement also moved quickly to North America. But here it was much more inclined to engage in social reform than was the case in England. According to Kathleen Woodroofe, 'The whole concept was broadened out to include all aspects of neighbourhood and community welfare, and ... resulted not only in local improvements in these fields, but also remedial legislation.'[6] The work in the cities of Canada and the United States also involved settlement workers directly with immigrant communities and all that this implied regarding intercultural relations as well as those of class.

The settlement house movement is associated with community organization and social action rather than with the casework that evolved from the COS. In the early years, settlement workers were at the forefront of advocacy for better working conditions, public health measures, recreational facilities, decent housing, and education for women as well as men. Despite the obvious class and ethnic bias of the settlement workers, there was a radicalism about the early settlements that provided a rich training in political action for many social workers before the influence of the movement dissipated after the First World War.[7]

Although the COS and the settlements differed significantly in their approach, they shared responsibility for encouraging the early training schools that evolved into present-day schools of social work. In Canada the establishment of the first schools at the University of Toronto (1914) and McGill University in Montreal (1918) was particularly influenced by settlement workers.[8] These early schools were firmly tied to the charities and settlements from which their students came and to which they would return. As such they were imbued with the importance of practical education and although the approach was 'scientific' in the sense that the curriculum attempted to apply the knowledge that social science offered, it

was not theoretically grounded as would become the case when a graduate degree became the requirement for professional practice.[9]

The social and urban reform background of Canadian social work was
tightly bound up with a pervasive and profoundly important movement
in the Protestant churches known as the social gospel. Indeed, Ramsay
Cook in his study of social dissent in late Victorian English Canada
argues persuasively that social work was the secular replacement of this
essentially religious movement.[10] It is quite likely that the majority of
the workers who filled the ranks of the profession in its early years came
by way of the social gospel, bringing with them its orientation to social
change.

The social gospel rested on a theology of an immanent God, and
preached social rather than individual salvation. The movement was a
direct offshoot of Christian Socialism, which in turn was a blend of ideals
drawn from the Owenite cooperative movements, radical labour, and
reform Darwinism that intermingled in Great Britain in the mid- to late
nineteenth century. This last was an important departure from the more
popular ideas of the social Darwinists who based their theories of society
on a belief in the value of competition and survival of the fittest. In contrast, reform Darwinists conceived of the natural world as interdependent
and survival as dependent on cooperation rather than competition. The
social gospel blended the values of cooperation, direct democracy, and
worker control with ideas of Christian brotherhood, and when combined
with the theological ferment within the Christian churches, it became a
potent force calling on Christians to save their society. 'The Social Gospel
addressed the whole problem, not just of individuals, not just of informal
social groups, but of institutions and institutional relationships in society.
Therefore, it became very deeply involved in virtually every promising
reform of the time.'[11] The result was the swelling of the ranks of reform
by many Christians who took up the cause of a new social order with the
religious certainty that God was on their side.

Canadians absorbed the social gospel along with much else of British
origin, but unlike the British, the Canadian movement developed a radicalism through exposure to Western agrarian populism and industrial
unionism. It was in the West that social gospel reformers such as J.S.
Woodsworth, William Irvine, and Salem Bland developed their ideas, subsequently bringing them East to Ontario and English Quebec. The radical social gospel, typified by Salem Bland, preached a 'new social order'
based on 'two great Christian principles of democracy and brother-

hood.'[12] The earthly kingdom of the radical social gospel was the antithesis of, and the antidote to, the materialistic, competitive, and unequal economic order of industrial capitalism. What was sought was nothing less than the abolition of capitalism and its replacement by a society based on values of cooperation and radical democracy.

There were two principal points of contact that directly tie Canadian social work to the social gospel. The first is in the early charities such as the urban missions and the myriad of infant homes and orphanages, many of which were founded by women and men as instrumental expressions of their social gospel beliefs. Canadian settlements in particular were the creation of the social gospel wing of the Presbyterian church, which hired an American Quaker to establish a series of settlement houses across the country. The second point of contact for the profession lay in the Social Service Council of Canada, which between 1914 and 1925 provided the organizational leadership to a national network of social welfare reformers and charitable organizations. Founded by the churches in 1907 and originally named the Moral and Social Reform Council of Canada, the council changed its name in 1914, forged an alliance between the churches, labour, and social reform groups, and began to lobby government and others for its agenda of social change. Its network of local councils, its annual national conferences, and it periodical, *Social Welfare*, were the chief sources for discussion and promotion of social welfare ideals until the emergence of secular social work organizations during the twenties. After 1925 the Social Service Council of Canada was displaced by the Canadian Association of Social Workers (1926), the Canadian Conference of Social Work (1928) and a network of 'cooperative welfare bodies' such as the Toronto Federation for Community Service that is the focus of study here.[13]

As a profession, social work declared itself to be rigidly secular, requiring its practitioners to replace moral judgment with 'judgement based on fact.' Nevertheless, it was 'permeated by individuals of social gospel persuasion,'[14] a factor that made it possible for social work to carry the values of the social gospel while at the same time eschewing the application of religious and moral principles. Social work was seen as a means of replacing the moral fervour and evangelical objectives of organized religion with a secular and scientific practice, and at the same time, not requiring the complete abandonment of faith. It is important to note that one of the hallmarks of the 'new professional' was seen to be an ability to separate the professional, scientific part of their lives from the religious and moral. The hindsight of modern scholarship shows us that this is not possible; nevertheless it was a major canon of professional practice and one that survives in some quarters today.[15]

Mariana Valverde has argued that moral reform and social reform were inseparable in the early decades of the twentieth century. She insists that preoccupation with moral purity imbued virtually all reform efforts, and that the two were inextricably linked.[16] Certainly, from the records of the early reform organizations such as those studied here, there is a clear and important overlap between the moral purity movement, which she examines in detail, and social reform. Nevertheless, there were those who resisted the powerful and persuasive impulse to link the two despite its legitimation by the dominance of the Christian church and the fear of 'heathen' (read non-white, non-Christian) influence on Canadian society. The change in name from the Moral and Social Reform Council to the Social Service Council of Canada was not made casually. Rather, it was a sign of an element of the reform movements that sought to distance itself from moral reform. This resistance was particularly characteristic of the emerging profession of social work. While many early social workers were certainly on the leading edge of the social purity movement and indeed may have dominated it in the beginning, professionalism and a professional discourse that placed a high value on technology, technique, and efficiency altered the nature of both their goals and the means for social change. Professional social workers and the agencies for which they worked consciously moved away from church affiliation, proclaiming themselves as secular and professing a new faith in science and its application.

It is important to note that while the overt Christian morality of the older social reform movement was fading, it did not mean the absence of any morality. One of the basic premises of this book is the importance of recognizing the values and moral ideals that underlie all efforts at social change. As Charles Frankel has pointed out, social welfare itself is an essentially moral idea.[17] If it were not so, then we simply would not concern ourselves with human well-being. As such, it is impossible to strive for any form of institutional or organized effort at promoting social welfare that does not rest on some belief about a moral order. Like many of their professional contemporaries, early social workers professed objectivity and neutrality of values, when in fact they were adopting a new morality in a modernism that worshipped science and technology.[18]

The professionalization of social work was intrinsically tied to the emergence of social science both as a discipline and as a tool for social change.

Both Canadian and American social workers were heavily influenced by the Chicago School of Sociology and the theories about community and social environments that emanated from the social scientists located there. But, the influence of the 'Chicago School' had a companion influence in Canadian social work history. Social science research was an important tool of the British Fabian Society, and Fabian socialism was the philosophical foundation of liberal reform in Great Britain. The intellectual home of the Fabians was the London School of Economics, and the discipline of social administration developed there provided the theoretical foundations for the development of a welfare state. This also transferred easily to Canada. Fabian socialism and its use of social science research for the purpose of social reform helped shape both the social work profession in Canada and the Canadian welfare state.

Marlene Shore's study of social science at McGill University in Montreal provides a fascinating account of the influence of social science on Canadian social work and social reform.[19] Events at McGill in the twenties foreshadowed the replacement of the early reformism of social work by a scientific and technical approach to social change. The Department of Social Study and Training was founded at McGill in 1918. It was urged on the reluctant overseers of the university by local businessmen, assisted by Professor James A. Dale, whose interest in popular education and settlement work came from his previous experience in London, England. Dale was instrumental in founding the University Settlement in Montreal, which was adopted by the university and figured in the establishment of the new school.[20]

The first director of the McGill school was John Howard Toynbee Falk. Falk was a passionate social reformer and a controversial figure. In addition to training social workers, his intention was to use the school as a centre for coordination of agency services and social reform in Montreal. The social activism and the emphasis on 'practical social work' advocated by Falk made him unpopular with the conservative scholars at McGill. He was eased out of his job and replaced by Carl A. Dawson, a theoretical sociologist, born in Nova Scotia but trained at Chicago.[21] Dawson shifted the emphasis of the school from practical social work to one that relied on research, and the role of the social scientist as purveyor of the facts necessary for social improvement. As Shore's analysis suggests, Dawson and the school he headed represent another direction in the secularization of early Christian reform.

Scholars at the Chicago School of Sociology where Dawson trained regarded values, culture, and institutions as creatures of their environ-

ment, and rejected ideas of genetic predisposition and inherent differences between races and nations. They called their discipline 'scientific
sociology' and developed theories of human and social ecology that
focused on the interaction of people and their environment. Scientific
sociology relied on a faith in scientific discovery of natural phenomenon
to describe and explain change and flux in human relations parallel to
that observed in the plant and animal world. In this respect social science
overlapped with Darwinism (both social and radical) in assuming that
natural laws governed human behaviour. The assumptions social scientists
made about the importance of environment and their approach to people in social settings had a profound influence on the approach of early
social workers to community organization and planning.

Purists trained in social science methods rejected involvement in the
direct activities of social reform, which they saw as diverting the scientist
away from the attainment of 'objective knowledge.' They envisioned their
role as one of impartial provider of scientifically derived information and
assumed that given the 'facts,' rational actors would behave in appropriate fashion. They also combined their theories with the radical democratic theories of John Dewey to create the assumption that social
improvement would follow naturally from the education of workers and
ordinary people in their communities. Reliance on a combination of
social science research and techniques of popular education became the
preferred method employed by many social workers engaged in community organization practice.[22]

The belief that people were affected by their social environment had
much to offer the profession in its search for the cause and cure of poverty. As such, community work was regarded as the other side of the casework coin by early practitioners. It was not until the end of the thirties
that social workers separated community work from casework and began
the process of developing community organization and social planning as
a practice method on its own.[23]

McGill's second major influence on the professionalization of social
work emanated from its Social Science Research Project headed by
Leonard Marsh. The project was established in 1930–1, funded by a grant
from the American Rockefeller Foundation. While it cooperated with the
Department of Social Science, the project departed in some significant
ways from Dawson's rigidly apolitical stance. First of all, the Project was
interdisciplinary, following international enthusiasm among some scholars for collaboration and a hesitancy to encourage too much specialization. In this regard it differed from American experience generally and

challenged the vested interest of the sociologists in establishing their own discipline in particular. Second, Marsh was trained at the London School of Economics (LSE) under Sir William Beveridge, an expert on employment policies and later the chief architect of the British welfare state.[24] Marsh's background at LSE led him to select for study subjects such as unemployment, housing, and population, revealing an interest in the kinds of social problems that were the concern of social reformers. His studies became a major source of research on health and unemployment for Canadian social workers and others in the interwar years. And third, Marsh was a Fabian socialist.[25]

Fabian socialism, like scientific sociology, regarded science as the necessary basis for progress, but departed from sociology by encouraging political action based on the facts. To this end, the Fabian Society sponsored social surveys and published a steady stream of pamphlets. Fabians advocated limited use of state power to mitigate the adverse affects of unbridled capitalism and bring about social harmony. This essentially liberal form of socialism underlay much of socialist thinking in Canada and was a major ideological current within social work.[26]

Thus while the scientific sociologists eschewed political action, their theories were adapted by others whose political inclinations led them to act on the information they were creating. At McGill, it led to conflict between the Social Science Research Project and the scholars and businessmen who controlled the purse strings, ultimately leading to the project's demise and the departure of Marsh. But this did not happen until Marsh had completed his studies on social conditions during the Depression of the thirties and laid the groundwork for his 1943 report for the Canadian government's Committee on Post-War Reconstruction. The Marsh Report became the basic blueprint for the Canadian welfare state.

The faith in science and rationality as the road to social improvement was in direct opposition to the Christian uplift of early social work. Social science provided yet another avenue for social workers who sought a replacement for the moralistic reform of their predecessors. They did not wholly reject reform and activism along the line of the 'pure' social sciences, but they sought to distance themselves sufficiently from subjective involvement through the use of scientific methods and through carrying a role as educators and enablers of people in communities.

The reliance of social work on science, rationality, and expertise reflected acceptance of utilitarian philosophy, one of the most important and pervasive ideologies of the progressive era. Utilitarianism begins with the belief that individuals are primarily motivated by the desire to maximize pleasure and minimize pain. It proceeds from this to use the calculus of efficiency as a tool for measurement of success in all human endeavour. For utilitarians, the ultimate goal of a well-ordered society is the achievement of social efficiency, expressed as 'the greatest good for the greatest number.' In order to achieve this ideal, they advocate state intervention as a means of ensuring the right ordering of social relations. As such, utilitarian belief is a secular system of morality, with the state replacing the authority of the church.[27]

Utilitarianism was originally a modification of classical liberalism that departed from the earlier philosophy with its belief in the use of state power to achieve social harmony. Its disciples did not reject freedom of individual action in a market economy, they simply added to it. Utilitarians justified state intervention in social affairs by reliance on the separation of politics, which they regarded as subjective and emotional, and management. With an expert civil service, sound decisions could then presumably be based on rational decision-making grounded in scientifically derived facts. This supremely rational and efficient order was the utopian ideal from which liberal reformers constructed the welfare state.[28]

While utilitarianism was essentially liberal, the emphasis on state intervention in social affairs and the explicit agenda for reform opened the door for incorporation of utilitarian beliefs into socialist thinking as well. Fabian socialists in particular were utilitarian to the core, seeking reform of government and stopping short of fundamental change in the economic order. Marx also drew on utilitarian philosophy, but one of the important differences between his theory of the economy and that of the Fabians is his rejection of the separation of the economy from the moral and social order. Nevertheless it is important to recognize that a utilitarian core, with its emphasis on rationality and efficiency, remained in both socialist and liberal streams of thought.[29]

Historians suggest that the dominant image of late nineteenth-century society was one that 'increasingly mirrored the total rationalization and the functional interdependence that characterized the machine.'[30] This image reflects a world view that placed science, technology, and industry at the heart of human progress. Utilitarianism, with its central motif of efficiency, is congruent with this view, and it may be argued that it was the most pervasive and influential belief system in late nineteenth- and early twentieth-century European and North American culture. The metaphor of the machine pictured social affairs and individual identity as functioning parts of a vast social machine, and progress became inevitably linked to personal, economic, and social efficiency.[31]

This was the society from which social work emerged. Social workers embraced the new 'gospel of efficiency,' and absorbed ideas of personal and social efficiency as primary values and something for which social workers should strive as individuals, collectively, and for their clients.[32] It is unthinkable that they could have done otherwise, given the pervasiveness and importance of efficiency and technocratic thinking in the society of which they were a part. But the achievement of a state of efficiency does not address issues of democracy or social justice. Indeed there is a fundamental contradiction between efficiency and other broad humanitarian and social goals. Efficiency is served by central authority and defeated by democratic participation and diffusion of power. The greatest good for the greatest number not only masks inequality, it explicitly accepts it. Furthermore, given the patterns of power in Western industrial societies, the 'greatest number' is inevitably white, male, and with capital.

Utilitarianism is not only blind to differences of gender and race, it actively perpetates oppression of women and minorities through its reliance on authority and state power. Utilitarian values, with their emphasis on central authority and the supremacy of expertise, are intrinsic to patriarchy and support the patterns of male dominance that characterize industrial societies. Its reliance on expertise ties the professional and managerial ranks to an oppressive class structure. Of all the admittedly conflicting values that inform social work, utilitarianism was probably the strongest and paradoxically, the least consistent with the humanistic and social justice goals of the profession. Both women and men in social work absorbed these values from their own dominant middle-class culture. In so doing, they blindly imposed them on those they sought to assist – primarily working-class and immigrant or aboriginal people.

The profession of social work is by its very nature divided by issues of gender. Because it is a 'caring' profession, it has attracted women to its ranks from its earliest days. Like teaching and nursing, social work was seen as a natural extension of women's work, although, as was the case in other female dominated professions, it was subject to supervision and control by men.[33] But social work differed in that the community work aspect of practice required interaction at the political and community level.

Charity work, the forerunner of social work, grew rapidly as a public activity in the nineteenth century. As a private activity, it had long been the responsibility of the local benevolent society or church parish. But the spirit of the British Poor Laws, which governed attitudes towards charity in English Canada, sought to place responsibility for regulating the giving of alms and deterring pauperism in public or institutional hands.[34] As the industrial revolution progressed and poverty grew, the roles both of local government and of voluntary agencies became much more important. Originally, charity work was carried out almost exclusively by men who made little distinction between establishing and operating charitable organizations and other civic responsibilities.[35] This blurring of public and private roles came easily for men, but it also provided opportunity for women. When women entered public life later in the nineteenth century, it was primarily through participation in religious organizations.[36] The male church leadership condoned and encouraged women's involvement in charity out of a belief that women possessed superior nurturing capabilities, and as charity became organized through community agencies it continued as a legitimate role for upper-class and middle-class women.

While encouraging women to take up charity work did not extend to giving women administrative responsibilities, there are examples of capable women working around the strictures of the church hierarchy to manage the early charities.[37] Eventually women not only did most of the visiting that was the backbone of social casework, they also carried much of the responsibility for managing organizations such as day nurseries, orphanages, and missions. While formal responsibility for management may have rested with men serving on boards of directors or in the hierarchy of a sponsoring church, women did much of the day-to-day work. The settlements in particular were dominated by women and provide a prime example of the organizing and managing skills of early women social workers.

Although women in social work quietly worked around and sometimes struggled against the domination of their male colleagues, they nevertheless concurred with the belief that women possessed unique and inherent maternal attributes that not only better prepared them for social work, but also were the key to 'social salvation.'[38] The essentially conservative ideas about family and women's role that were central to these beliefs were the assumptions that guided the efforts of social workers to restore family life or rescue abused children when that family life was seen as inadequate. A clear example of how the assumptions of maternalism were applied is found in the role of the teaching homemaker. Crucial to the strategy for the prevention of poverty and a preoccupation of social workers in the twenties and thirties, Middle-class caseworkers and 'visiting housekeepers' shared responsibility for instructing their lower-class women clients in techniques of health, hygiene, and nutrition. Women's domestic role was seen as the key to family health and to the continued ability of men to support women and children through participation in the labour force.[39]

While maternalism had much to do with the role of women in case-work, it also was very much part of social reform, extending these ideas about women's capabilities to the realm of community and ultimately society as a whole. These values were clearly articulated in the 1930 annual report of the Toronto Child Welfare Council: 'The love of a mother for her child is an ageless phenomenon, and the organization of society with the will to care for many mothers' children is, I think, but an extension of that mother love on a wider, or the widest possible scale ... We do not deal with material things, but in social ideals. We are not concerned with changes in skirt lengths, but we *are* deeply concerned with changes in mental attitudes and in social criteria.'[40]

This is a statement of philosophy that clearly reflects a desire to transcend the values of materialism and competition that characterized the capitalist ethic and to create a new society based on social values of caring and cooperation. These values added special meaning to the concept of community. Interdependence, circles of caring, and networks of mutual support have long been fundamental to the way in which women interact and are distinctly different from the dominant individualistic views of social relations more commonly preferred by men. Thus community work as seen at this time was congruent with values of cooperation and mutual aid and with ways of organizing favoured by organizations dominated by women, such as the Child Welfare Council.

In many respects, maternalism within social work was clearly responsible for a conservative approach to working with families. In community work, it was also at least partly responsible for the imposition of middle-class values on immigrant and working-class people through the work of women in the settlement houses and YWCAs. But there was also a minority of women who combined their maternalism with a different concept of familial relations and a radically different view of how society ought to be organized. Social work contained within its ranks a small but significant core of activist women for whom social work offered a means of working for social change consistent with their beliefs.[41]

The overwhelming opinion among feminist historians who have examined the work of women in social work and social reform is clear. The vast majority were white, middle-class, and consciously or unconsciously engaged in work that strengthened the liberal, and largely Anglo-Saxon,

Protestant power structures of Western society. From the evidence given, the reproduction of patterns of class and race that flowed from their efforts is incontestable.[42]

Acceptance of traditional values regarding the relations of women in the nuclear family is also seen by scholars as the underlying premise of women reformers. Most argue that the weight of influence in a conservative paradigm of maternalism and subordination to a male-dominated system of production and community relations was overwhelming. This is not surprising, and where scholarly differences do lie, they seem to be in positions regarding the nature of criticism and whether it is fair to judge the beliefs and actions of the past based on the standards of the present. But despite the seeming agreement on the pervasiveness of maternalism, there is also a seemingly universal acknowledgment that there were a few individuals who resisted the conservative assumption of a women's sphere within a private and domestic world of family. This is where a revealing uncertainty lies. We are led to the possibility that a radical influence did indeed exist, a possibility that has yet to be seriously examined.

The uncertainty is heightened by differences among feminist scholars on what constitutes a 'radical' perspective. For some, nothing short of seeking to dismantle the institution of the traditional nuclear family qualifies an individual or a movement as radical. For others, the transformation of the relations of production (and therefore reproduction) is the requisite characteristic. Yet others are attempting to integrate notions of class struggle and the social construction of gender with anti-racist strategies. All have wisdom to offer while at the same time they raise major contradictions. The question that is posed here, in the context of social work with its contradictory political underpinnings, is whether it is possible to carry a radical perspective alongside one that affirms traditional maternalist notions or beliefs. How do we categorize, if that is what we must do, beliefs that combine conservative notions of family with a desire to transform political and economic relations – a maternalist approach that does not buy into the liberal paradigm of individualism and capitalist modes of production and distribution?

Lori Ginzberg, in her analysis of women's charitable and benevolent activities in nineteenth-century America, raises an interesting point when she argues that moral reform contains within it both conservative and radical tendencies. While maternalism can lead to a female separatism that reinforces women's domestic role, it can also lead to a more radical view that seeks to transform both men and women and the way in which relations between the sexes are organized. Ginzberg's study identifies a new professional class of women in the latter part of the nineteenth century who scorned the 'moral suasion' of a previous generation and allied themselves with a business approach that sought efficient ways of organizing charity and embraced male ways of exercising power. She argues that their belief in sameness of the sexes led to liberal practices associated with the welfare state. Thus a non-maternalist perspective can also lead to very conservative ends. Significantly, Ginzberg also found a minority of women who opposed this new liberalism, as they had opposed the strict moralism of an earlier time, and continued to support a radical and transformative approach to social change.[43]

Ginzberg's primary thesis is that both separatist and sameness ideologies of gender obscure issues of class. In other words, we cannot disentangle gender from class. What we are left with is a clear picture of the class bias of women reformers, and, I would add, no doubt about the predominance of race – and a murkiness on the subject of gender.

More recently, Seth Koven and Sonya Michel, in their overview of a series of comparative studies on women and welfare politics internationally, reject a simplified definition of maternalism as being no different than an oversimplified definition of feminism. They define maternalism as a plurality of 'ideologies and discourses that exalted women's capacity to mother and applied to society as a whole the values they attached to that role: care, nurturance, and morality.'[44] They found notions of maternalism informing the actions of both women and men and having significant influence in the emergence of welfare states, albeit in varying degrees. But they make no claim that either women or the ideologies of maternalism ever had the upper hand. What they do point out is a fundamental dilemma for women caught between the ideals of a reordering of society in a uniquely female way and the pragmatic necessity of playing by the existing rules.

The women in this study are no different from Ginzberg's nineteenth-century women or Koven and Michel's twentieth-century women. They articulated the classic maternalist ideologies while simultaneously accepting the pragmatic realities of male power and welfare state (although they varied on where to draw the line between public and private responsibility). And as in Ginzberg's study, a few were radically different. While the evidence in this study is inconclusive, it points to the possibility of a greater element of radicalism than we have been given to believe. But the extent and nature of that radicalism is yet to be explored.

Barbara Taylor argues that nineteenth-century socialist feminist ideals that stemmed from the Owenite cooperative movement and other forms of utopian socialism survived into the twentieth century.[45] The radical social gospel had it roots in these early movements and undoubtedly provided one of the conduits on this feminist grapevine. Given the importance of religion to social work, it is inconceivable that women coming into social work would not be aware of those social gospellers whose beliefs were rooted in the cooperative ethic and who sought the demise of capitalism and the attainment of a new social order. They combined their maternalism and their radicalism into what Joan Sangster calls 'militant mothering.'[46] Social work offered an opportunity to apply these ideals in a vocation. Furthermore, the radical social gospel was preached from the pulpit of Canadian churches, and the fact that a call to work for a transformed society could be combined with faith made it all the more legitimate.

Sangster's study provides repeated examples of an inter-mingling of women in social work with women in the radical left around issues related to family and child welfare. Her analysis provides evidence that there was a socialist feminist minority within social work that is circumstantial, but strong. She argues that 'unemployment and relief – either experienced firsthand or viewed secondhand – were radicalizing forces for many women.'[47] Social workers were clearly in one of the best positions to view poverty and injustice secondhand, and her biographical cameos of individual women frequently include experience doing social work. Indeed, some of the most prominent women on the left were trained social workers.[48]

Sangster also discusses the collaboration that took place between the social democratic CCF and the communist Popular Front during the thirties and forties. Women in both parties took up issues such as day care and the adequacy of relief, issues that were also central to the women social workers in the Toronto welfare councils studied here. A later study by Susan Prentice confirms this collaboration specifically within the day-care movement in Toronto following the Second World War, one in which the Toronto Welfare Council, successor to the Child Welfare Council participated heavily. The day-care movement was lead by radical women on the left and eventually defeated by the virulent red-baiting that was going on in Toronto in the early 1950s. Prentice notes the contradictions that existed within this movement, one that articulated the conservative ideas of family and women's domestic role alongside their acceptance of women as workers. She provides a clear example of the possibility of a dual and contradictory commitment that is both conservative and radical.[49]

Canadian social workers were strongly influenced by developments in the United States during both the pre-war and postwar periods. A radical socialist group known as the Rank and File Movement made up an estimated 10 per cent of social workers in that country during the Depression.[50] Rank and Filers were anti-professional and sought to ally social workers with the working class. They supported the worker movements of the thirties and opposed the support given by the American Association of Social Workers to President Roosevelt's New Deal, declaring that the contributory aspect of its social insurance provision placed the burden on the already oppressed workers. Like so many other socialist movements on both sides of the border, the American Rank and File Movement was stamped out and its members driven from their jobs in the purges that followed the Second World War.

The radical Rank and File was not a feminist project per se, although it included women among its most vocal and visible members. It is the combination of its influence on Canadian social workers and the existence of some evidence of feminist social action among early social workers that leads to the conclusion that there was probably a radical element among women in Canadian social work before the Second World War. Social work was never revolutionary in the strict sense of the word, and those whose politics ran along these lines would not be among those who entered its ranks. But there were women who struggled against the mainstream values of society and sought fundamental change along peaceful lines. For these women, social work was a means to an end. It not only provided a legitimate means of livelihood, which is something that cannot be ignored, it also provided a potential platform for social action and access to the power structures of society. While they lacked the present-day analysis of patriarchy as it relates to class, they saw women's ways as a necessary ingredient for the transformation of society into a just, humane, and peaceful social order.

The values of cooperation and social democracy, and the activism of many women social workers, brought them into conflict with some of their colleagues. In particular, cooperation and democracy contradicted the utilitarian values of efficiency and central control that governed the practices and beliefs of their male colleagues who were the administrators of social agencies and the gatekeepers between social work and the businessmen who controlled the funds. Social activism jeopardized the support of the business community and was opposed by the male social work hierarchy if only for pragmatic reasons. These differences were not a dichotomous split between men and women in social work. Women held to the values of efficiency, as did men to the values of cooperation. But on the whole, there was a gendered difference in the approaches to social work that prevailed during the early years before the Second World War.[51]

The Second World War was a watershed in the evolution of social work in Canada. The rise of corporate power, the cold war attitudes towards any activity that was deemed communist, and the reintroduction of traditional conservative norms regarding family and women's role[52] all had an enormous impact on the profession. In the face of massive economic, political, and cultural resistance to much of what social work had been trying to accomplish, social workers retreated into a narrow professionalism, relying on scientism and technique, and worrying about their status among an array of competing professions in science, health, and planning. Casework absorbed the renewed emphasis on traditional family life and turned to Freudian psychology for theoretical justification and support. Community work became separate from casework, focusing on social science and comprehensive community surveys as the rational basis for maximizing resources to meet community needs. In the face of a hostile corporate hegemony, social reform and social action clung to a bland form of community development, where the appropriate role for a social worker was seen as solely that of 'enabler,' never that of partisan.[53]

Most important for community work in particular was a preoccupation with urban reform that returned after the war. The building boom that occurred in the postwar period and the influx of immigrants opened up by the cessation of hostilities led to concerns for controlling urban growth. The migration of black Americans into the cities of the northern United States had also resulted in vast urban slums that became a major focus of concern in that country once the war was over. While Canadians did not experience the phenomenon of urban slums in the same way, American experience nevertheless spilled over the border and Canadians too became involved in a movement for urban renewal. The efforts to address urban poverty were accompanied by the strengthening and legitimizing of urban planning as a profession, and with it the interest of social workers in combining physical and social planning. The result was the legitimizing of social planning as a major part of social work practice and a displacement of women in community work by men who rushed to involve themselves with the power structures that were developing around urban planning.[54]

None of this bode well for women in social work generally and, by inference, for the profession as a locus for radical practice. The loss of a visible radical element has indeed been the fate of the profession, which has participated primarily in the liberal mainstream of Canadian and North American society since the Second World War. Even in the so-called radical sixties, social workers adhered to strategies of comprehensive planning and a social action that rested on liberal assumptions about the economic order.[55] Awareness of the existence of a vigorous and sometimes radical approach to social change and the ideals of working for a new social order that lay within the early profession was lost in the historical amnesia that characterizes modern society. The story of Toronto social workers involved in their struggle for social change turns a light on part of that forgotten past.

CHAPTER THREE
_____

The Organization of Charity
in Toronto

The provision of charity was the focus of widespread concern in Toronto
in the opening decades of the twentieth century. Civic leaders bent on
eradicating poverty, disease, and crime saw charity not as a remedy but as
a cause. Burgeoning relief rolls and the proliferation of organizations dispensing charity were considered major sources of 'the social problem.' In
1911 a Charities Commission established by the municipality to survey
the field and recommend reform counted 307 missions, institutions, and
other relief-giving organizations. This was a sizeable number for a city of
376,538, and neither the threefold increase in Toronto's population since
1881 nor the economic recession that had begun three years earlier provided city fathers with a satisfactory explanation.[1] The Charities Commission blamed 'indiscriminate giving' on the part of citizens, and poor
management practices on the part of the charities.[2] Both those who gave
money and those who ran the charities sought to eliminate perceived
duplication of effort and impose standards of management and service.
In so doing, they sought to contain the proliferation of charitable organizations and to control the manner in which relief was provided.

In 1918 businessmen and leaders in the emerging profession of social
work joined together to found the Toronto Federation for Community
Service. Their alliance was fostered by a common commitment to efficiency, which in the field of philanthropy was associated with joint fund-
raising, proper standards of management, and perhaps most important,
coordination of effort among local charities. As the head resident of
Toronto's Central Neighbourhood House put it; 'One social agency too
often does the work in its own restricted field, without becoming

informed about what is being done by another agency working among a slightly different group in the same locality. This tends to produce overlapping, and represents a very wasteful expenditure of effort and money.'[3] In the eyes of businessmen, coordination would result in cost savings. In the eyes of social workers, coordination was related to conserving their time and improving services. Their concern was much more for ensuring that the needs of their clients were met than for economy.

Thus while social workers and businessmen joined together in various approaches to organizing services, their alliance masked an important difference. The rhetoric of efficiency appealed to both groups in its promise of reducing wasteful expenditures of time and money. Neither the donors nor the workers wished to see scarce dollars spent to no avail. But social workers were also concerned with emerging standards of professional practice and effective ways of meeting the needs of families and communities. The result was a struggle for control, with the business community seeking to contain costs and the social work community seeking professional autonomy. The primacy of one or the other became a major underlying source of conflict between those who gave funds and those who provided service.

Like other financial federations, the Federation for Community Service in Toronto was not the first attempt to control charity organizations and contain costs, but it was the first truly collaborative effort between business and social work. Two earlier attempts to organize charity in Toronto were particularly noteworthy for the resistance they evoked among social workers. The first of these was Toronto's version of the Charity Organization Society (COS), the second a particularly coercive version of an 'endorsement bureau' popular among businessmen of the early boards of trade. A review of the experience with both the COS and the Board of Trade endorsement movement helps explain the enthusiasm with which social workers allied themselves with the business community to help found the Federation for Community Service.

The Charity Organization Society is best known for sending 'friendly visitors' into the homes of impoverished families. But as noted in Chapter Two, there was much more to the COS idea than friendly visiting and moral uplift. Of equal importance was the goal of coordinating and regulating all charitable efforts in the community.[4] Each COS was organized according to city districts for the purpose of coordinating all the charitable work in that particular area. District conferences provided a means for charity workers to exchange information, and as the organization grew, employed agents oversaw administrative affairs and helped recruit and supervise volunteer visitors. The maintainance of a central registery of all applicants for relief, intended as a clearing house to ensure that no duplication of work took place, was another major feature of COS work. Originally the intention had also been to audit the accounts and inspect the annual reports of each charity, and to require each to pay a fee according to their annual income. This threatened the autonomy of the charities and not surprisingly met with little enthusiasm and cooperation. Even the idea of a central registry, which survived well into the twentieth century, met with little actual cooperation. In the face of widespread non-compliance, only the practice of coordinating efforts on a district basis survived alongside the practice of friendly visiting.[5]

Toronto's COS was founded in 1888 under the name Associated Charities. Modelled on the COS in London, England, its purpose was to bring the charities together into district groups in order to regulate their activities and to address the perceived problems of pauperism. And like their counterparts elsewhere, Toronto charities declined to cooperate. At best, Associated Charities oversaw a loose affiliation of organizations and struggled to keep alive the hope that it might some day 'evolve into a "more systematic plan of relief."'[6]

In Toronto, regulation of public relief was also seen as desirable, and Associated Charities pressured the city to assume a greater responsibility. Civic authority was seen as necessary to assist in curtailing abuses, to fix final authority somewhere, and generally to help in regulating the whole charitable enterprise. Unlike Britain, Ontario did not have any central authority to regulate local relief, and Goldwin Smith, the wealthy British intellectual who was the chief power behind Associated Charities, lobbied the province for a poor law modelled on that of Great Britain. Smith sought the power of the law 'chiefly because he thought that official authority was needed to deal effectively with such "semi-criminal" forms of behaviour as "imposture, vagrancy, and mendancy." Armed with police power, a [municipal] poor law office might cleanse the community of pauperism.'[7]

None of this was particularly successful, and by 1900, Associated Charities had virtually ceased operation, causing considerable concern to civic leaders impatient with the inefficiency and growing cost of relief. In 1908 the churches established a renewed version of Associated Charities, apparently in favour of rooting charity in a religious tradition and in opposition to the new scientific approaches introduced by the emerging profession of social work. It quickly became the fourth-largest dispenser of relief in the city, but in attempting to establish a central registry in 1911 it once again evoked the resistance of the other charities.[8]

The fact that the revived Associated Charities, along with so many other Charity Organization Societies, gave relief was a departure from the early intention that friendly visiting would replace the need for relief. By this time, experience had taught that dispensing relief could not be wholly avoided and well over two-thirds of the Charity Organization Societies in North America had taken on this task. Now the intention was to provide small amounts of relief to deserving cases with the intent of helping the individual regain independence. But public 'outdoor relief,' that is, non-institutional relief, for the most part was still viewed as fostering dependency and the role of the state continued to be seen as one of punishment and coercion. Only the judicious and well-orchestrated provision of relief in the private sector was seen as acceptable.[9]

While many upper-class Torontonians and charity workers shared the beliefs and sentiments of the COS, the resistance of the charities themselves provides some evidence of opposition. By the early part of the twentieth century, social reformers were increasingly conscious of the environmental causes of poverty. Some undoubtedly also rebelled at the idea of refusing food for a hungry family as a means of instilling the virtues of thrift and hard work. Increasingly, this opposition came from the ranks of the new professionals, who coupled their humanitarian instincts with the desire for a much more 'scientific' approach to determining the causes of a family's distress. They were still a long way from recognizing poverty as a structural feature of industrial capitalism, but they had moved a considerable distance from the views of Goldwin Smith and Associated Charities. At the very least, scientific social work sought to distance itself from the overt religiosity and moral uplift of the nineteenth-century COS. In some respects, the conflict between the church-sponsored Associated Charities and other charities may have been a Toronto-specific reflection of the vigorous debate in England at the time. The British Royal Commission on the Poor Laws and Relief of Distress that reported in 1909 had publicly pitted the London COS and its adherence to the punitive philosophy of the 1834 Poor Law against the newer Fabian ideas that favoured scientific investigation and a humane system of public and private welfare.[10]

Whatever the cause of the differences in Toronto, civic leaders remained determined to find a way to coordinate and regulate all charitable efforts in the city, both public and private. If Associated Charities was not the answer, some other means of achieving the efficient management of charity and eliminating unnecessary and wasteful relief had to be found.

In North American cities, one of the chief alternatives to the coordinating function of the COS was a system of endorsement of 'worthy charities' initiated by local boards of trade. This too became a source of friction between charity workers and those who sought control over their work. Endorsement bureaus were created as an attempt on the part of the business community to use their collective ability to grant or withhold funds as a lever to introduce standards of efficiency into the management of charitable organizations. The endorsement movement was particularly appealing to businessmen in Toronto, where the search for control over charity had so far yielded little result. The Toronto Board of Trade used the idea to create a municipal Social Service Commission that would make up for the inability of Associated Charities to coordinate charitable work. Resistance to the commission was one of the major contributing factors to the alliance of business and social work that created the Toronto Federation for Community Service.

Boards of trade, or chambers of commerce as they are more commonly known today, grew rapidly in North American cities in the latter part of the nineteenth century. They were on the leading edge of civic reform, becoming a centre of power for small entrepreneurs, businessmen, and industrialists who formed the economic elite of the urban community. The reform of local government was a primary concern of the boards, and they gradually gained considerable influence over local elected councils, which they used for their own interests.[11] Among their objectives was the elimination of perceived inefficiency and fraudulent practices of charitable organizations.

The system of endorsement established by the boards of trade required that the charities meet rigid standards of management in order to qualify. Charitable organizations were required to hold regular board meetings and to use accepted methods of raising and accounting for funds. They were also required to 'cooperate with other charitable institutions in preventing duplication of effort and in promoting efficiency and economy of administration in the charities of the city, as a whole.' With a system of investigation in place, a board of trade would then make every effort to convince would-be donors to confine their giving to approved charities. No distinction was made between donations provided through the municipal levy or by private donors. All were considered public funds and all required public accountability on the part of the charity that received them.[12]

The extent to which a board of trade endorsement bureau might go to ensure compliance was clearly coercive: 'As a condition of endorsement the committee may each year require evidence of a constantly increasing standard of excellence ... methods may be carefully studied, conferences held with boards of management, and if necessary, fundamental changes insisted upon to bring about the very highest standard of service.'[13] On the whole, the endorsement movement was governed by men of power and influence who exerted their authority with little regard for the social welfare objectives of the charities or for the experience of the social workers who managed them. The actions of the business community were seen not only as trampling on the rights of the charities, but also since there was little regard given to standards of service, as stifling innovation and improvement of services.[14]

To ensure its effectiveness, a sprinkling of American boards of trade extended the system of endorsement by using the authority of municipal government to force coordination and standards of efficiency on reluctant agencies.[15] It was this ultimate measure of coercion that was adopted in Toronto. The Toronto Board of Trade was active on the 1911 Charities Commission noted above. The Charities Commission recommended the establishment of a municipally appointed Social Service Commission to which the city agreed in 1912. The new commission conformed in every respect with the model for an endorsement bureau developed by the American boards of trade.[16]

Toronto's Social Service Commission was made up of five members, one each from city council's board of control and the Board of Trade, and three appointed citizens. Its membership was deliberately constituted so that 'no member of that body should be directly or indirectly interested in any of the charitable institutions of the City,' reflecting a decided lack of confidence in Toronto charities.[17] The commission issued cards of endorsement to inform private donors, and as a municipally appointed body, it also advised the city regarding charitable grants. The commission's rigid standards of administration and non-duplication of service were enforced through regular inspections by members and an employed staff whose findings were published in an annual report. In its own words, the Social Service Commission was a 'central bureau to distinguish between deserving and undeserving institutions.'[18]

The coercive intentions of the commission met with massive resistance from the Toronto social welfare establishment. Social workers and public health professionals, charity leaders and social reformers drew together in opposition. Their target was the abolition of the Social Service Commission and reorganization of all charitable work in the city. The essential tool for accomplishing their goals was the establishment of the Federation for Community Service, a joint fund-raising organization in the private sector that would replace both the commission and the city's role in funding private charity.

The Federation for Community Service in Toronto was part of a broad movement towards financial federation that essentially replaced the endorsement bureaus. The first of these federations was organized in Cleveland in 1913, with others following soon after in several large American cities.[19] The initiative came from Cleveland's Chamber of Commerce, whose intention was to refine the idea of endorsement, softening its overt coerciveness and drawing social work administrators into a collaborative arrangement that would eliminate the resistance of local charitable organizations. Financial federation brought charities together in association with each other, and with the business community. Its first purpose was efficient fund-raising, and the prospect of having a greater and more stable source of funds was a powerful incentive for the otherwise reluctant charities.

With the involvement of the agencies, financial federations also took on a direct role as the centre for coordinating all charitable work in a local community. The idea of coordination replaced the earlier and simplistic desire of the endorsement bureaus and the COS to simply eliminate unnecessary or ineffective charitable organizations. Specialization among agencies had grown as 'scientific social work' gained hold, and with it, the problem was seen by the professionals not so much as outright duplication, but more as the problem of overlapping services or of discontinuities in service between agencies that left the needs of people unmet. At the same time, coordination also held out the promise of more efficient operation, which appealed to the businessmen whose philanthropy paid the bills.[20]

Thus the goal of coordination of services, with its promise of both improved service and efficient operation, was central to the common cause that held the alliance of businessmen and social workers together. As a collaborative effort, federation satisfied the same concerns as the endorsement movement while ostensibly ensuring cooperation from the charities themselves. The combined raising of funds was efficient, as was the opportunity provided by controlling their distribution for ensuring that recipient agencies were properly administered. Through central control over funding, federation also held out the hope for improved services by coordinating all charitable effort on a community-wide basis.

In their attempts to avoid the mistakes of the past, financial federations introduced a number of important innovations that accompanied joint fund-raising. Preparation of an overall budget for anticipated needs in the community, methods of budget control for charities, and widespread use of volunteers to solicit money were all unprecedented. In the long run perhaps the most significant difference introduced by financial federations was a requirement that participating charities not solicit money from anyone who had already contributed to their campaign. This requirement redressed a flaw in earlier attempts at joint fund-raising and, in effect, tied the fortunes of the charities to that of the federation. It made cooperation imperative in a way that the crude coercion of earlier attempts could never have achieved.[21]

The organization most responsible for promoting the establishment of a financial federation in Toronto was the Bureau of Municipal Research. The first bureau of municipal research was established in New York City by a group of businessmen and professionals dedicated to bringing about civic reform by applying the principles of scientific management to local government. These principles were first promoted by Frederick W. Taylor, an engineer whose scheme for applying the principles of efficiency to industrial management became a model for the management of the whole of society. Taylor's original scheme included much that pertained only to the factory floor, but it also included systematic management procedures and production control through establishment of a central planning department. It was these latter attributes that reformers adapted to civic government, placing sound management based on science and expertise, planning and rational decision-making at the core of all reform. By substituting 'knowledge for indignation' scientific management became a panacea among a generation of reformers who promoted 'social efficiency' as the key to resolving all the social problems of the day.[22]

The Toronto Bureau of Municipal Research was founded in 1913 following a review of the administration of local government carried out by the New York Bureau at the request of a committee of local businessmen.[23] The New York organization had a strong interest in the reform of charity. Three of its directors had previously worked in philanthropic organizations, and they viewed civic government as similar to that of a 'welfare agency,' with responsibility for measuring and taking into account 'those community needs that were not yet satisfied.'[24] This intermingling of civic responsibility and community welfare was reflected in the pronouncements of the Toronto Bureau: 'A community is more than its government – which is only its best established committee – inasmuch as the whole is greater than a part. The community must develop some all-embracing co-operative administrative method, governmental and non-governmental, to meet the needs of human conservation and development.'[25]

The language of cooperation, and the lofty goals of 'human conservation and development' had appeal for social workers. Equally appealing was the Bureau's commitment to the use of professional expertise in the management of civic affairs, which was easily translated into the management of charity organizations. The efficiency ethic that underlay everything the Bureau espoused was especially appealing for the agency managers, most of whom were men acting as gatekeepers between the profession and the wealthy businessmen upon whose money and civic power their agencies depended. The Bureau of Municipal Research's appearance on the scene and its proposals for a financial federation were welcome indeed for agency workers searching for an alternative to the coercive tactics of the city of Toronto's Social Service Commission.

The alliance of the Toronto Bureau of Municipal Research with the social agencies was fostered by the personal involvement of its director, Horace Brittain. Brittain had come to Toronto from a position with the New York Bureau and was considered an expert in public administration.[26] In addition to his role as director of the Bureau, he was superintendent of Toronto General Hospital in 1917–18, which was a time when hospitals were dependent on charitable donations for services to the poor. He was therefore considered a manager of a charitable organization, and as such was active in the Canadian Conference of Charities and Corrections and taught at the Department of Social Service at the University of Toronto. Perhaps more important, he was also a member of the Rotary Club, which was, the men's fraternal organization that provided the initial funding to launch the new federation.[27]

In 1917 the Bureau of Municipal Research published a scathing attack on the Social Service Commission in a pamphlet entitled *Toronto Gives*. Its lengthy subtitle summed up the underlying philosophy: 'Can A Community Plan Its Giving For Community Purposes Or Must Individuals Continue to Give Without a Knowledge of the Community Needs and What Resources Exist To Meet These Needs? A Discussion of Haphazard Versus Planned Philanthropy Based on a Study of the Facts.'[28] The pamphlet set out a detailed plan for a financial federation, and the following year the

Federation for Community Service was founded precisely along the lines recommended.

The new idea of community needs and the notion of planning in order to meet those needs, both emanating from the Bureau of Municipal Research philosophy that associated civic government with welfare, suggest that poverty was no longer attached to moral failure. But in its pamphlet, the Bureau also deplored the 'casual giving' of Toronto citizens as an 'extremely wasteful and often harmful mode of giving.' Alongside the new philosophy lay the still active nineteenth-century belief that indiscriminate giving would lead to duplication of relief and would foster dependency among the poor. The whole idea was not so much an appeal for largesse and meeting community needs as it was an appeal to eliminate waste, and as such was part of the Bureau's general crusade for efficiency.

The Bureau of Municipal Research also believed firmly in separating public and private responsibility for charity, taking the position that private agencies should be controlled by the private sector, and public services by the public sector. In the Bureau's view, the coordination of public services should be in the hands of professionals in the public service and not in the hands of politically appointed commissions. This view reflected the utilitarian belief in objective science and rational decision-making as a necessary corrective for the corruption and self-interest that was observed in the political realm. The Social Service Commission violated these principles, and the Bureau championed transferring the responsibilities for coordinating public relief from the commission to the Department of Public Health and moving the coordination of private charity to the proposed Federation for Community Service.

The idea that relief should come under the control of public health was not controversial in 1917 as it would become in later years. Since the previous century public health reforms had been at the forefront of attempts to eradicate poverty along with disease. In Toronto there was a history of amiable cooperation between social workers and public health nurses, and Charles Hastings, Toronto's influential medical officer of health, was an active supporter of the growing professionalism among social workers.[29] The Bureau of Municipal Research's campaign for reform of charity was the visible edge of a powerful alliance among an influential segment of the business community, public health professionals, and social work leadership. The alliance supported fully the new profession's struggle for legitimacy and at least on the surface, the desire for agency autonomy.

Following the establishment of the Federation for Community Service in 1918, the agencies, in alliance with the Bureau of Muncipal Research, campaigned to rid the city of the Social Service Commission. They succeeded in 1921, but it was not an easy victory. One of the arguments for retaining the commission was its stated objective of ultimately eliminating all municipal financing of private charity. Also, the nominal control of the Federation by the agencies, however weak in reality, was undoubtedly sufficient to raise scepticism among those who sought assurance that business was in control. These concerns understandably appealed to the politicians, and Toronto City Council's powerful board of control opposed abolition of the Social Service Commission. The two-thirds vote in city council needed to overturn the recommendations of the board of control required vigorous lobbying on the part of the Bureau, the Federation, and its member agencies.[30]

In clear contrast to the Social Service Commission, the structure of Toronto's Federation for Community Service was designed to give the agencies control over its affairs. Delegates of fifty-four of the city's charities formed a majority on a central council that determined policy for the Federation. In addition, a group of associate members representing the contributors was elected by the central council. In 1919 this group included representatives of the Board of Trade, the Canadian Manufacturers Association, the Local Council of Women, the Trades and Labour Council, and the Rotary Club.[31] The intention was that the Federation gradually reach out to include all organizations which had an interest in charity, including services provided by the churches. As one of the initiators of the new organization, the Bureau of Municipal Research was also included, but plans were approved for its automatic retirement from active membership at the end of 1921.[32] (A list of charter agencies is contained in Appendix 1.)

A budget committee was responsible for both raising and distributing money. The budget committee and the central council, roughly representing the dual functions of fund-raising and service provision, met together over important matters in the early years. Although in principle the central council held the ultimate authority, the necessity for joint meetings with the budget committee indicates the power that the financial side of the organization held.

Results of the campaign for funds in the first two years were impressive for a city the size of Toronto at the time, even by today's standards. Collections rose from $282,696 in the first campaign in 1919 to $346,986 in January 1920, and $378,000 in November of the same year. The goal for 1922 was an optimistic $450,000. The number of donors also increased, from 8500 to 30,000. This increase, which was similar to experience in the United States, reflected success in securing donations from working people. Their contributions were small in comparison to the philanthropists of the past, but their numbers certainly increased both participation in and awareness of the charitable work of the agencies.[33]

Despite the initial success in raising funds, the Federation soon began to present problems for the social agencies. Lack of input into the business-dominated budget committee and the tendency for the central committee to make decisions on financial rather than service grounds was causing considerable unrest. One of the early concerns was over the refusal of the Federation to add agency staff to the budget committee. The agencies sought a direct means of providing 'expert advice' when decisions were made on the allocation of money raised. More to the point, their absence at budget meetings meant that important decisions affecting the agencies were once again solely in the hands of businessmen. An agency-dominated policy committee was established in December 1923 to assist the budget committee by providing advice on service standards, problems of duplication, and personnel policy. Ostensibly created to relieve the budget committee of some of its workload, the policy committee in reality served to offset the deteriorating influence of the agencies in budgetary matters. Nevertheless, it did not have the influence that direct participation on the budget committee would have provided, and so agency unhappiness persisted.

The difficulties emerging in the Toronto federation were not unusual. Some social workers in the United States were sharply critical of the whole idea of financial federation, which by the end of the First World War had blossomed into the Community Chest movement. Frank Persons of the New York Charity Organization Society, one of the more vocal critics, expressed the widespread fear of loss of agency autonomy, declaring the Chest plan was 'equivalent to putting the individual agencies in the hands of a receiver.' Others feared that joining in the movement meant placing social work in the hands of financial interests whose primary concerns were to keep costs down and to suppress 'troublesome movements.' Still others saw the federations as promoting mediocrity, moulding the agencies to a single average standard.[34]

Looking back in the fifties, Frank Bruno, a prominent social work educator, suggested that the opposition of social workers to the financial federations was even stronger than the written record seemed to indicate. In his opinion, the federations succeeded because the proliferation of agencies and consequent demands of funders made them the only solution in large cities. The pragmatic reality was that 'many social workers ... did not welcome the Chest; but they accepted it as the way out of a difficult situation.'[35] It appears that the alliance between business and social work in the financial federations of the era after the First World War was a marriage of convenience.

The perceived solution to the threat of loss of agency autonomy from a business-dominated financial federation was the organization of a council of social agencies. An agency-controlled council was seen as providing a means for collective promotion of agency work, and for defence of agency interests when threatened, and a way for social workers and volunteers to work collaboratively on the social problems and issues of the day. In contrast to the efficiency goals of the financial federations, and even clearer contrast to the endorsement bureaus, the councils of social agencies espoused a set of values that emphasized cooperation, democratic participation, and agency rights.

The advocates of the council of social agencies have particularly emphasized its lack of authority, and the necessity for joint action by the separate boards of the respective agencies engaged in any communal undertaking. They have a fear of coercion from some more closely centralized authority with true power, and believe it is possible to bring the light of public opinion to bear upon recalcitrant agencies without surrendering any of their own control over themselves. They believe greater, if less speedy, results come from agreements reached by discussion and ballot than by any dominating leadership.[36]

This may be regarded as a kind of 'organizational populism,' which for many social workers guided beliefs about the proper organization and governance of charity. It reflected a rejection of central authority, a reliance on direct democracy, and shared responsibility rather than hierarchical power, all characteristic of early twentieth-century populism. In the organization of charity, the populist belief in democratic rights of citizens was transposed into democratic rights of individual agencies. Cooperation was a primary underlying value of populist thinking and was consistent with the comradeship of a reform movement. The values of cooperation and democracy that underlay the councils of social agencies contrasted sharply with the authoritarian and hierarchical approach taken by the business-dominated financial federations.

The early councils of social agencies were autonomous and separate from the financial federations. But despite the differences in approach, by the late twenties many had joined together in a single organization. William Norton, a pioneer in the 'cooperative movement' in social work, reasoned that the councils were limited by lack of funds and lack of staff, a situation that gradually drove them into the arms of the financial federations. He observed 'how one council of social agencies after another, after struggling with the task before it, has turned eventually to the financial federation as a supplemental power for reaching its ultimate goal.'[37] The pragmatic need for funds would continue to be the deciding factor in the coming decades as social agencies and their councils weighed the contending desire for autonomy and the need for resources to carry out their work.

Merging of councils of social agencies and financial federations brought an additional and unintended potential advantage. Although they were initially reluctant, the financial federations sought the advice of the councils for their budget committees, believing that 'their duty to contributors to insure a just allocation among the different agencies of the funds so raised was of equal importance to money raising itself.' From this perspective, the federations depended on the councils for 'valid advice,' and the assurance this gave donors that their money was well spent.[38] While control over the funds gave a federation considerable control over agency work, the public nature of the joint fund-raising task required justification of their actions. Thus from the very beginning the relationship between the funding organization and the council of agencies was legitimized by a perceived reciprocity in the allocations process.

Councils of agencies served one more very important purpose in that they were a forum for fostering professional knowledge and skills. They were organized initially by agency managers and volunteers whose concerns went beyond agency autonomy, to include service standards and professional methods. The councils were structured to provide an opportunity for workers in similar areas of work, both paid and volunteer, to meet together in 'functional councils,' and thus were an important tool both for coordination of effort and for discussion and propagation of professional standards. The councils of social agencies in the early years played a role similar to that played by a professional association, although it may be argued that their attention to reform and social action was significantly greater than that given by many professional associations of a later day.

In Toronto both the Neighbourhood Workers Association (NWA), in the field of family work, and the Child Welfare Council, which is the subject of the following chapter, fulfilled the function of providing a meeting ground for professionals and volunteers with similar interests. But they were part of the structure of the Federation for Community Service rather than coming under the umbrella of a council of social agencies as was the case in many other cities. While Toronto was different in this respect, the essential contradictions between the objectives of the social workers and the business community were the same. Not surprisingly, the agitation for a separate council of social agencies that began shortly after the Federation was founded came from the growing professional subculture that was fostered by the NWA and the Child Welfare Council.

The NWA was already in existence when the Federation was founded. It had been established in 1914 at the request of the city, which was seeking ways to improve the coordination of all relief in the community, a task that the Social Services Commission, like Associated Charities before it, was proving unable to fulfil. In Toronto, 'outdoor relief' to the unemployed, able-bodied poor was administered by the House of Industry, which was considered a private charity although virtually all of its funding came from the city. The House of Industry was Toronto's version of the poorhouse, providing not only institutional (indoor) relief, but also relief to poor families living in their own homes (outdoor relief). It was regularly under attack from other charities for its inhumane practices, and since the city was its source of funds, critics frequently directed their complaints to city council. The request in 1914 followed one of these periodic episodes and was an attempt on the part of the city to exert control over the House of Industry without becoming directly involved. The NWA's role was greatly enhanced by a mandate from the municipality to screen all first-time applicants for outdoor relief. The city also 'recommended and requested' that all organizations receiving city grants become members of the NWA.[39]

Thus the coordinating role proposed for the NWA was not new when the Federation for Community Service was founded in 1918. The difference lay in the fact that the Federation was expected to provide funds to enable the NWA to carry out these responsibilities. This arrangement dovetailed nicely with the objective of the Bureau of Municipal Research to place coordination of public relief under the Department of Public Health and to retain coordination of private relief in the private sector. The existing collaboration between the public health sector and social workers would then serve to provide further coordination between the two sectors, helping to achieve the Bureau's goal of a perfectly efficient community.[40] The actual tasks of coordinating services were carried out by district secretaries on the NWA staff whose salaries were paid by the city through the Social Service Commission in the beginning. This not only violated the Bureau's principle of separating public and private responsibilities, but also meant that both organizations claimed authority to supervise the district secretaries and the resulting confusion became another source of conflict between the Social Service Commission and the agencies.

It is essential for understanding the evolution of social work in Toronto to recognize the community work origins of the NWA. While it did indeed become the Family Service Association of Toronto, and it may easily be assumed that it evolved out of the COS movement, this was in fact not the case. The NWA was originally a creation of the settlement houses in Toronto and, if anything, was seen as an alternative to the coerciveness of Associated Charities.

The NWA was itself an organization of organizations, created by bringing together several district conferences that had been established by the settlement house workers to coordinate their work with other agencies in their neighbourhood. Its original organization on a district basis persisted, and this, together with its mandate for coordination, was among its most important characteristics. As such it was still very much a part of the general desire to organize and coordinate services on a city-wide basis, but unlike Associated Charities, it was under the control of professional social workers.

In its early years, the NWA's role did not include the direct provision either of relief or of casework services, although this changed very quickly for several reasons. One was the growing importance of social casework as a method of professional social work practice. Another was continued conflict over the procedures of the House of Industry, which created the necessity for private charities such as the NWA to distribute relief directly. Where previously, private charities could send their clients to the House of Industry to obtain relief, casework and relief now went together.[41] But the addition of casework services did not replace the community work tasks of the NWA's professional staff. Social workers simply assumed that both were part of their practice.

The executive secretary of the NWA was Frank Neil Stapleford, who was a major figure, along with Brittain and Hastings, in the organization of charity in Toronto. Stapleford was hired in 1918 with the help of a donation from the Rotary Club to reorganize the NWA and to organize the Federation for Community Service. He was a Methodist minister who had left the pulpit to work in the Fred Victor Mission in Toronto. His work at

the mission led him to become active in settlement work and he participated in the early district conferences that preceded the formal establishment of the NWA. Stapleford's social gospel persuasions gave him a keen
sense of mission in the reform and reorganization of social welfare. Like
Brittain, he was an avid Rotarian, and it is probable that this connection
was responsible for drawing the Rotary Club into participation in the
founding of the Toronto Federation. Stapleford relinquished his responsibilities as 'organizing secretary' of the Federation at the end of the first
year, but from then on his name appears on the list of almost every important committee within the Federation. Easily one of the most prominent
and influential persons in Toronto social work, Frank Stapleford continued as the general secretary of the NWA until his death in 1952.[42]

The existence of the NWA, and harmonious relations between social work
and business fostered by the campaign against the Social Service Commission seem to have precluded the need for the agencies in Toronto to
develop a council of social agencies alongside the Federation for Community Service. But, as already noted, friction between the social work interests and the financial interests of the Federation emerged very quickly.
The preoccupation with financial matters on the part of the Federation's
central council and lack of agency input into the budget committee
prompted a growing desire for an organization that would better serve
the agencies. Toronto social workers, like their counterparts elsewhere,
began to advocate the establishment of a council of their own that would
counterbalance the domination of financial interests and allow concentration on improving service standards.
   Poor relations between the agencies and the Federation were aggra-
vated by the fund-raising woes that emerged following the Federation's
initial success. In 1922 the estimated shortfall was $22,665, six per cent of
approved agency budgets of $372,471. While 1923 saw some improve-
ment, the campaign returns took a downward turn again the following
year. Toronto experienced a sharp economic recession in the early twenties, which provides part of the explanation for the poor financial picture.
More likely, the problem was simply a stabilization of fund-raising capacity
following the surge of goodwill generated by the Federation's optimistic
claims at its inception. Whatever the reason, a shortfall in campaign proceeds meant making unanticipated financial decisions. The Federation
decided to reduce expenditures by making all agency budgets subject to
revision by the budget committee based on the agencies' monthly financial statements. Any sense of reciprocity in the allocations process had

clearly disappeared. This was the ultimate in control and could only have increased the agencies' desire for genuine participation in the budget committee. The response of the Federation was the establishment of the policy committee noted above.[43]

The tension between the agencies and the Federation was further intensified by the growing professional concerns of the social workers over standards of service. In this regard, the importance of councils of social agencies for introducing and encouraging professional standards became the issue. One of the approaches for raising standards of service popular with social workers at this time was what was called the survey method. It relied on scientific methods in gathering information as well as on social work expertise in that a survey was conducted by a senior practitioner called in to advise the community on what changes were needed to improve services. Two successive surveys carried out in Toronto by highly respected social work experts from the United States came out with strong recommendations for an agency-controlled council of social agencies.

The first of these surveys was carried out by C.C. Carstens, executive director of the Child Welfare League of America, and was finished in the spring of 1925. Part of Carstens' concern centred on the lack of attention given by both the central council and the budget committee of the Federation to service issues. He criticized both bodies for their single-minded concentration on financial matters: 'We heartily commend the care and patience with which financial decisions are arrived at, but the question must be raised as to securing vitality for the common deliberative process on other than financial questions.' In Carstens' view, an independent council of social agencies should 'match the unified financial plan of the community with a unified planning and deliberating body.'[44]

The Carstens report provided a detailed design for such a council including the recommendation that the central council of the NWA become a committee of a council of social agencies. The central council was the umbrella for the district councils that brought NWA social workers together with other workers in various neighbourhoods throughout the city. In effect, Carstens was proposing transferring the coordinating function of the NWA to the new organization. He noted that the NWA had paved the way for the Federation and placed its stamp on the Federation's organizational character, but he suggested that the NWA central council no longer filled the need for 'a common city-wide meeting place for all agencies.'[45]

The NWA was indeed experiencing major changes in its role and function. Frank Stapleford was thoroughly committed to the importance of professional methods in social work. Under his guidance the NWA had added social casework to the coordinating functions of the district secretaries. In many respects, the NWA had become an all-purpose social work agency, and social work in Toronto had evolved as a practice that placed community work and casework back to back as two sides of the same coin.

Carstens had conducted his survey in haste, with little input from the local social work community and without consulting Stapleford, who was out of town at the time. His report reflected the emphasis on specialization that characterized the training of social workers in the United States and assumed that the NWA was primarily a family agency. Toronto social workers were outraged. They welcomed the idea of an independent council of social agencies, but they rejected out of hand the details of Carstens' recommendations because they failed to retain 'all that is valuable in the NWA – especially the local district groups.'[46] Toronto services had continued to organize themselves around district councils, which were in effect gatherings of professional workers and volunteers from many different agencies and organizations to exchange information and coordinate their efforts. The gathering of the district councils under the umbrella of the NWA's central council was an important local institution and not one to tamper with.

Despite the anger over Carstens' recommendations regarding the NWA, the idea of a council of social agencies for Toronto was considered a good one. A request was made to Francis H. McLean early in 1926 to survey family welfare work and to report on the 'need for a General Council of Agencies in Toronto' adapted for 'local conditions.' McLean was field director for the American Association for Organizing Family Social Work and a leading advocate of the idea of a council of social agencies to carry out community welfare planning and coordination.[47] McLean was undoubtedly familiar with the criticisms directed at the Carstens report. His own report did not have the kind of detailed recommendations made by Carstens, and he was very careful in his discussion of the work and structure of 'that unique district organization of the Neighbourhood Workers Association,' which, he observed, was already known to his organization.[48] But his report was very firm on the need for a council of social agencies to protect the rights of the agencies to be heard and to be directly represented by their own board and staff.

With the establishment of a Community Chest the need for a Central Council [of Social Agencies] becomes greater because of the temptation that comes to a Chest in the absence of a Council, to resort to coercive methods ... The great big danger in Community Chests today is the wielding of great power by a comparatively small group, even though some of them are trained social workers ... The Council of the Federation for Community Service has never and could never have functioned as a Council of Social Agencies, because the individual agencies are not therein represented.

This was the direct democracy of organizational populism. In McLean's opinion, a council of social agencies would offset the lack of representation and central control of the Federation's central council, and also overcome its preoccupation with finances.[49]

McLean was generally critical of the fund-raising side of the Federation, suggesting that 'Toronto has a better opportunity for social work than the support it receives from the community.' Appealing to the booster instincts of business, he observed that 'Toronto because it stands as a city of influence not only in the province but in all Canada, has a special obligation to keep its mind receptive to good ideas.'[50] He saw an 'outstanding need' to secure greater understanding of the services provided on the part of an increasing number of men and suggested what must have been a novel idea of establishing case committees of young businessmen in conjunction with the Board of Trade loan fund. This loan fund had been established in the recession of 1921–3 to assist family agencies on a case by case basis when relief clients were unable to pay utilities and rent.[51] McLean was certainly not suggesting a businessman's committee to review each request as a measure of control. Rather the suggestion reflected his belief that the business community was unaware of and therefore unconcerned about the extent and nature of service needed. He assumed that given the 'facts' of the matter, support would follow.

The reception given the McLean report was warmer than that given Carstens, although it was not without its critics. The Federation for Community Service formed a constitution review committee, which proposed a watered-down version of McLean's suggestions that virtually eliminated agency control. This prompted the agencies to raise the spectre of non-cooperation with the Federation unless there were safeguards that made clear 'the supremacy of the council element over the financial.'[52] With this fundamental principle made clear, plans proceeded for a vote on a new constitution at the annual meeting to be held in the spring of 1927.

At this point, plans for reorganizing the Federation to include a council of social agencies came to a complete halt. A major conflict that had been brewing for several years between the professional social workers and the church-controlled Roman Catholic agencies exploded into the open. The outcome was the rupturing of the Federation with the departure of the Catholic agencies and the abandonment for the time being of plans to re-organize. Once again it was the recommendations of C.C. Carstens that led to the crisis. In this instance however, his recommendations had struck sympathetic chords in the professional community.

The issue of participation of Roman Catholic agencies in the Federa-tion went back to 1922 when concerns were expressed at the annual meet-ing that 'certain agencies' should be entirely supported from denomin-ational funds. This vague concern grew to specific criticism by 1924 when the policy committee reported that there was an 'impression in the mind of the public that the Roman Catholic organizations receive too large a proportion of the funds distributed; that Roman Catholic organizations duplicate others doing a similar type of work, thus defeating some of the fundamental aims of the Federation.'[53]

Attempts were made to try to convince the Catholic agencies to forgo their autonomy and merge with their Protestant counterparts for the sake of unity and the principle of federation. Meetings held with the arch-bishop and with the agencies concerned to resolve the issue before the upcoming campaign were unsuccessful. It was not until the following fall that the budget committee agreed to fund Carstens' survey.[54]

Up until this point, the primary rationale for attempting to merge the Catholic and non-Catholic agencies was the perceived efficiency that would result and, perhaps more important, the effect that negative public attitudes would have on the campaign. Anti-Catholicism was strong in Toronto in the 1920s and the fund-raisers were convinced that any appearance of sectarianism would result in plunging campaign results. No one questioned the underlying Protestant bias of the so-called non-sectarian agencies.

Carstens was a booster for professionalism. His report was adamant that all services come under the control and supervision of professional social workers to ensure conformity to proper standards of practice. He not only criticized the Catholic agencies for duplicating the work of the 'non-sectarian' agencies, he was scornful of their use of 'kindly volunteers' rather than trained workers, which he saw as being fifteen to twenty years behind the times. Carstens proposed bringing all volunteers under the supervision of the new professionals, and this meant merging Catholic agencies with the mainline Protestant-supported agencies since that is where the trained social workers were found.

Carstens was not simply being insensitive and arrogant. He reflected the narrow professionalism that characterized social work's struggle to shift from a moral crusade to a secular and scientific pursuit. Stapleford, despite his social gospel roots, typified this shift when he suggested that 'undue importance' was being attached to the need for Catholic workers and that social casework could 'be done quite apart from religious considerations.'[55] But the substitution of professional workers and scientific method for Christian guidance ran contrary to Catholic beliefs about the need for religious influence. Furthermore, Carstens had advocated separation of child and family welfare, which violated Catholic approaches to working with the family, and his scorn for 'kindly volunteers' had dismissed the centuries-old Catholic practice of volunteering to work with the poor. The Catholic agencies were not without standards of service; their standards simply rested on a different set of values. It is little wonder that they decided to withdraw from the Federation rather than see their values overrun by the secular science of social work.

The antipathy towards sectarian agencies seems to have receded during the period of the McLean survey. Once that was finished, the issue surfaced again at a most inopportune moment. In May 1927, just at the point when the agencies were considering who their nominees might be for the proposed council of social agencies, the Federation's budget committee received a letter from the chairman of the campaign committee advising of widespread opinion that the Catholic agencies received a larger share of the funds than was publicly shown. He suggested that this had led to a decline in contributions and advised an 'amiable withdrawal' of both the Anglican- and Catholic-sponsored agencies, leaving no church-affiliated agencies in the Federation. The response of the Federation was an acknowledgment that 'the presence of Roman Catholic organizations in the Federation is a barrier to securing adequate funds for the support of the work.'[56]

This incident precipitated another round of special meetings, consultations with major donors, and a review of American experience. Talks were held with the Anglicans and some petty grievances resolved, but it was the Roman Catholic agencies that were the chief target. The member agencies expressed concern that the Catholics had not contributed their share of money, but they were more concerned that they had not been cooperative 'in attaining the best standards of work with children, and in duplicating general services.' Neither the fund-raisers nor the social workers were happy with the recalcitrant Roman Catholics. In the end, a 'statement' was sent to the archbishop. Its contents are not part of the record, but the annual meeting of the Federation held in January 1928 reported the separation of the Catholic from the 'non-sectarian' agencies.[57]

The withdrawal of the Roman Catholic agencies brought the plans for establishing a council of social agencies to a halt. Bad feelings that had undoubtedly been generated between the agencies made organization of a new cooperative venture impossible, at least for the time being. Significantly, the departure of the Catholic agencies resulted in the appearance of another financial federation in Toronto and badly compromised the ideals of comprehensiveness in the coordination of services. Where previously there had been two federations – a Federation of Jewish Philanthropies had been established in 1917 just before the founding of the Federation for Community Service – there were now three.

What stands out during the first decade of federation is the social workers' struggle for legitimacy and eagerness to establish norms of a secular and scientific practice. As an agency-based profession, social work also sought autonomy for the organizations for which they worked, and struggled to put in place forms of democratic control that flew in the face of the hierarchical and businesslike approaches of the financial federation. What they failed to recognize in the rush to escape the overt morality of an earlier time was the new morality of science and efficiency.

The union of social work and business interests that remained under the umbrella of the Federation for Community Service moved into the depression years in a very fragile condition. The desire for a separate council of social agencies would continue. So too would the desire on the part of the business community to bring all of the charitable activities in Toronto under the control of one central organization. The economic crisis, which affected both agencies and business deeply, would simply exacerbate the problems, and conflict inevitably returned.

CHAPTER FOUR

Direct Action versus Slow Interpretation

Efforts to establish a council of social agencies in Toronto were renewed early in 1931. Toronto was one of the few large cities in North America that did not have such a council, and continued concern over professional standards, agency influence on budgetary matters, and coordination of services kept the idea alive. But the economic and social climate of the thirties added a dimension that had not existed in the twenties. The strain on agency budgets, the increasing activism of some social workers, as well as the increasing attention given to social issues by the business community all heightened the desire for such an organization, while at the same time adding complications and slowing the process down. The perceived purpose and motives for establishing a council became sharply differentiated, affecting not so much the question of whether a council was needed, but how it should be organized.

Part of the contention lay in the long-standing question over whether such a council should be part of or independent of the Federation for Community Service. Added to this was a growing concern within social work over whether it was proper to engage in direct social action as opposed to 'slow interpretation,' a question of importance for an organization expected to carry the responsibility for leading the profession in its work in the community.

The conflict between these two approaches to social change was clearly political. 'Slow interpretation' reflected the belief in the objectivity of science and the idea that a professional should provide scientific knowledge in a 'neutral' and 'non-judgmental' way. It was consistent with utilitarian notions of expert guidance for rational decision-making. Slow interpretation was the preferred approach for many, if not most, social workers, who believed that societal improvement would result from providing the facts and ensuring opportunities in the community for learning and participating. It linked with the growing interest in adult education and, like other earlier approaches to reform, had both radical and conservative potential. Direct action, on the other hand, was rooted in the belief that there are fundamental conflicts within the social and economic order that can be resolved only through direct and deliberate intervention in the political system. As a youthful Saul Alinsky put it to the National Conference of Social Work in 1938, 'We must ... forsake our technical trowels and turn to the steam-shovel of social action.' It was a contentious issue among social workers at the time, causing considerable debate and difference of opinion.[1]

In Toronto, this conflict took on a gendered aspect that flowed from the debates over whether a community-wide council of social agencies could be developed on the base of the existing Child Welfare Council, which was largely a women's organization. While it was seen by some social workers as the natural organization to assume the broad function of a council of social agencies, others were opposed to the direct action approach to social change taken by its leadership. The women who led the Child Welfare Council challenged the conservative and safer route of slow interpretation favoured by their male colleagues, who stood between the Council's interests and the powerful business-dominated financial federation. Direct action also required a degree of autonomy not possible if a council of social agencies was to be an integral part of the Federation. It was a protracted struggle that finally ended, at least temporarily, with the laying down of the Child Welfare Council and founding of the independent Toronto Welfare Council in 1937.

In the fall of 1918, Frank Stapleford, in his capacity as organizing secretary of the Toronto Federation for Community Service, convened a meeting for the purpose of organizing the Child Welfare Council. When it was created, the Federation had two ready-made 'functional councils' to do the work of agency coordination. The central council of the Neighbourhood Workers Association (NWA) coordinated the work of several district councils and through them the work of family agencies. The Federation of Settlement Houses concentrated on services for immigrants and poor people in the working-class districts of the city.[2] But the lack of a formal organization of agencies in the field of child welfare left a serious gap, given the attention that child welfare matters were receiving at the time.[3] The meeting was well attended by thirty-one women and men, most of whom were prominent leaders in Toronto's child welfare circles. The Federation for Community Service promoted the new organization's importance in businesslike terms: 'The Child Welfare Council is a newly-formed and much-needed organization for the purpose of co-ordinating the child welfare work of the city. The children constitute the greatest asset of the community. The Council exists to prevent the loss of any of this asset, and 57 organizations are co-operating in the work.'[4] The Council's importance was also reflected in the number of organizations that joined, many of which were not members of the Federation but nevertheless felt the need to participate in such a council.

The new Council's objectives were consistent with the prevailing emphasis on coordinating charitable work and improving standards of service. Sections on health, dependency, delinquency, and education were established to facilitate discussion and interaction between workers with similar interests. The word 'dependency' replaced 'pauperism' in the discourse, although it had much the same meaning, and child-care workers came at the issue from the perspective of the effects on children of parental poverty and unemployment, and of inadequate wages and relief. Raising professional standards was also viewed as important, leading to events such as the sponsorship of a lecture by American social work expert Edith Abbott, director of the U.S. Children's Bureau, and the survey by C.C. Carstens of the American Child Welfare League discussed in the previous chapter.

At first the Child Welfare Council was effectively under the supervision of the Neighbourhood Worker's Association. Indeed the lines between the Federation, the NWA, and the new Council were unclear in the beginning, since the same people were active in the leadership of all three. Reverend Peter Bryce, founding president of the Federation and president of the NWA, also served on the Child Welfare Council. Frank Stapleford, general secretary of both the Federation and the NWA, was on the executive of the Council, and a number of the NWA's senior social workers were also active. A new constitution and the appointment of an executive secretary in 1923 marked a turning point for the relative independence of the organization. In January of that year, membership stood at sixty-seven persons, representing thirty-three agencies plus eighteen associate (individual) members; by the annual meeting in May this had risen to eighty-seven persons, representing forty agencies and twenty-seven associates. At this point, Stapleford and Bryce retired as officers, confident that the Child Welfare Council was finally 'on its feet,' leaving Robert Mills, a statistician and administrator who had recently taken up the position of general secretary of the Toronto Children's Aid Society, to head its activities as president.[5]

The male leadership of the Child Welfare Council in the early years reflected the prevailing norms and assumptions about the necessity of having men in charge. But child welfare in the twenties, while not exclusively a woman's issue, was certainly dominated by reform-minded women. The Council's rank and file included many of the most active and prominent women in Toronto's child welfare movement. It would not be long before they asserted their hold on the organization, taking positions of authority and responsibility on the Council's executive. Nevertheless, men like Mills and Stapleford would continue to have influence out of all proportion to their numbers within the Council, primarily because of the links they provided between this essentially female organization and the male-dominated Federation.

From the beginning, the Child Welfare Council had strong ties with the Local Council of Women, undoubtedly because of overlapping membership and areas of mutual concern. Florence Huestis, one of the prominent leaders in the National Council of Women of Canada and a president of its Toronto branch, participated in the organizing meeting and served as chairwoman of its section on dependency. In 1928 the Child Welfare Council became an organizational member of the Local Council of Women, and its president convened the Local Council of Women's child welfare committee. Together, the two organizations formed joint committees and mounted exhibits at the Canadian National Exhibition held in Toronto every summer.[6]

A very active and dedicated core of women provided strong and sustained leadership during the Child Welfare Council's brief existence. One of the most prominent was Barbara Blackstock, who took over from Robert Mills as president in 1925. Her professional training as a nurse and midwife was taken in England, and was an unorthodox education for a woman of her class. Blackstock's primary interest was in the need for home services, and she was instrumental in founding the Red Cross Visiting Housekeepers (later Homemakers) Association. Her efforts to organize housekeeping services provide early evidence of her unconventional activities. She worked in the face of opposition by her own profession of nursing, which, in an attempt to consolidate its position as handmaiden to the male-dominated medical profession, fought 'untrained' services in the home.[7]

In 1933 Blackstock married H.J. Cody, bishop of the Anglican church, president of the University of Toronto, and former minister of education in the Conservative government of William Howard Hearst. Although she resigned as president of the Council upon her marriage, she remained at the centre of activity. While fitting the stereotype of the conservative upper middle-class woman in many respects, Blackstock Cody was no conformist. She fully supported the direct action stance of the Council, and used her position in Toronto society to great advantage in the pursuit of unorthodox ends.

Barbara Blackstock Cody was followed in the presidency by Lois Fraser, whose husband, Kaspar Fraser, was a well-connected corporate lawyer.[8] Fraser held an MA in physiology and had a particular interest in nutrition programs for children in day nurseries. Her leadership of the Child Welfare Council continued throughout its difficult final years to its demise in 1937. Unlike Cody, she remained active and eventually resumed her position of leadership in the new Toronto Welfare Council.

Another central figure was Margaret Gould, who became the Council's full-time secretary in 1930 and remained in that position until the end. Gould was a social worker and journalist with an interest in labour. She had worked as a writer for the Canadian Brotherhood of Railway Employees and was a member of the growing democratic left in Toronto. Along with several other members of the Council, she was a member of the Toronto branch of the socialist League for Social Reconstruction.[9] In 1934, Gould visited Russia to learn and write about its system of health care, a trip that left her open to charges of being a communist. She was both idealistic and articulate, and these attributes along with her position as executive staff meant that she was very influential in shaping the Council's philosophy and work. When the Child Welfare Council was disbanded, an eventuality for which some held her responsible, Gould took a position as journalist and editorial writer with the Toronto *Star*. From that position she continued to wield influence, reputedly writing most of the *Star*'s left-leaning editorials on social issues in the late thirties and forties.[10]

In general, the Child Welfare Council attracted a group of social workers who may be described as leaders in their profession. Agnes McGregor, the lone woman and only full-time person on the faculty of the University of Toronto's School of Social Work in 1918, was among the founders and served as the Council's first secretary. Another woman active from the beginning was Ethel Dodds Parker. Parker was executive secretary of the Council from 1925–7, active on its committees throughout the thirties, and a staff member and eventually director of the city's Division of Social Welfare, and also a president of the Canadian Association of Social Workers. The Council's executive consistently included social workers such as Mrs J.S. Driscoll and Kathleen (Kay) Gorrie who held senior positions on the staff of the NWA. Three of these women later became agency executive directors, Parker of the national YWCA, Driscoll of the York County Children's Aid Society, and Gorrie of the Protestant Children's Homes. Gorrie was also to serve briefly as the first executive secretary of the Toronto Welfare Council when it was established in 1937. Their career paths lend credence to a Child Welfare Council claim to being a training ground for professional women seeking to assume a public role.[11]

The Child Welfare Council placed social reform goals among its priorities at an early stage. This was in spite of the fact that activism was generally at an ebb during the twenties. The annual meeting in 1924 divided the work of the Council into three general areas, one of which was 'concerted action.' Communication and sharing among the members with a view to raising professional standards, and the dissemination of information and 'inspiration' to the public comprised the other two. This last function served both the struggle of the profession for legitimacy and the need for public support for the Council's social reform objectives.[12]

At the same annual meeting, the Child Welfare Council reported a major initiative, undertaken in cooperation with the Social Service Council of Ontario, to seek reform of the province of Ontario's responsibilities for child welfare. Charlotte Whitton, who had recently left the position of assistant secretary of the Social Service Council of Canada to work towards the establishment of a national child welfare organization, was invited to speak. She focused on the 'lack of unity in Social Welfare laws' and the need for 'centralized administration' of the province's responsibilities for child welfare. Ontario child welfare legislation was not only criticized as inadequate, it was seen as inconsistent and fragmented, and the objective was to convince the province to consolidate its responsibilities and place them under the control of a central administrator, preferably a social worker.[13]

While this objective certainly reflected the more conservative desire to coordinate services, it also had elements of political activism. The Child Welfare Council took an active and influential part in a coalition of organizations that successfully advocated establishment of the Royal Commission on Public Welfare in Ontario in 1929. Known as the Ross Commission, it led to the organizing of the Ontario Department of Public Welfare in 1931. While the Toronto Child Welfare Council cannot take sole credit for these provincial developments, the overlap in leadership and the relative status the Council was given on the inter-organizational group that was established to interact with the royal commission are indicative of its influence.[14]

The interest in reorganizing public services for children and families reflected a major preoccupation with legislation and the role of the state in social welfare. From the beginning, the Council based its actions on a philosophy of 'fundamental rights of childhood' and a comprehensive scheme of services and benefits that it envisioned as available in any community. The philosophy implied at least a regulatory role for the state and, in the case of child welfare, direct public provision of benefits such as mothers' allowances, and indirect benefits such as support for day nurseries. While state regulation has conservative implications insofar as it could be (and is) used to reinforce and enforce class and traditional family structure,[15] the idea of children's rights was nevertheless a real departure from older notions of charity and the sacrosanct family, and its promotion marked the Council as a 'ginger group' in the welfare politics of the twenties and thirties. The Council kept a sustained watching brief on all legislation pertaining to children, and was particularly active in promoting changes to the Children's Protection Act, Deserted Wives Act, Unmarried Parents Act, and Adoption Act at the provincial level.

At the local level, public health, recreation, and education also received a great deal of time and attention. Interests were divided between what were perceived as the different needs of 'normal' children and 'handicapped and delinquent' children. Promotion of healthy family life was a chief concern, and availability of maternal and infant health care, day nurseries, playgrounds, and public health programs in the schools were seen as important. School attendance was a particular concern in the twenties and the Council lobbied for 'vocational guidance' programs, regulation of child labour, and increasing the school leaving age. In the interest of prevention of delinquency, the Council worried over such things as what children read, what they saw at the movies, and supervision of dance halls. A sustained interest in 'illegitimacy' also pertained to both family life and reducing delinquency. On one hand, mother and child needed care, and adoption placement was critical. But there were also undoubtedly overtones of prevention of immoral behaviour on the part of young women who mostly shouldered the blame for the sin of pregnancy out of wedlock. And finally, when all else failed, the Council concerned itself with standards of institutional care of children, raising the juvenile age, and strengthening the role of the juvenile courts.

When the effects of the Depression took hold in the thirties, the Council's attention concentrated largely on concerns for the health of mothers and children in families where the male breadwinner was unemployed. Nutrition became the major plank in a vigorous campaign carried out in alliance with the Red Cross Visiting Housekeepers to maintain the health of families and stave off the worst of the effects of unemployment and underemployment. The Council actively promoted school meals and as described in Chapter 5, laid the groundwork through its alliance with the Red Cross Visiting Houskeepers for a major campaign both for adequate relief benefits and for minimum wages to allow families to maintain a life of 'health and decency.'

Through all of its public efforts, the Child Welfare Council found it necessary to fight a constant battle on behalf of professional social work. Their efforts in this regard were aimed at promoting professional standards within the agencies and at convincing an increasingly sceptical public that trained workers were needed in every 'social work post.' Referring to the call of the Ross Commission for 'follow-up work' with people coming out of institutions, the council despaired: 'For all social work there should be a corps of trained social workers in Ontario. There is practically no such thing. This work cannot be done by anyone who has merely the inclination and goodwill to do such work. It requires, in addition, special training and experience.'[16] The solution seen by the Council was support for schools of social work in all universities in the province and for graduate education for social workers in addition to four years at the undergraduate level.

While the Child Welfare Council had a relatively independent life of its own, it nevertheless was organizationally tied to the Federation for Community Service. The upheaval that followed the departure of the Roman Catholic agencies from the Federation in the late twenties necessitated a constitutional rearrangement, including a board structure that had not previously existed.The membership of the Federation board of directors, which held final authority over all matters of substance, was clearly the locus of business interests. In 1930 its ranks included J.E. Atkinson, publisher of the Toronto *Star*; C.L. Burton, President and general manager of Simpsons; M. Ross Gooderham, vice-president of Manufacturer's Life Insurance Co.; W.C. Laidlaw, president of Laidlaw Lumber Co.; John J. Gibson, vice-president and general manager of the Chartered Trust and Executor Co.; and J.H. Gundy, president of Wood Gundy and Co. Once formed, the Federation board grew steadily throughout the thirties in size and in the prominence of its members. From 1930 to 1937, the board tripled in size from 14 to 47 members. In 1939, after the Toronto Welfare

Council was formed, the Board membership leaped to 102 members and represented not just a cross-section of Toronto's business community but a cross-section of a national corporate and political elite. The proportion of women remained the same, growing from 2 to 15.[17] In short, the Federation for Community Service became a large, influential, business-dominated organization holding considerable power over the development and funding of social services in Toronto. As such, agency participation and influence became a critical issue.

The source of agency participation lay primarily in the functional councils of the Federation, which at the end of the twenties comprised the central council of the NWA and the Child Welfare Council. But these two organizations, while representative and vibrant, were remote from the formal centre of decision-making within the Federation. A large Federation council on which all agency members had one vote was also in existence, but had little authority. The agency voice, where it had any hope of being heard, was through the social policy committee, which carried the primary responsibility for advising the Federation board on matters concerning agency relations and service issues. The makeup of the board, from which social workers were conspicuously absent, meant there was a lack of basic information about service issues, forcing it to rely on the social policy committee for information and opinion. In effect, this committee was in the position of broker between the two major interest groups making up the Federation – the business and agency communities.

The social policy committee was also an arena where gender differences inevitably came to the surface. In the beginning it had a balance of men and women, including strong representation from the Child Welfare Council. The committee membership of fifteen was predominantly professional, nine of whom were women, including Council activists Cody, Parker, and Gorrie. The six men included Stapleford, Mills, and Edward J. Urwick, director of the Department of Social Work at the University of Toronto.[18] In contrast, the membership of the Council's executive committee, stood at twelve in 1930, only one of whom was male. Social workers such as Mills and Urwick, who served on both the Child Welfare Council and the social policy committee, were particularly influential, standing between the men of the business community, who were certainly more inclined to listen to other men, especially if they held administrative positions, and the women in the Child Welfare Council, who regarded them as professional colleagues.

While the social policy committee carried an important role on behalf of social workers and the agencies, it clearly did not do the work of a council of social agencies. One of the principal motives for such a council was the recurring dream of having a vehicle for coordination of services. Both the business and social work communities regularly voiced this desire, although as pointed out in the previous chapter, for the very different reasons of cost efficiency and service effectiveness. In order to coordinate services, it was thought necessary to involve all the services in a community, both public and private. It was commonly agreed, therefore, that one reason for having a council was the need for an inclusive organization that would involve the Catholic and Jewish agencies, the civic departments of health and public welfare, and agencies not currently part of the Federation for Community Service. This included large and important agencies like the YWCA, the YMCA, and the Red Cross with its Visiting Housekeepers.

The matter was given added urgency by Toronto's mayor, William J. Stewart, who was agitating for amalgamation of the three financial federations. The mayor's concern came from a desire for greater efficiency and was no doubt related to the efforts at the time to contain municipal costs as the economic crisis deepened. There was an assumption early in the Depression that properly organized private charity would take the strain off the relief budget, partly because it used philanthropic rather than tax dollars, but mostly because of the persistent belief that unemployment was a matter of individual circumstances and that 'good' casework would result in putting people back to work. Entering the Depression, many social workers shared this faith in individual causes of unemployment and believed fervently that their professional interventions would result in reducing relief rolls.[19] For most, this belief did not last for long, but the political and economic interests in the community clung to the idea throughout the decade.[20]

Given the recent debacle, the Federation for Community Service was reluctant to enter into negotiations with the Federation of Catholic Charities. Rather than wasting time on the unlikely prospect of bringing the three financial federations together, and refusing to oppose the mayor publicly, the Federation focused on a council of social agencies that would presumably accomplish many of the same objectives.[21] From this point of view, the primary purpose of a council was to coordinate services and improve cost efficiency, a purpose better accomplished from within the Federation, where it could be backed by the power of the purse. It diverged from the view that saw a council of social agencies representing agency and professional interests, better accomplished from an independent position.

The Federation for Community Service gave the social policy committee the task of re-examining the need for a council of social agencies. The
committee began by identifying existing organizations carrying a social
planning function. It was a fairly long list, including the Federation council itself, the NWA, and the Child Welfare Council. In addition, it was also
understood that both the Council of Jewish Social Agencies and the Federation of Catholic Charities were considering some kind of coordinating
body. Barbara Blackstock, president of the Child Welfare Council at the
time, declared this fragmentation of effort a waste of time, and advocated
a central planning organization that would preserve the values of the
existing organizations but provide central leadership.[22] This point of view
added weight to the argument for an independent council of social agencies, given the unlikely prospect of the Jewish and Catholic federations
agreeing to become part of a planning body that was within the Federation for Community Service.

The social policy committee responded by asking two prominent members of the Child Welfare Council, Margaret Nairn and Ethel Dodds
Parker, to draw up a proposal. Nairn had been a volunteer assistant to
Francis H. McLean when he carried out his survey in 1926. Parker was
currently a member of the Council executive committee. The model, presented by the two women in February 1931, contained a number of
important differences from previous proposals, including a new name,
Toronto Welfare Council.

Unlike McLean's proposal, which had left the question of the relationship of a council to the Federation wide open, Nairn and Parker were
clear on the need for it to be separate. Nor did their proposal avoid the
issue of fundamental change for the NWA that had been suggested by
C.C. Carstens in 1925 and vigorously rejected. The new proposal recommended that the central council of the NWA become the 'family section'
of a council of social agencies and the district councils of the NWA
become 'district branches.' The Child Welfare Council would become a
section on children, the Federation of Settlements a cultural section, and
provision was made for a section on health 'if and when' the health agencies agreed.

The proposal assumed that funding would come from all three financial federations. Interestingly, although a new council would include the
proposed municipal Department of Public Welfare, city funding was
deemed not advisable. This may not have been because of distrust of the
municipality. The agencies were actively involved in planning for the new
department, and the Child Welfare Council had been active in promoting

the establishment of the newly established provincial Department of Public Welfare. It is more likely that the principle of maintaining a clear distinction between public and private sector responsibilities that had guided the establishment of the Federation for Community Service in the beginning remained paramount. The introduction of municipal funding would have violated this principle.[23]

The proposal drawn up by the two women contained all the elements considered ideal by many social workers. It was comprehensive in scope, organizationally independent from the three financial federations, and controlled by professionals and the agencies for whom they worked. Nevertheless, initial reaction when the proposal was presented to a special meeting of the social policy committee was not encouraging. The objection was raised that a separate organization would result in 'completely divorcing Federation for Community Service from social planning,' just when the Depression made critical its social planning functions. This objection revealed the importance of coordination of services, with its underlying assumptions of cost efficiency. The alternative suggested was to simply broaden the membership of the existing Federation council, but this merely represented tinkering with the status quo. The conflict between the two approaches – a separate council versus one integrated with the Federation – was beginning to heat up. The proposal was tabled in favour of the earlier issue of helping organize a municipal welfare department.[24]

The plans for a council of social agencies were seriously affected by funding considerations at this point. By 1932 the deepening economic depression was having a severe effect on both fund-raising and the need for services, and by the following year, the Federation and its agencies were suffering a financial crisis. Campaign returns for 1933 were only 91 per cent of the previous year, necessitating drastic measures to deal with the shortfall.[25] This demanded extraordinary effort on the part of everyone, and, if for no other reason, the sheer quantity of work and the problems involved made the effort required to organize a separate council of social agencies an intolerable burden.

The economic crisis also fed concerns that funding a new council would siphon scarce dollars away from the agencies. These were serious obstacles in the path of those seeking a separate organization. In tight financial times, the natural tendency of financial federations is to restrict the admission of additional agencies. This view was expressed by Robert Mills, who went on record as opposing the admission of any new agency to the Federation, including a council of social agencies, on the grounds that it would adversely affect the funding of existing members.[26] As general secretary of the Children's Aid Society, he was expressing the view of agency administrators. But Mills was also opposed to any sudden or drastic change in the status quo. He advocated allowing a council to grow gradually from the base of an existing small group, and withdrew from the planning committee for a council of social agencies, stating that he had always believed there to be 'unusual and important difficulties' that made such a council in Toronto a difficult proposition. This appears to be a version of the 'unique Toronto' argument that revolved around the role of the district councils of the NWA. While this was certainly part of the problem, his letter of resignation also reveals that he was under pressure from those who were impatient with his slow and cautious approach.[27] Mills's position as administrator of one of the largest agencies in the Federation meant his view was influential. His membership in the Child Welfare Council made him a particularly formidable opponent when he chose to disagree with the approach of its leadership.

While financial matters were important in slowing the plans, Nairn and Parker's proposal had also reopened the controversial suggestion that the NWA be stripped of its community responsibilities. At a meeting held in the fall of 1931 in Frank Stapleford's office, discussion focused on the future position of the NWA central council and its district associations. It was agreed that a new Council should encourage agencies to continue affiliation with existing organizations.[28] There obviously was to be no suggestion that the NWA relinquish its community work. As Stapleford later explained:

The NWA was intended from its foundation to be a community movement. It was not founded as a case working organization to deal with cases, but largely to assist churches and other organizations in the community to deal with these problems and to form a central clearing house through which this work could be done effectively ... Our roots are in community soil. We would be untrue to our whole tradition to turn our back upon that. The NWA must always take the view point of the community as a whole ... If we depart from that tradition I believe that a great deal of the value and power of the organization will also go.[29]

This was the view that saw casework and community work as two sides of the social work coin. Stapleford's commitment to this ideal was so deep and his influence so entrenched that the idea of a council of social agencies taking over the NWA's central and district councils was not seriously raised again until after his death.

Nor was the idea that a council be built on the foundation of the NWA an issue, despite its routine discussion and the planning and coordinating mandate that the Federation had originally given the agency. This too would have meant unacceptable change for the NWA in that a council of social agencies was by definition more comprehensive than a family agency. Stapleford acknowledged the relatively narrow focus of the NWA, but he could not accept any interference with the approach to family work that he had developed in his agency.

Stapleford's opposition to expanding or changing the NWA was to be expected. But he was also opposed to the alternative of expanding the Child Welfare Council, which was gaining favour in some quarters. A council of social agencies was seen as an organization that would provide leadership to other agencies and professionals, and there is evidence of Stapleford's unwillingness to see women in such positions. In a letter which chastised him generally for his resistance to change, Margaret Rich, the assistant general director of the Family Welfare Association of America, suggested that his solidly male board of directors would benefit from opening its ranks to women. Her comment also reveals the control Stapleford exercised over his own board: 'Whether in the long run the Board would be even better if you gradually added some women to it is something, of course, to which you will be giving your own attention.'[30]

Stapleford acknowledged his position in a letter to A.D. Hardie, executive secretary of the Federation for Community Service, which he was prompted to write in response to accusations that he was responsible for slowing the development of a Council. He acknowledged that 'Mills and I have never shared the somewhat extravagant hopes' of some regarding a council of social agencies, but he suggested it was 'childish' to classify those who saw difficulties as opponents. His letter went on to lay blame on the actions of the Child Welfare Council.[31] Stapleford was complaining about the direct action stance of the Council, which met with his disapproval, especially in light of the controversies described below. His patronizing references to extravagant hopes and childish behaviour also reflect the patriarchal disdain with which he and Mills regarded the ideals of a women's organization.

Despite the reservations of some, the idea that a council of social agencies be created by expanding the base of the Child Welfare Council was gaining acceptance. Paradoxically, it was encouraged by the financial considerations that favoured a council as part of the existing Federation, as well as the laying to rest of any consideration of building a new council on the base of the NWA. Issues concerning the welfare of children logically required its involvement, and the Child Welfare Council was given an increasingly active role in the affairs of the Federation, serving on committees such as the one struck in 1933 to consider amalgamation of Toronto's day nurseries along with the idea of family allowances.

But all was apparently not well with this arrangement. A committee to sort out the responsibilities of the Child Welfare Council relative to those of the Federation was struck. It was acknowledged that both the Child Welfare Council and the Federation were carrying responsibility for 'liaison work' with agencies and that both were needed. But it was suggested that the Child Welfare Council become more closely tied to the Federation.[32] Yet the idea of tightening its ties to the Federation was clearly not favoured by the Child Welfare Council. A report prepared by a special committee of the Council reveals the differences that were growing. It laid bare the conflict between the ideals of the socially conscious and activist Child Welfare Council and the narrow focus and controlling methods of a fiscally conscious Federation: 'Control is not a socially desirable method of bringing about improved social standards ... The Child Welfare Council is the only unit which stands for city-wide social planning with a membership based on absolute equality, and with co-operative thought and education as its main object. It cannot be suspected of autocratic or individualistic aims.' Furthermore, it was pointed out, the Child Welfare Council's broad membership base, much broader than the Federation's, meant that it was a good training ground for a future 'city-wide, all-inclusive council.'[33]

Distrust of the Federation for Community Service was in part a reflection of the resentment and anxiety of the member agencies of the Child Welfare Council over the stringent fiscal constraints placed on them by the Federation. The cutbacks in their budgets were severe, and the Federation, through its social policy committee, was also attempting to amalgamate or eliminate agencies in an effort to save money.[34] The move to amalgamate the day nurseries is an example of this kind of action, and the involvement of the Council, noted above, gave its members an intimate knowledge of the Federation's objectives and methods. But there was also a reluctance that had little to do with the financial crisis. Fear of loss of their autonomy of action, a fear that was rooted in a fundamental difference of opinion on the propriety of direct action lay behind the Council's rejection of the overtures of the Federation. If the Child Welfare Council was to become a city-wide, all-inclusive council of social agencies and still maintain its social reform activities, autonomy would be critically important.

Reflecting back, when the struggle was nearly over, a committee established to handle the difficult question of the relationship between the Child Welfare Council and the proposed council of social agencies listed the problems. First were the difficulties of building an organization that was 'active and homogenous and at the same time broadly representative.' Second was the problem of adequate finances. Last and most important was a conflict between the 'conception of a Council of Social Agencies as a medium of slow interpretation [and] the conception of its function as one of direct action.' The committee noted that in the opinion of some, these were mutually exclusive views on the basic purpose of a council. The first conformed to the slow developmental approach favoured by administrators such as Stapleford and Mills. The second saw a council as an instrument for intervening directly and purposefully in community affairs – an approach favoured by the ideals of the Child Welfare Council.[35]

The direct action stance of the Child Welfare Council became highly controversial in 1934 when it took up the cause of reforming the management of the York County Children's Aid Society (CAS). York County included the City of Toronto and a number of municipalities and townships that surrounded the city on all sides. Population growth outside the city boundaries had been substantial since the First World War, and inaction on the part of both the city and the province on matters of annexation and rationalization of assessment bases had resulted in the creation of a patchwork of small municipalities within the county, some of which were working class and quite poor.[36] The York County CAS carried responsibility for all areas other than the city; however other social services would not have been so neatly divided. Family agencies throughout the Toronto area would have occasion to refer children from 'the Townships' to the county CAS.

In the course of their work, many caseworkers had become convinced that the superintendent of the York Children's Aid Society was responsible for abusive treatment of children in his care. As early as 1930, agencies had begun to refuse to refer children living in the county who were in need of protection. Repeated efforts to evoke action from the CAS board and county council had failed.[37] Leading a coalition of local townships, child-caring organizations, and women's organizations, the Child Welfare Council formally petitioned the Ontario cabinet for a public inquiry into the administration of the York County CAS. Drawing on thirteen case examples of administrative laxity and glaring abuse of children, the Council charged the Society with 'failure to discharge its functions pursuant to the provisions of the Children's Protection Act.' The petition was signed on behalf of the Council by Barbara Cody, Lois Fraser, and Margaret Gould.[38]

While political action could frequently be carried out quietly and behind closed doors, in this instance there was no avoiding the publicity. The chairman of the board of directors of the York County CAS, and the person most likely to be held responsible was George Henry, premier of Ontario. Furthermore, the province was heading into an election, so the timing left the Council wide open to charges of partisanship.[39] The furore that followed resulted not only in putting the plans for a council of social agencies on hold once more, but also added immeasurably to the misgivings held by some over the methods employed by the Child Welfare Council.

The immediate response of the Ontario attorney-general was to with-hold the details of the Child Welfare Council's petition from the public and to conduct a quiet internal investigation. Pressure for a public inquiry came from the Opposition in the legislature and the Toronto press. In an effort to forestall these demands, Henry appointed Senior County Court Judge James Parker to head a judicial inquiry – still to be closed to public scrutiny. Not to be deterred, the Council petitioned the Ontario Court of Appeal and won their case. Chief Justice Sir William Mulock ruled that the Parker inquiry should be public and open.[40]

The actions of the Child Welfare Council were completely vindicated by the findings handed down by Judge Parker in the fall of 1934. He ruled that the York County CAS had indeed 'conducted its work in a "negligent, incompetent and ineffective manner."' The superintendent was found to be incompetent, with no experience, no guidance, and in the habit of drinking on the job. Parker faulted the Society's directors for a situation they knew existed, yet had failed to remedy. He commended the Council whose actions, he admitted, he first regarded as 'over-zealous' but later found to have been motivated 'solely by interest in child welfare.' The Toronto *Star*, which had supported George Henry's Liberal opponents in the recent election, took direct aim at Henry, 'champion pooh-pooher of Ontario,' and congratulated the Council for its persistence. The new provincial administration dissolved the York County CAS board and fired its chairman, by now the ex-premier of Ontario.[41]

Despite Judge Parker's vindication of their actions, the Child Welfare Council could not possibly have emerged from this controversy un-scathed. It was simply too political. Any controversy, however justified, tended to be eyed with alarm by the fund-raising arm of the Federation. One with partisan overtones that could antagonize large numbers of the businessmen who contributed to the Federation was completely unacceptable. Furthermore, the Council's actions offended the views held by many social workers that political activity was at all times unprofessional, and all the more so during an election campaign that saw the defeat of the government. Thus the actions of the Council not only met with the disapproval of the Federation leadership, they also angered many social workers.

The controversy over the York County CAS had serious consequences for Margaret Gould. Part of the debate over the plans for a council of social agencies focused on the question of 'leadership.' This generally was a euphemism for executive staff, and in part the debate reflected concerns that insufficient money would be budgeted to attract a skilled professional on a full-time basis.[42] But the leadership question also reflected criticism in some quarters of Gould's radical style. If the Child Welfare Council was to continue and expand, the continuation of Gould as executive secretary was implied. Thus, disbanding the Council rather than simply expanding its membership and purpose to create a council of social agencies was a potential strategy available to those who wished to replace Gould and her supporters.[43]

Rumours that Gould was a communist began circulating during the Parker inquiry. She later insisted that the rumours had been spread by those who hoped to stop the Parker inquiry by suggesting that the charges against the York County CAS were no more than partisanship on her part. Gould was particularly bitter that the rumours had been circulated by members of her own profession.[44] Censure of this kind rose from the deep divisions that existed within social work in the politically volatile thirties. The face of social work was changing significantly under the pressure of hard times and struggles for legitimacy. The retreat into scientism was well under way and many social workers were now convinced that practice could and should be carried on in an 'objective' fashion, ruling out any participation in politics. This meant rapid retreat on the part of some from social action, separating casework from community work in the process. If reform was to take place, it would be through 'interpretation' of the facts and the slow process of changing public attitudes. Hence the disapproval from within the ranks of social work of Gould and the direct action approach of the Child Welfare Council.

The combination of the controversy over the action against the York County CAS and the malicious rumours being spread about its executive secretary altered the debate over the future of the Council. Up until the time of the Parker inquiry, it appears that its conversion to a more comprehensive council of social agencies, either by attaching it to the Federation or by simply building on its current membership, had been under serious consideration. Once the inquiry became a matter of public interest, the idea that the Child Welfare Council be disbanded and replaced by a new organization became the preferred option. Lois Fraser, the Council's president during the entire controversy, later charged that this option had been handed down as a forgone conclusion. She blamed a 'self-appointed group' that had long sought the demise of the Child Welfare Council.

Whether it was a forgone conclusion or not, dissolution of the Council presented particular difficulties in 1934. It was justifiably pointed out that such a move could be interpreted by the public 'as an act of censure and punishment of the Child Welfare Council by the social workers of Toronto, for its activities in connection with the York County Children's Aid Inquiry.' As well, current proposals for a new council did not budget for full-time staff. This in itself was unacceptable, but as Fraser pointed out, it also meant releasing Margaret Gould, an action that 'would inevitably leave the impression in very many quarters that her services were no longer required.' Fraser argued that this would have a lasting effect on the social reform activities of all social agencies. The Child Welfare Council executive asked for and was granted time.[45]

Once the York County inquiry was safely over, negotiations over the relationship of the Child Welfare Council to the development of a council of social agencies began again. In March of 1935 a meeting was held in the office of A.D. Hardie, executive secretary of the Federation for Community Service. It was attended by the leading volunteers of the Council: Barbara Cody, Lois Fraser, Margaret Nairn, Agnes McGregor, and Kay Gorrie. The record contains two reports of this meeting, the first indicating agreement to disband the Child Welfare Council. The Council requested that this report be withdrawn and destroyed. The second report replaced the agreement to dissolve with an agreement to consider the 'quality of leadership needed,' undoubtedly referring to Gould's position. This was not a real agreement. The Federation for Community Service was handing down an ultimatum.[46]

A month later, reporting to her executive committee on the progress of plans for a council of social agencies, Fraser warned that there was need for safeguards to assure continuation of the programs and quality of work of the Council: 'Some members of that [planning] committee made it quite clear that it was not their intention to retain anything of the Child Welfare Council but its budget.' Despite her concerns, the executive voted to go out of existence in favour of a council of social agencies, with only the proviso that they receive six months' notice.[47]

A moratorium appears to have taken place over the next year while the planning committee was reorganized to include agencies outside the Federation. The public Departments of Health and Welfare had been members from the beginning, but important voluntary agencies such as the YWCA had not been included. This step was necessary if comprehensiveness was to be achieved. The involvement of major services outside the Federation also increased the need for an autonomous council. Whether for this reason, or because the federation could not tolerate additional conflict, the issue of independence appears to have disappeared from the agenda, at least for the time being.

Plans seemed to progress smoothly, and early in November 1936, the social policy committee of the Federation held a special meeting to consider details for a new council of social agencies. A broad membership was proposed, with participation on the democratic basis of one unit, one vote, and with each agency paying fees based on the size of its operating budget. There was a relatively minor fuss over the issue of large agencies and public departments being placed on an equal footing with small agencies, but on the whole, plans seemed ready for implementation. The Child Welfare Council was to be disbanded, but reassurance was given that its past efforts would not be lost: 'The Social Policy Committee went on record as re-affirming appreciation of the work of the Child Welfare Council, in its efforts towards creating better conditions for the children of the City. It was strongly felt that every care should be taken to safeguard the projects of this Council, and to make sure that in grasping for the shadow of a Council of Social Agencies, the substance of the Child Welfare Council is not dropped.'[48]

The assurances were evidently not sufficient for the membership of the Council. In a general meeting held the following day to ratify the proposal, fifty-six agency representatives, all but two of them women, rejected the earlier decision of their executive committee to disband and demanded that the idea of building a council of social agencies on the base of the existing Child Welfare Council be reexamined. They saw the decision to dissolve the Council as capitulating to the opposition of 'some of the leading social agencies.' This was probably a reference to the opposition of Stapleford and Mills, executives of two of the largest agencies in Toronto. Their fears were not helped by Reg Hopper, one of the two men present, who was chosen to explain the purpose of the proposed council of social agencies. Hopper was executive director of the Ontario Society for Crippled Children and a member of the Child Welfare Council, but on this occasion he was identified as representing the Rotary Club. For an audience devoted to non-material ends and the distinction between the 'world of business and our own,' his choice of words was unfortunate: 'Social work today is not just an enterprise of an individual agency, but a community enterprise. A Council of Agencies helps social work to be such an enterprise.' Enterprise was the last thing the women in his audience envisioned for a new council. As one observer commented, the agencies of the Child Welfare Council were 'disinclined to commit suicide.'[49]

The arguments prepared by the Council executive for the follow-up meeting reveal the pragmatic basis of their original recommendation to dissolve. They presented three options: the membership could refuse to dissolve and thus obstruct the establishment of a council of social agencies; it could agree to dissolve to further the development of a such a council; or the Child Welfare Council could be broadened into a general council. The third option was rejected by the executive on the grounds that, in the judgment of the planning committee, an expanded Child Welfare Council would not have the necessary support.[50]

The first meeting to reconsider the question coincided with the farewell broadcast of King Edward VIII, and had to be adjourned. In the interim, the executive wavered. They decided there were 'no insuperable difficulties for the expansion and development of the Child Welfare Council into a general council' provided they had the support of a majority of the agencies.[51] The Council executive neither trusted nor accepted the authority of the planning committee established by the social policy committee to develop a council of social agencies. Notes probably made by Barbara Cody in preparation for her role as chairperson of the Child Welfare Council membership meetings show a lack of confidence that the planning committee would present all the facts.[52]

At an emotional meeting in January 1937 the Council executive got the mandate they needed. Requests for someone to identify the advantages of starting afresh met with no response. Suggestions that an expanded Council would retain the experience of the past met with applause. The actions of the agencies demonstrated widespread support for the activities of the Child Welfare Council. It was not simply a case of a few radicals taking an extreme position in their approach to social planning. It was determined opposition to the conservative approach of the Federation and its social policy committee.[53]

The matter was then placed before a meeting of all agencies who might be concerned about a council of social agencies for Toronto. Invitations were sent to 175 organizations, 97 of whom were members of the Child Welfare Council. The official minutes record impassioned speeches in favour of having a council, and the forgone conclusion of a vote in favour. But the creation of a council of social agencies was not the issue. Unofficial transcripts of the meeting reveal a frustrating debate over the issue of expanding the Child Welfare Council. With Cody in the chair, no one was willing to be too specific, but clear allusions were made to the narrowness of the Council's executive and the unwillingness on the part of some agencies to join on this account. Others refused to vote on the grounds that the meeting did not have any authority. On one hand there was too much authority in the hands of a few, on the other, not enough authority in the hands of many. Stapleford finally broke the stalemate by suggesting that the alternatives be formally presented to the agencies and a referendum held.[54]

Approximately 160 agencies and public departments were polled. They were asked to choose between Plan A, which was to build a new organization from the ground up, and Plan B, which was to expand the membership, executive, and committee structure of the Child Welfare Council, retaining its current staff. Eighty-four agencies replied, thirty-eight in favour of Plan A, twenty-seven for Plan B, and nineteen who decided not to vote. The result mirrored the divisive nature of the question, but it was sufficiently conclusive.[55] A second general meeting of agencies held on 14 June 1937 voted for a provisional board, which was given the responsibility for making all arrangements for the operation of a new council of social agencies.

Although she had chaired the previous meeting as well as the committee which had prepared and supervised the referendum, this time Barbara Cody was not in the chair. The meeting, held at University of Toronto's Hart House was chaired by Edward (E.J.) Urwick, director of the School of Social Work. Urwick's opening comments show that he sought reconciliation through a balance of interests in the makeup of the provisional board. He asked the assembled delegates to exercise care when voting 'to secure a good representation of men ... and to see that lay persons elected outnumbered professional workers in approximately the proportion of two to one.'[56] The issue of lay versus professional control was an important and perennial concern, but one over which there was rarely disagreement, at least in principle. The need for men on the board was a different matter. The overwhelming participation of women in the Child Welfare Council had been a major drawback in the eyes of its critics. The 'narrowness' of its executive was not one of interest, but of gender. Critics saw the need for the idealism of the women involved to be tempered by the pragmatism and caution of their male colleagues. It was not by accident that Urwick was chairman of both the provisional board and the board of the Toronto Welfare Council established the following autumn. His presence gave assurance that a new council of social agencies would not be an organization dominated by women.

Not only were these events guided by the assumption that administrative matters are a male domain, men were also claiming primacy over the community work aspects of social work practice. As the Depression dragged on, increasing emphasis was being placed on coordination of services and comprehensive social planning, rather than social action and social reform.[57] Social planning required skills and legitimacy for negotiating with agency managers and funders, a task closely associated with administration. Furthermore, social planning and coordination of services were framed as politically neutral activities, grounded in objective science and resting on a belief in the efficacy of rational behaviour. This was a thoroughly utilitarian approach to social reform, and consistent with the prevailing values of business and, increasingly, social work. Women may have been given grudging approval for providing advice on matters related to developing services for children and families, but it was a supportive role, and such activities were regarded as provision of information and facts needed for an interpretive function, not for use in direct political activity.

Equally important for the status of women in social work was the separation of casework and community work that accompanied this shift from social action to social planning. As a technical and expertly driven process, social planning was seen to require different skills and authority from casework. By the end of the decade, 'community organization,' defined as the 'balancing of resources to meet identified needs' by the influential National Conference of Social Work in the United States, was acknowledged as a distinct practice method. The separation of community work and casework opened the door for male dominance in the field of community work and confined women in social work to the casework aspects of professional practice.[58]

The establishment of a provisional board for a new council of social agencies was accompanied by a decision to close down the Child Welfare

Council by the end of June. Margaret Gould used the occasion of the final meeting to deliver a spirited defence against the accusation that she was a communist. She also accepted the suggestion made by some that her actions had been responsible for the outcome of the referendum: 'I have heard ... that this vote does not signify disapproval of the work [of the Council], but of myself personally ... I am glad therefore that their efforts and aims have been endorsed really, and that the recent vote indicates censure of me only.'[59]

It is unlikely that Gould was the sole target of the move to dissolve the Child Welfare Council. She had the vocal and visible support of many of her colleagues and her emotional farewell at the last meeting of the Council was given with the foreknowledge and blessing of the executive. Barbara Cody, who could not attend, joined in the praise by letter in which she made her admiration for Gould a matter of record: 'I feel no one has made a more valuable contribution during the last ten years to the development of constructive social thought and activity in Toronto than she has.' A full statement, including Gould's address, was sent to the press. Gould represented an approach to community work and social action that may have been a minority view, but nevertheless had significant support within the Toronto social service community.

The disbanding of the Council and the events that surrounded it provide a graphic illustration of the growing gender inequality within social work. But it was a process in which some women unknowingly participated.[60] Toronto's Child Welfare Council drew together some of the most prominent women in social work in English Canada at the time. They were educated, competent, and as noted above, many moved on into executive or other positions of influence. They joined with other professional and activist women, many of whom served on the boards of the agencies for which they worked, to seek change in their society's response to the human misery they observed every day. As with modern feminists, some sought radical change, although the majority undoubtedly sought reform limited by the parameters of the existing order. Yet despite their expertise, and despite the ideals they stood for, which had long been integral to social work, they were, in effect, voted out of office. Social work had shifted fundamentally into a professional pursuit guided by an hegemony of technocratic values.

CHAPTER FIVE

A Measured Minimum

The Toronto Welfare Council played an influential part in the changes that were taking place in social welfare in Canada during the Second World War. While wartime turned everyone's attention to the national effort to contribute to victory in Europe and the Pacific, behind the scenes there was much planning geared towards ensuring an orderly return to a peacetime economy. Fears of massive unemployment as had occurred following the First World War, and acknowledgment of the failures of public policy regarding relief and unemployment during the Depression set the tone.

The Council's approach to community work mirrored the widespread adoption of Fabian principles by social workers as the profession emerged from the economic crisis of the thirties. A faith in research as the foundation for progressive reform of society, coupled with a humanitarian ideal of establishing a 'social minimum,' below which no citizen could fall, was the cornerstone of professional values. The fervour of the social gospel and of maternalism had receded into the background, replaced by a faith in science and rationality. Fabian economists such as Leonard Marsh of the McGill Social Science Research Project and Harry Cassidy, who was the dean of the Toronto School of Social Work during the forties, were leading figures in the education of professional social workers and also in the high-level efforts devoted to the construction of a Canadian welfare state.[1]

The Toronto Council's influence in national affairs belied its local base. During the forties primary responsibility for social welfare in Canada shifted from local to national and provincial levels of the state. While delivery of most personal social services remained at the local level, the policy and funding was increasingly being determined elsewhere. This created a dialogue between social workers, who used their local welfare councils as a means of participation, and the politicians and professionals working in the Dominion and provincial governments. The experience and expertise of Welfare Council staff and volunteers contributed directly to the national planning process.

Corporate interest in social welfare was also shifting from local to national levels. Where formerly relief was entirely a local affair governed by an uneasy coalition of social workers, local politicians, and small businessmen, it was now a matter of national interest and of much greater substance. As Alvin Finkel has pointed out, the corporate elite began to support state participation in social affairs in an unprecedented way during the thirties.[2] As will be seen, this support became containment and control during and after the Second World War. Toronto, which was rapidly overtaking Montreal as the locus of corporate power in Canada, became a centre from which the corporate agenda was developed. It placed the Toronto Welfare Council in the middle of the conflict between corporate business interests and the Fabian ideals of the social work profession.

When the Toronto Welfare Council was established in 1937 its purpose, structure, and activities reflected the latest professional thinking with respect to community practice. The Council saw itself as the spearhead of a comprehensive attack on social conditions. The very choice of name, welfare council, rather than the traditional one of council of social agencies, was intended to indicate the broader focus embracing 'all communal efforts for social improvement.' Its interests included not only those fields that traditionally fell within social welfare, but also education, recreation, and housing. Nevertheless, the Council remained very much an instrument of the agency community, intended to bring 'closer co-operation between the many and diverse organizations in the city,' and to become 'a centre for the study of common problems and for joint efforts toward their correction.' The centrepiece of this vision was research, and more than ever before, the Council was focusing its activities on generating research that would provide the basis for collective reform activities.

Seventy-two organizations became members during the first year, all of them in the voluntary sector with the exception of the city Departments of Public Welfare and Public Health, which participated as 'special members.' A board of directors was elected by the member agencies, each having one vote regardless of size or status. There was no provision for individual membership.[3] (A list of member agencies is in Appendix 2.)

In the beginning, the Toronto Welfare Council was not only structurally independent of the financial federation, it was intended to be financially independent as well. The fundamental fear of external or central control was expressed in the desire to finance the organization fully from membership fees and to avoid any large grants from a single source. It was expected that agency members would carry the load, an expectation dependent on anticipated fees from participating government departments. While each agency had only one vote regardless of its size, this equality did not follow with respect to membership fees, which were set according to the size of an agency's operating budget. The Federation for Community Service was expected to provide funds only as a supplement to agency fees that would otherwise be excessive. Contributions from individuals were 'acceptable,' but did not constitute membership. It was above all intended as a democratic and self-supporting organization of agencies.[4]

The Council adopted three objectives for carrying out its work of improving the welfare of the community: first, the provision of information, grounded in research and scientific fact, for use in planning activities; second, the 'creation of Public Opinion,' the interpretative approach preferred by most social workers; and third, the 'promotion of social legislation,' a discreet version of direct action in the interest of social reform.[5] In general, the Council saw itself as a resource of information, expertise, and inspiration for the planning and reform activities of organizations in the local community. This clearly reflected an approach to social change that rested on a faith in science and rationality. It also relied on the assumption that research was a politically neutral activity and that its use as a basis for planned changed by interested citizens and elected officials would follow.

Notable for its absence was the objective of coordinating services. During the years of financial stringency, coordination had emerged as a process related to efficiency and economy of effort rather than improving standards of professional service. As such it was associated with the business of allocating funds and was seen as the responsibility of the financial federation. Social planning on the other hand was seen as being concerned with the nature and quality of services throughout the community as a whole. Thus the new Council did not replace the social policy committee of the Federation for Community Services, which, despite some fear of overlap, continued in its primary function of advising the Federation on matters related to funding its member agencies.

In the first two years, the new Council nearly collapsed under the weight of activities it was expected to carry. The first expectation was that it carry forward the work of the defunct Child Welfare Council. In addition, the Federation promptly referred all other social service matters not directly related to the allocation of its funds. This in itself was quite sufficient for an organization still in its infancy, without the flood of requests that poured in from the community. These ranged from requests for advice on agency development to requests for assistance in approaching the police about their failure to enforce the Child Protection Act. By February 1938 nineteen program committees had been appointed, and the Council was seeking the assistance of 'volunteer secretaries.'[6] (A list of committees is in Appendix 2.)

By the end of the first year, the Welfare Council was fending off 'rumours of financial instability.' Membership fees had proved to be totally inadequate, causing some concern that it would be better to quit than to try to continue with insufficient funds. Appeals were made to prospective members, including city departments, and to all three financial federations, Catholic, Jewish, and Protestant. The membership drive proved reasonably successful, and approaches to the Federations produced a modest response, although not the hoped-for agreement to cover the required fee for all of their member agencies. But approaches to the city met with failure and were regarded as a potential disaster. The matter of City support involved acceptance of full membership by the Departments of Public Health, Public Welfare and possibly Recreation, plus agreement by the board of control to pay a substantial fee. Since bringing together public and private agencies was fundamental to the principle of comprehensiveness, the council was forced to accept the city departments as non-paying 'special' members rather than compromise this all-important feature. Eventually, further compromises involved approaching individuals for donations and the Federation for Community Service for a grant. Thus financial necessity began a process that would culminate in reuniting the Council with a financial federation.[7]

The Welfare Council hired Kay Gorrie as its first executive secretary in the summer of 1937. Probably because of the perceived agenda to ensure male leadership, together with the shift in perceptions of community work as a male pursuit, the Council considered whether it could afford to hire a man. But the limited budget made it necessary to hire a woman, although the board resolved to seek a higher amount to lessen the distinction between what could be offered men and women. The small budget meant not only a low salary, it also meant no money could be found to support staff participation in social work conferences, a major source of personal support as well as information needed for guiding a new welfare council into place. Gorrie was given a salary of $2500 and paid her own way to national conferences in Canada and the United States.[8]

The burgeoning workload and financial pressures were intolerable. Gorrie's frustration was reflected in a letter to the chairman of the Canadian Conference on Social Work that was planning to meet in Toronto. Recognizing that she would be expected to carry much of the administrative burden, Gorrie pleaded for another arrangement: 'A Council for a city the size of Toronto should not have such a limited staff, but the financing of even our small budget is so difficult, I cannot see how we can increase the staff for some time to come.' Eventually an exhausted and overextended Gorrie was forced to resign because of 'ill-health and nervous strain,' and the board made a note to consider the workload carefully for the future.[9] The issue of sufficient funding to support staff requirements was an issue that would plague the Council during its entire existence.

The year 1939 ended on a desperately low note. Edward J. Urwick, the Council's president since its inception, also resigned; board elections had resulted in a loss of several 'valued members'; the Council was evicted from its office; and the declaration of war brought recognition that 'radical change' in the planning and provision of social services was about to happen.[10]

From this low point, the fortunes of the Council began to rise. Lois Fraser returned to the board of directors after a brief retirement and was elected president early in 1940. Fraser and Beatrice Kirkpatrick, who had served as vice-president of the Child Welfare Council alongside Barbara Cody, provided the volunteer leadership over the remaining years of independence.

Shortly after Fraser's return, the Council hired Bessie Touzel as its new executive secretary. Touzel was well on the way to becoming one of Canada's most respected social workers. She was a graduate of the University of Toronto School of Social Work and had worked as a district secretary in the Neighbourhood Workers Association (NWA). This alone made her well known to Toronto social workers. She went from the NWA to a position as chief of staff in the Department of Public Welfare for the City of Ottawa, an unusual position for a woman at the time. Touzel's commitment to ideals of social justice and the strength with which she held to her convictions led her to resign that job in protest against the harsh policies of the Ottawa Public Welfare Board when it fired forty women social workers and replaced them with male inspectors under orders to root out the 'chisellers' on the relief rolls. Touzel was incensed by the injustice this perpetrated on both workers and recipients alike, and it brought into glaring prominence the disregard with which professional social workers were held. Her resignation became a *cause célèbre* among social workers, whose struggles for legitimacy were intense and painful as the economic situation worsened.[11]

Touzel came to the Toronto Welfare Council from a position with the Canadian Welfare Council that she had been offered following her sensational stand against the City of Ottawa. Her work in Ottawa had brought her in contact with many of the persons influential in the development of a welfare state in Canada, which together with her municipal experience brought an added and important dimension to the work of the Toronto Council. Touzel's experience and professional stature also meant that she was much in demand as a consultant in the planning for postwar arrangements for social welfare. Her advocacy for a strong public role and her own public activities became a source of strain between the ideals of the Welfare Council and the anti-welfare sentiments of the business leadership in Toronto.[12]

While support for planning at a national level was one source of friction, many of the local activities of the Council during Touzel's tenure contributed even more to placing it in the midst of controversy, not all of them attributable only to Touzel. The issue of adequate levels of relief that the Council inherited from the Child Welfare Council was only one of a wide range of activities. Wartime brought to the fore issues of housing, day care, and recreation. This last arose in part because of plans for 'rehabilitation' of the armed forces, and in part as a concern for children and youth left unsupervised by mothers engaged in war industry.[13] Regarding housing, the Council undertook a major survey of needs in Toronto. The study documented substantial overcrowding and disproportionately high costs forced on the poor in order to gain shelter. The Council advocated public housing as the only solution, a position that did not endear it to those sectors of the community committed to private enterprise.[14] Regarding day care, the Council took a position that was initially simply unpopular, and eventually made it subject to considerable red-baiting. At the end of the war governments immediately ceased funding day care, assuming no further need. Despite findings that identified widespread need among families with children in the Toronto school districts, the Council was unsuccessful in convincing senior and local governments, including school boards, to continue both preschool care and junior kindergartens.[15]

The Council was also deeply involved in the issue of the administration of public welfare, which became a major preoccupation of civic organizations during the war. Relief rolls were low and reorganization was considered timely and necessary before the arrival of an expected postwar crisis in unemployment.[16] This was the only issue that constituted a partial victory. In a drive for administrative efficiency, the Board of Trade, the Bureau of Municipal Research, the mayor and several of the city's councillors advocated the amalgamation of the Department of Public Health and the Department of Public Welfare. Fearing domination by the medical profession and lack of attention to the principles of social work, the council won its argument that public welfare was much too complex to combine with the equally complex field of public health. However, it lost an important part of the battle when it championed the appointment of Robena Morris, assistant commissioner of public welfare at the time, to the position of commissioner. The Council argued that the position should not only go to a professional social worker, but also to a woman, since a woman would be better able to deal with the humanitarian aspects of working with people on relief. Instead, the city appointed Howard S. Rupert, the former assistant in the Department of Public Works who had headed the civic review of the plan to merge the two departments.[17]

In the summer of 1940, three years after the founding of the Welfare Council, the Toronto Board of Trade renewed its longstanding campaign to establish one fund-raising organization that would meet all of the charitable needs in Toronto.[18] Not only were there three Federations coexisting in the city, there were a significant number of large agencies such as the YMCA, the Salvation Army, and the Red Cross campaigning on their own. The proliferation of appeals was an annoyance for the major contributors and added to their perennial suspicions of service duplication and inefficiency: 'The multiplicity of separate appeals for charitable funds had long been a bugbear of the commercial community, and the Board [of Trade], with other organizations, had for years urged their co-ordination as a means of reducing the overall number, effecting administrative economies and defining with more clarity the actual fields of social activity in which the numerous agencies were operating.'[19] The Board of Trade's persistence eventually succeeded and the various appeals agreed to join together on a trial basis in 1943 under the name United Welfare Fund.

Response among social workers to the idea of one central campaign for funds was decidedly mixed. The Community Chests and Councils of

America (the Three Cs) was vigorously promoting community chests, which were intended to be a comprehensive replacement of the fragmented and sectarian fund-raising that had evolved from the earlier financial federations. The Three Cs also promoted close association between Chests and Welfare Councils, an association that was opposed by some influential social workers in the United States who argued that independent councils were better able to secure the confidence of public agencies. The massive entrance of state governments into the administration of public welfare in the United States during the Depression drew many American social workers into government service, intensifying the debate in that country over the relationship between public and private planning. Canadian opinion was heavily influenced by the perceived negative influence of the Community Chest that accompanied that debate, particularly among those Canadian social workers who were committed to increased state involvement in the provision of social services. Touzel, in particular, was a strong advocate of state participation in social planning, and both she and Fraser were opposed to the idea that the Welfare Council become part of a Community Chest.[20]

Despite the opposition, there was strong support among some social workers for the Council joining the Chest. Professional social workers within the three Federations as well as the Welfare Council encouraged reluctant agency boards and volunteers to support the establishment of a Community Chest on the grounds that central planning needed central funding if the needs identified in the community were to be met. For the Welfare Council and the agencies, there was the added rationale of need for a stable and expanding source of funds, plus the pragmatic recognition that the approval of the business community was essential if this were to happen.[21] All of these arguments appealed to the male agency administrators and planners. But given the heightened importance of planning during wartime, and the concurrent efforts to construct a welfare state, it had wide appeal among female social workers as well.

Nevertheless, agency autonomy remained an important consideration. This included a relatively recent anxiety that the Welfare Council not become dependent on any one source of government grants, adding to the importance of seeking private sector financial support. Paradoxically, this became an issue because of vastly improved relations between the Welfare Council and Toronto City Council. This was partly a result of Touzel's experience and interest in municipal affairs, and partly due to the election of Fred Conboy as mayor in 1941. Conboy was a dentist who had been active in the Welfare Council of Ontario, serving as its president in

1936. He was well known and sympathetic to the social work community in Toronto.[22] Under his leadership, the City finally agreed to assume paying membership in the Council, and began to provide funding for specific projects such as the housing study completed in 1942–3. This led to demands that the Welfare Council meet its increased need for funds with public money. The Council refused, taking the position that work done at all three levels of government would be compromised by lump sum grants.[23] The desire for sustaining funding from the private sector was a risky business, since the need for experienced staff to carry out its range of activities and the sheer quantity of work meant that the very existence of the Council and its ideals depended on its adequacy. An unsympathetic Community Chest could spell serious trouble, a risk which did indeed become reality.

In 1943 the Welfare Council requested that their allocation be more than doubled for the coming year. This was the year for which the first joint campaign was conducted, and requests required agreement from both the Federation for Community Service and the newly established United Welfare Fund, both of which proposed to hold the Welfare Council allocation at the same level as the previous year. The Council saw the issue as raising the question of 'the whole role of the Council,' and threatened to pull out and conduct their own campaign if their request was refused. The United Welfare Fund, facing its critical trial year, was in no position to bargain on that point and acceded to their request. It was probably the only time in the entire history of the relationship between the planning and fund-raising organizations in Toronto that the planners had the advantage.[24]

With the enthusiastic participation of the Board of Trade in its campaign, the United Welfare Fund was very successful. The next step was the establishment of a permanent Community Chest for Toronto. The general chairman of the Fund, in correspondence with the agencies, gave assurance that this would not mean control of their affairs:

Membership in a Community Chest does not mean undue control of a welfare organization, nor does it mean the loss of its name or autonomy. It does assure each organization and the public that the work of every organization is examined with a view to showing that the complete programme and services are being maintained without over-lapping and without waste. Those who have had experience in Community Chests feel that this type of organization has generally meant an assurance of adequate financial support, and has carried the approval of the giving public.[25]

In short, coordination and efficiency held out the hope of greater support from the business community and the prospect of more money to go
around. In the face of an expanded professional role and a growing need
for funding for a professionally trained staff, the issue of independence
from a united fund paled in comparison.

Along with other agencies, cautious approval for participation in the
Community Chest was given by the Welfare Council's board of directors.
But concerns were clearly expressed that the safeguards of adequate representation on the board and budget committee of the proposed Chest
be secured to ensure that financial concerns would not once again domi-
nate those of planning. Over twenty years of experience coupled with lack
of agency input into budget decisions within the financial federation left
a residue of justifiable anxiety over how easily concerns for efficiency and
cost containment could become paramount.

Despite this anxiety, the hope that a combined organization would provide better opportunity for influence over funding decisions had invariably been a deciding factor for agencies when faced with the question of
relationship with a financial federation. When coupled with the emerging
professional ideals that associated comprehensive planning with comprehensive funding, this hope once again carried the day. After a six-month
courtship in early 1944 the Council agreed to become a department of
the new Community Chest on a trial basis.[26]

The new partnership immediately brought requests from the Chest for
staff assistance. The Council agreed to lend its assistant secretary and
resolved to look at the need for increased staff so as 'not to fail member
agencies.'[27] This was a harbinger of things to come. The Council, from
the time it rejoined the fund-raising organization, was faced with conflicting pressures – from the Chest for assistance in the coordination of services and allocation of funds, from the agencies for assistance, and from
its own activities as a comprehensive, scientific, and proactive planning
organization.

One of the advantages of an independent welfare council had been its
perceived freedom and flexibility to advocate improved public services.
The experience of the Depression had demonstrated the inadequacy of
relief, and there was support from business as well as social work for a proposed campaign to seek improvements in public welfare. In the months
before the Welfare Council was formed, the Federation for Community
Service had devoted considerable time to the issue, and plans to
approach the City of Toronto dominated the agenda of every meeting in

the first half of 1937. Nevertheless, there remained strong resistance to improvements in relief and the approach of the Federation was uneasy and cautious. In September, as soon as it was organized, the matter was turned over to the new Welfare Council. The rationale was the Council's ability to involve non-Federated agencies. Undoubtedly it also had the advantage of placing the issue at arms' length from the Federation and thereby avoiding possible negative publicity during the campaign for funds.[28]

The Welfare Council established a committee on public-private relations under the chairmanship of Lois Fraser. The Council gave the committee a mandate to include 'all matters involving the relationship between public and private services,' and invited senior public officials, education and nursing professionals, and representatives of the townships and the province to participate. The first task was a major public education campaign to influence public opinion in favour of an increase in food allowances, which, along with fuel, made up the core of relief benefits.[29]

Opposition to increasing the amount of relief given began immediately. Horace L. Brittain of the Bureau of Municipal Research complained that increased relief allowances would result in either increased taxes or worse, the borrowing of money by the municipality to which he was 'utterly opposed.' Brittain, who joined the Bureau in 1914, was now regarded as one of Canada's experts in public administration. He suggested the only avenue for increasing levels of relief was through administrative savings, a position that reflected the long-standing concern of the Bureaus of Municipal Research to encourage efficiency in civic government, as well as his own entrenched views over how public affairs ought to be managed.[30]

A.W. Laver, Toronto's commissioner of public welfare since the department was established in 1931, was also opposed. Although he agreed that food relief was inadequate, at least in the winter months, he also favoured the idea that recipients could supplement their low benefits with odd jobs, and denied charges that his department was deducting all extra earnings once the rent was paid.[31] The medical officer of health, G.P. Jackson, with considerable disregard for current knowledge in the field of nutrition, conducted a survey comparing the weight of individuals on relief with that of those who were not. He interpreted his findings as suggesting virtually no difference in rates of malnutrition and suggested that 'generous quantities' of bread and milk accounted for an increasing incidence of overweight among relief recipients.[32]

Recognizing that the province had ultimate authority over the level of relief allowances, the Welfare Council arranged a meeting with Eric Cross, minister of public welfare. Cross had previously opposed any increase in relief on the grounds that employment was increasing and food costs were down. The Council argued that food allowances in Toronto were a full 26 per cent below the lowest of three generally accepted standards for adequate nutrition set by the Ontario Medical Association, the Canadian Council on Nutrition, and the League of Nations. Citing the opinion of the medical officers of health that there was no evidence of poor nutrition, Cross suggested that higher levels of relief would endanger family responsibilities and be a disincentive to the unemployed taking odd jobs. He lectured the Council on the 1834 British Poor Law principle of 'less eligibility,' which insisted that relief never exceed the wages of the lowest paid workers: 'If the relief allowances were brought too close to the lower wage levels there would be the great danger of encouraging inertia. People would not make an effort to get off relief. At the present time men are refusing to go out to work on farms, preferring to remain on relief.'[33]

This clash of 'expert' opinion signalled the perils of assuming that empirical data and rational arguments will sway policy change. When it comes to matters of social welfare and the role of the state, ideology and power will inevitably guide the ultimate outcome of policy debates, and the use of expert opinion can be selected according to which expert has the view most favourable to the position of those in power. This manipulation of empirical data and expert opinion would become a major strategy on the part of opponents who were eventually successful in suppressing the Council's campaign for higher relief benefits.

In the summer of 1939, a year following the meeting with Cross, the Toronto Welfare Council published a landmark study, *The Cost of Living: A Study of the Cost of a Standard of Living in Toronto Which Should Maintain Health and Self-Respect*. It was presented at a public meeting to which the Council invited representatives of trade unions and the unemployed, service clubs, the Board of Trade, local and provincial politicians and the heads of surrounding municipal welfare departments plus the provincial Department of Public Welfare. The conference attracted between 200 and 250 people, making the decision to print 500 copies of the report a modest one.[34]

The Cost of Living Study was intended to define what material goods made up a minimum standard of living for 'health and self-respect' and what those goods cost at current Toronto prices. The idea of identifying and publishing the essentials to maintain a decent standard of living was not new. Its origins lay in the Fabian 'Doctrine of Minimums,' which declared each individual to possess an inherent right 'not only to live but to live after a decent fashion.'[35] Following the First World War, reformers began to seek information on the nature and cost of such a minimum: 'A standard of living in each community might be tabulated by women home-makers. Such information should be available to all classes in the community. How are workers – girls, boys, men or women, – to know on what sums individuals and families can live and maintain health and efficiency in one district or another if these matters are not studied, determined, and published for their use?'[36] Implied was both the assumption that a standard would vary from one community to another and that the information itself should be available to everyone. It also reflected the prevailing assumption that responsibility for family health rested in women's hands.

The view that this was women's work was significant. Poverty was being linked with poor health, which in part was seen as a result of inadequate nutrition. The prevention of poverty therefore rested not only on protecting the health of the breadwinner, it also depended on the ability of women to bear healthy children and to care adequately and properly for their families. As such it was a cause that had found its way onto the agenda of women's organizations and social agencies concerned with the well-being of the family. Its broad preventive focus held out a vain hope that the well-being of people, no matter what their social or economic standing, could be ensured by adequate diet. Thus the most important component of a decent standard of living became the purchase and preparation of food, universally regarded as the responsibility of women.

Since working-class housewives were considered 'notorious' for their lack of knowledge and skills to ensure proper nutrition,[37] the work of visiting housekeepers was regarded as a much-needed service. In order to provide these workers with the necessary scientific information, efforts to develop standardized budgets for household needs began. The pioneer work of the Montreal Council of Social Agencies, with its ties to the empiricism of the McGill School of Social Science, provided a model for Toronto agencies. The Montreal council published a scientifically derived budget in 1926, and when the Depression began, it was but a short step to develop comparisons between minimum budgets and levels of public and private relief.[38]

The Toronto Child Welfare Council took up the cause in 1933 in cooperation with the Red Cross Visiting Housekeepers Association. A joint committee established four objectives: the publication of a position identifying 'essentials for satisfactory living' to include nutrition, housing, clothing, health, [household] upkeep, recreation, and savings; determining the cost in Toronto of these essentials; the recording of actual expenditures by families in Toronto; and observing the effect on families who 'fall below these essentials.' The committee, which was later transferred to the Welfare Council, was chaired by Marjorie Bell, executive director of the Red Cross Housekeepers. Bell was also a member of a committee established by the Ontario Medical Association to investigate the adequacy of 'relief diets.' The Medical Association committee was founded at the request of 'various relief organizations for scientific information,' and was chaired by Dr F.F. Tisdall, an associate in paediatrics at the University of Toronto.[39] It was the beginning of an association between Bell and Tisdall that, with the added expertise of Dr Alice Willard of the Household Science Department at the University of Toronto, would become the research team behind the Council's Cost of Living Study and subsequent studies for the municipality and eventually the province.

The goal of achieving a minimum standard of living for all went beyond adequate relief to include the question of a fair wage. The Federation for Community Service, when it took up the cause late in 1936, entered into a joint study with the Board of Trade to look at the question of minimum wages in relation to a minimum standard budget. Bell was asked to provide the information and when she reported early the next year, it evoked immediate interest and reaction. Bell and her colleagues had calculated a minimum weekly budget for a family of five at $25.30. In 1935 the families surveyed by Red Cross visiting housekeepers and by caseworkers in the NWA earned average wages of $15.80 in 1935 and $17.85 in 1936. Toronto relief allowances for a family of five for food alone was $6.04 compared to a minimum adequate budget of $8.00. It was obvious to anyone who cared to add it up that neither wages nor relief was sufficient to provide the basic needs of families in Toronto. Even the Board of Trade took a position in favour of a minimum wage law, which was under consideration by the provincial government of the day.[40] Thus in the beginning, scientific study of the cost of living was sanctioned by business as well as the social work community.

The immediate objective of the Cost of Living Study was to provide needed information to caseworkers in social and health agencies, to employers for comparison with prevailing wages, and to the general public for assessment of proposals for minimum wage legislation. The membership of the study committee included Tisdall, Bell, and E.W. McHenry, chairman of the School of Hygiene at the University of Toronto. McHenry was later appointed a consultant for the province on nutrition and wrote a report, largely based on the work of this committee, that was used as the basis of provincial policy on food allowances. Lois Fraser, who was also trained in nutrition, participated, and she and Bell held the responsibility for raising the money, $2000 of which came from the London Life Insurance Co., to pay the salaries of the researchers.[41] Support from the insurance industry for efforts to improve nutrition and health was logical. Support from an increasingly powerful insurance lobby for the wider social purpose of the Cost of Living Study would prove to be fragile indeed.

The study was carefully designed and exhaustive for its time. It was supervised by the Red Cross visiting housekeepers and employed three of their staff. One hundred and sixteen low income families agreed to participate, forty of whom persisted for the entire year, during which the weight and content of their diet was carefully recorded each week. McHenry supervised the calculation of its nutritional content. While this was underway, subcommittees for each of the categories of life's necessities debated the level of sufficiency that would become the minimum standard, and then surveyed the actual cost. The final result was a minimum cost for a family of five of $28.35 per week for only the barest necessities. The report carefully pointed out that this included little recreation, no alcohol or tobacco, no telephone, and no pension. The committee also surveyed prevailing wages. The average wage of breadwinners in the study was $19.64 per week, and a check of the wages of other agency clients revealed that the vast majority earned less than $22.00, and almost 30 per cent earned between $15.00 and $19.00. Clearly, the income of the agency clients, even though they were employed, was not sufficient to maintain a decent standard of living.[42]

Along with providing the facts and figures, the final report attempted to counter the widely held belief that failure to make do on a low income was the result of poor management, implicitly on the part of women in the home: 'The statement is frequently made that some families "get along very well" on a low wage, and that the ability to manage is the most important factor. Those who have detailed knowledge of the situation are convinced that the ability to manage well, while valuable, is not sufficient, and they have constantly before them the evidence of harm resulting from the low standard of living made necessary by inadequate income.'[43] For social workers who were confronted daily with the reality of poverty, it was a constant and frustrating struggle to convince the sceptical public of the impossible plight of the poor.

The experience of social workers also lay behind a decision to concentrate the study on the needs of a family of five. While it was not the average size family for the population as a whole, this was the size family most commonly encountered by agency caseworkers and homemakers. This information therefore suited the needs of the agencies. But in order to also meet the needs of the general public for information, the study included a chart for easy calculation of the minimum cost for families of different sizes. Thus the intent of the early reformers to make such studies useful for 'all classes in the community' was fulfilled.

There was little action towards encouraging higher levels of relief for about two years following the publication of the Cost of Living Study. The Council was preoccupied first with finding an executive secretary, and then with the commencement of the Second World War and a general hostility towards relief recipients, many of whom were summarily declared ineligible and expected to join the army.[44] But by 1941 the reform of public welfare generally was once again at the fore, and with the favourable climate at city hall noted above, the Council resumed its campaign for adequate benefits.

At the Council's urging, the City of Toronto commissioned Tisdall, Willard, and Bell to do a study of the level of food allowances required to sustain a nutritious diet for those on relief. Drawing on the previous work of the Cost of Living study, the trio established a scale for calculating food allowances according to size of family, sex of family members, and age of children. The Tisdall-Willard-Bell (TWB) report not only recommended increased allowances as was expected, it also recommended that allowances be adjusted with each 5 per cent change in the Dominion Bureau of Statistics Cost of Living Index. Where prices had been relatively stable during the Depression, the possibility of inflation was now evident.[45]

The mayor called a conference of agencies who were predictably enthusiastic about the proposed TWB scales. But what was an evident social problem during the Depression had become a matter of contention in the relative prosperity of wartime. Where previously the Board of Trade had approved of a minimum standard, it was now adamantly in opposition. The city delayed its budget for the coming fiscal year in order to bring the Welfare Council and Board of Trade together with the hope of reconciling their points of view. The Council was anxious to remain on good terms with the powerful Board of Trade, yet they were not prepared to relinquish their deeply held principles. The Council board adopted a 'non-compromise position,' maintaining that 'it was the function of this Council to provide scientific data on these questions and that it would be inconsistent for its representatives to suggest that less than that described in the report would at any time be adequate.' Council board members expressed the view that the Board of Trade was under the influence of prevailing anxiety about anticipated postwar unemployment, and attempted reconciliation by agreeing that municipal relief should not be required to meet this larger problem.[46]

The Welfare Council's unwillingness to compromise on its position was a statement of its commitment to research as a neutral and objective basis for planning. It was in contrast to others, such as the Canadian Medical Association, who had bowed to 'constant pressure for cheapness' and modified their standards to reflect what was considered possible rather than desirable.[47]

Although it was unable to convince the Board of Trade, the Welfare Council had little difficulty persuading the city's public welfare advisory committee, whose advice on the matter would precede any decision by city council. This committee had finally been established under Mayor Conboy's administration after several years of fruitless lobbying on the part of the Council. Lois Fraser was appointed to conduct a watching brief of the committee's proceedings in cooperation with the League of Women Voters, and the whole arrangement provided the Council with a useful channel of communication to City Council. The report of the public welfare committee that followed the TWB report reflected the theories that linked poverty and health and targeted improved nutrition as a major strategy for the prevention of poverty: 'Recent discoveries in the field of nutrition give grounds for the belief that by proper food, properly prepared, the physique, mental capacity, energy and health of the people can be materially improved, and the incidence of disease correspondingly reduced.'

On the committee's recommendation, the city approved the adoption of the TWB scales for determining the amount of food allowance, as well as the appointment of a professional nutritionist to city staff, the mounting of a 'forceful educational programme,' and the use of cash vouchers – which had also been a matter of long standing debate and controversy. In an attempt to mollify the opposition, the city also included a policy of 'rigid control' of eligibility and abuse by recipients, and the coordination of all agencies involved.[48]

The adoption of the TWB scales for relief by Toronto City Council intensified the controversy. The Property Owners Association, in a letter to Mayor Conboy, insisted there was no evidence that the health of recipients suffered on the lower relief scales; that the new scales would be higher than the earnings of tax-paying working people; and that if vouchers were issued, some means must be employed to ensure that the cash was used for the purchase of food. Predicting a rise in the relief rates of 70 per cent, the Association declared the whole policy to be a 'raid on the City treasury which cannot be justified.' They repeated a long-standing position, and one that was widely held, that the province should take over all responsibility for the administration of relief, removing it from the realm of city politics and by inference, from the property tax base.[49]

The position of the Property Owners Association as well as the Board of Trade was fundamentally different from that of the Welfare Council and its supporters. It rested on the values of the work ethic and less eligibility and placed a priority on keeping the tax rates down. The position of the Welfare Council rested on the value of the social minimum and had as its priority ensuring a decent standard of living for all, regardless of cost. The insistence of the Property Owners Association that there was no evidence of poor health, despite the growing body of research to the contrary, demonstrated an indifference towards science and rationality as the basis for decisions, placing the controversy over adequate relief in the realm of contending values and political action.

The relief scales recommended by Tisdall, Willard, and Bell faced more than local opposition. They were higher than those allowed by the province and required lobbying at that level as well. Following a major conference on nutrition in which the Welfare Council participated, the province established an Ontario Nutrition Committee early in 1942. It was chaired by the provincial medical officer of health and brought together representatives of several provincial and national organizations concerned with health and nutrition. The provincial committee did not include the Toronto Welfare Council, but Marjorie Bell was appointed as a representative of the Canadian Dietetic Association. The purpose of the committee was public education and interorganizational cooperation. E.W. McHenry was appointed honourary consultant in nutrition to the Ontario Department of Health and was asked to provide the requisite expertise.[50]

The province also asked McHenry to prepare a report and make recommendations on food allowances and relief. Relief allowances in Ontario were still being updated simply by adding a percentage to the schedules that had been recommended in the 1932 Campbell Report.[51] Levels now stood at 'Campbell plus 60' and were obviously out of date.

McHenry finished his report on the eve of a general election that resulted in Ontario's government passing from the hands of the Liberal Hepburn administration to the Conservatives under George Drew.

Drew's minister of public welfare, Dr R.P. Vivian, did not release the report. Instead he announced an increase in the provincial relief rates.[52] The Welfare Council publicly protested the failure to publish the report, seeing the move as a failure on the part of Drew's government to consult with the community. Lack of consultation violated the principles of local input and wide circulation upon which the Cost of Living Study had been founded. Moreover, Toronto City Council, at the Welfare Council's urging, had taken an unprecedented step in assuming extra costs of improved food allowances, evidence of strong local involvement and support. The Council recommended that the city stick to its own policy and not adopt the McHenry standard until the report was released and the public had a chance to study and discuss its contents.[53]

Although it had not been released, the Council had obtained a copy of the McHenry Report and was unhappy with some of its content. The report was substantively similar to the one prepared for the Toronto Welfare Council by Bell's committee, but the suggestions in the earlier report were seen by McHenry as extravagant. He compared his own standards for nutrition and related costs with those of the Welfare Council, the Dominion Bureau of Statistics, and the Ontario Department of Public Welfare, rejecting the last two as inadequate. He acknowledged that his own standards and the Welfare Council's were similar, but he suggested that the Council had provided for excessive amounts of milk, fruit, meat, and fish, and their standard was therefore more costly. He pointed out that the main purpose of a food allowance should be adequate nutrition without extravagance.[54] One can surmise that McHenry's point of view, which carried the weight of medical expertise, was seized on by those whose first concern was to keep the rates down.

McHenry's report also referred to studies that appeared to support his own firm belief that there was a lack of nutritional knowledge and that cash allowances were often misspent. His report stressed nutrition education, although he was of the opinion that a better alternative, strictly from the point of view of nutrition of course, was to establish special restaurants for the poor that would ensure nutritious meals. It was an argument on the side of the soup kitchen. Despite the Welfare Council's disclaimer, the belief persisted that mismanagement on the part of the homemaker was responsible for the poor nutrition and ill health of the poor.[55]

Toronto City Council and the Welfare Council were caught in a political shift in attitude towards relief that had occurred following the change of government in Ontario. Shortly before the election, Farquhar Oliver, the Liberal minister of public welfare at the time, agreed to hear a delegation from the city and the Welfare Council requesting that the province assume its share of higher rates of relief recommended by the TWB Report. Now, the new Conservative minister stubbornly refused to give any consideration to the city's request or to the TWB Report.[56] The difference reveals how essentially similar research can reflect two very different views. Selection of supporting studies, interpretation, and conclusions were aimed at differing political ends. One view, that of McHenry, conformed to the desire to keep the tax rates as low as possible; the other, that of TWB, saw that rates must be sufficiently high to ensure a life of 'health and self-respect' for the poor. Admittedly both views incorporated the idea of a social minimum, and the Welfare Council's position may be regarded as only marginally different from their conservative opponents. But the TWB standard, had it been incorporated into provincial policy, would have made a very real difference to the lives of people attempting to live on relief. The legacy of McHenry remains as the underpinning of social assistance rates in Ontario today.

The province's approach went beyond arguments over levels of relief, encompassing a fundamental shift in thinking about nutrition education and the prevention of poverty. Despite the fact that information about the buying and preparation of food was traditionally provided by women to other women, control of the rapidly developing field of nutrition education was now being assumed by men. Shortly after it was organized, the Ontario Nutrition Committee approved plans for a provincewide program and the Department of Health appointed one of its male medical doctors to take charge. The Welfare Council and the Red Cross were outraged by the appointment. Through Marjorie Bell, the Nutrition Committee heard a formal protest from Lois Fraser as president of the Council. Referring to the war effort, Fraser suggested that physicians were needed elsewhere and pointed to 'the general trend of replacing men by women even in fields where they were not fitted for the work.' At issue was the entrance and domination of the field of nutrition by doctors and by men.[57]

In the discussion that followed, McHenry argued that nutrition was as much a part of the health concerns of the province as tuberculosis or venereal disease, and therefore needed the expertise of a physician. Janet Lang Ross, representing the Ontario Council of Women, and a physician herself, acknowledged that this position was quite contrary to the wishes of the Council of Women, but nevertheless sided with her professional colleague. William Anderson, whose appointment representing the insurance industry had been suggested by the Ontario Medical Association, agreed with the doctors. He observed that since women would be doing most of the work, the support of women's organizations was important and they should be represented on the committee. At the same time, the 'community organization' of the education program should be through the local medical officers of health, whose support was also needed and who would only accept direction from another medical man. The objections raised by the Welfare Council were overruled. Shortly thereafter, the province disbanded the committee, with its representative structure, and replaced it with an internal, interdepartmental committee.[58]

The education of homemakers had been the purview of women's organizations and the female profession of social work for decades. The assumption that nutrition was a matter of health needing the expertise of physicians had taken the matter out of the hands of women and shifted responsibility from social work to medicine. As the concern became entangled with public welfare and a matter of provincial policy, and as its importance rose, it was taken out of the hands of local communities and centralized in the provincial bureaucracy.

The loss of control over the traditionally female field of nutrition to public health and to medicine was part of a steady decline in the influence of women and women's organizations. While the Toronto Welfare Council had men at both the board and staff levels, it was headed by women and seen by many as a woman's organization. The idealism of the new Council was no more acceptable than the idealism of the old Child Welfare Council except that now the Council had raised the ire of both the Community Chest and the men who held the reins of provincial power. The response of the Federation for Community Service had been to curtail the reform activities of the Child Welfare Council and to place the women who led it in a position where male supervision was ensured. The response now was essentially the same.

The loss of control over nutrition education also revealed the strength of the values that placed responsibility on the individual, rather than with society. The approach of the Welfare Council was one of seeking fair wages for the working class, and adequate food allowances for those on relief. It placed the emphasis on social and community solutions to the problem of poverty and ill health. The approach of McHenry and the Ontario Nutrition Committee placed responsibility on the individual, and sought to solve the problems of the poor by instructing the homemaker on the efficient management of her household. Both approaches ostensibly relied on research, but the differences between them reveals the ultimate disregard it was given in the face of contending ideologies.

As the war progressed and plans for postwar reconstruction moved more and more towards the welfare state and ideals of a social minimum, the distance between these two positions widened. Initially, the Welfare Council was regarded as promoting extravagance and unnecessary expense. Eventually, it became caught in the postwar hysteria that regarded every social ideal as part of a perceived communist threat. Social workers in Toronto were publicly accused of communist sympathies and the board of the Community Chest found it necessary to respond to accusations by 'a group of management' that the TWC was engaged in political activity and being used as a 'propaganda organization.'[59]

Thus on several fronts, the reform efforts of the Toronto Welfare Council placed it in opposition to those who wielded power and influence. It is not surprising therefore that the Council's actions eventually brought it into direct conflict with the Community Chest.

At the end of the war, the Welfare Council's Cost of Living Study was seriously in need of revision. Wartime controls on both prices and wages were gone, consumer spending was compensating for years of constraint, and wages were going up in response to unprecedented union strength. Revised versions of the publication revealed that the weekly cost of providing for a family of five had risen from the 1939 level of $28.35 to $35.85 in 1944 and $40.11 in 1947. Food was second only to housing as the cause of the increase in living costs. But the Council did not include housing costs in its revisions, taking the position that provision of subsidized public housing was the only way to meet minimum requirements for shelter. The updated figures were considered much more reliable since the Council now had the advantage of considerable research activity in both the United States and Canada to support its figures. This was true for information on nutritional needs and also for medical and dental costs, which had been carefully calculated for Canadians in preparation for a planned national health insurance scheme.[60]

Copies of the revised study were in considerable demand. Five thousand of the 1944 revision were printed, ten times the number printed in 1939. Its original readership of workers in social agencies had broadened dramatically to include large corporations, trade associations, labour relations experts, and newspaper journalists. The labour unions in particular found its contents useful, since it provided ready reference to the relation between cost of living and wages. The Workers' Educational Association requested four hundred copies, requiring a motion of approval by the Council board. The Cost of Living Study had become a very effective instrument in meeting its original purpose, which, it will be recalled, went considerably beyond the information needs of agency workers to include employers and the general public interested in assessing the adequacy of minimum wages. It was for this last purpose that its format had been deliberately designed so that non-professionals could easily use it to estimate the needs of families of different sizes.[61]

The use of the Cost of Living Study by labour organizations precipitated a crisis. It was a time of rising labour militancy and the little red-covered booklet, now nicknamed the Red Book, was suddenly under attack by some of the large corporate supporters of the Community Chest. In the fall of 1947, Edgar Burton, chief executive officer of Simpsons' department store found his workers on a picket line handing out the schedules from the study that compared living costs to wages. Burton, who was also chairman of the board of the Chest, demanded that the booklet be withdrawn from circulation.[62]

Burton's demand unleashed a flood of complaints from business supporters of the Chest. The study itself was attacked by marshalling expert opinion that questioned the validity of the Council's research as well as the interpretation of its findings. There were complaints that the statistical weighting used by the Council was faulty; that the average family was made up of three (an inaccurate assumption) and not the five used as a base in the study; and that the highest incomes since 1929 and the obvious surge in consumer spending belied the study's findings that costs were higher than wages. In any event, the study was seen as duplicating the work of the Dominion Bureau of Statistics, and if not government, then a national organization such as the Canadian Welfare Council. The critics, many of whom were executives of large national corporations, made it very clear that they were angered by its use in support of increased wages by labour, and by political groups such as the CCF and the communist Labour Progressive Party. They objected to the Council 'assuming the function of producing such material,' suggesting the whole project was inappropriate for a local Welfare Council.[63] The concentration on national policy had become a handy tool for opposing the involvement of the locally based council.

The reaction of the Welfare Council board was unequivocal, echoing the 'non-compromise' position taken earlier when the Board of Trade had attacked the TWB report. Beatrice Kirkpatrick, the Council president, stated flatly that such research was entirely proper for a planning and coordinating council. The issue was seen by the board as reopening the 'fundamental question of Council autonomy' and a matter to be included in discussions currently being held on the Chest-Council constitution. The board resolved to continue with the preparation and distribution of the booklet and to take the matter up directly with Burton rather than to accede to a request for a joint meeting of the executive committees of the Chest and Council.[64]

The demand that the Cost of Living Study be withdrawn followed other less overt actions on the part of the Chest to suppress the reform activities of the Welfare Council. Critics of the Council had also sought an end to Touzel's work at the national level. Their complaints were accompanied by quiet assurance that the Council's budget requests would receive support only if her activities were curtailed.[65]

Touzel's knowledge and skills had been much in demand by senior civil servants and politicians who were in the process of building a welfare state. In 1941 Bryce Stewart, deputy minister of labour, drew her into the national Labour Coordinating Committee. In 1943 she had been loaned to Leonard Marsh for three weeks while he struggled to meet the demanding deadlines of the Advisory Committee on Reconstruction. Brooke Claxton, minister of health and welfare, consulted her in 1944 when drawing up the legislation for a family allowance. Furthermore, Touzel's work at the national level was instrumental in introducing the Toronto Council's Cost of Living Study and the TWB standards for relief to the national policy makers. Both the Marsh Report and the family allowances introduced in 1944 rested on the principle of a social minimum, and both drew directly on the Cost of Living Study in Toronto as an argument and an example for establishing such a minimum.[66]

Fears of potential damage to the annual campaign for funds because of lack of support from large corporations disgruntled over labour's use of the Red Book was therefore only part of Chest discomfort with its planning partner. Some of the large supporters of the Chest did not approve of the Council's social reform activities in general or of the activities of its executive secretary. The motive was as much to stop further development of state social programs as it was fear that the generally left-leaning activities of the Council would affect the campaign.

In November of 1947, less than a month after the Chest demanded withdrawal of the Red Book, Touzel resigned as the Council's executive secretary. Officially her reason was the career opportunity presented by an employment offer from the Canadian Welfare Council. Unofficially, she had tired of the constant criticism and underlying conflict that lay between the Chest and the Council. The atmosphere of distrust, innuendoes that she was communist, and the attitude of some of the businessmen, who were 'in the habit of persons taking their wishes as law,' did not allow her to pursue her personal beliefs or to use her knowledge and skills as a social worker.[67]

The reform role of the Welfare Council was seriously eroded by the loss of Bessie Touzel as its executive secretary. Sooner or later, she would have moved on to other tasks, but the circumstances of her leaving, within days of the Chest's demands, reinforced the limits that were being placed on the Council. Like her predecessor, Margaret Gould, Touzel was uncompromising in her ideals. Both women were highly skilled, respected by their colleagues, and able to provide the kind of leadership that a proactive and reform-minded organization needed. Both suffered the personal blows and professional frustration of unjust criticism and irrational censure. While they had the support of those nearest to them within the organization, most of them women, the inherent vulnerability of their position made their role untenable. It is debatable whether others similarly inclined would have been willing to move into their position; but it is unlikely that the Community Chest would have allowed its planning partner to hire another executive secretary with similar potential for attracting controversy.

Despite their initial stand, the Council withdrew the Cost of Living Study from circulation pending resolution of the conflict. With Touzel's departure and the perceived threat to the finances of both the Council and the Chest itself, the Council board was wavering under the pressure. Some members saw approaches to the Canadian Welfare Council as a reasonable compromise, and others insisted that they should stand on principle at any cost. Eventually the Council agreed to approach the national organization to take over sponsorship of the study, and to keep the Toronto figures, which were being updated by Albert Rose, the Council's director of research, for internal use only. But the board also resolved to begin using separate letterhead to reinforce the Council's independence, and acknowledging that this was a cosmetic solution, to ask that reconsideration be given to 'the whole joint set-up.'[68]

By the fall of 1948 the Red Book had been withheld from circulation for almost a year and Rose had left the Council's staff to teach full time at the University of Toronto School of Social Work. Following 'unfavourable' discussion in the Workers' Educational Association and charges in the local press that the Council was being 'suppressed by the financial interests in the Community Chest,' the Toronto Trades and Labour Council made a formal request that the study be updated and reissued. The Chest could no longer postpone the decision to reissue the study, and approval was given subject to the format being vetted by a 'representative citizens committee,' to include appointees from labour and the board of the Chest.[69]

In the spring of 1949 the Cost of Living Study reappeared as the *Guide to Family Spending in Toronto*. The new title of the publication represented the fundamental difference between the old and the new. Rather than a measure to help determine a community standard that would 'maintain health and self-respect,' it was now a guideline for individual and family responsibility. It remained useful to caseworkers, teaching homemakers, and the nutrition programs of public health, but services such as these depended more on the view that incompetency on the part of the homemaker was the problem to be addressed rather than any income policy of the wider community. To be fair, it was still intended for use by advocates of a decent standard of public welfare. But the controversy had choked off the wide circulation that it had previously attained and its format was complex, restricting its usefulness to professionals and persons familiar with technical reports. It was a compromise that no longer met the original goals of providing a wide readership with factual information that would help citizens at large assess the impact of low wages and inadequate levels of public welfare on working people.

The controversy generated by the Cost of Living Study revealed the fundamental clash of values between the social workers who controlled the Welfare Council and the businessmen who controlled the Community Chest. The Fabian values of the Council may not have been widely understood or popular, but there is no evidence that they were considered radical by the majority of the population in the postwar period. They were unpopular primarily with a corporate elite, the sector of the philanthropic community that was concentrated in the Community Chest movement. The corporate executives who attacked the Cost of Living Study did so because it added weight to union demands. They did so also because they were fundamentally opposed to the socialism of a welfare state. The issue was complicated by the anticommunist hysteria of the cold war period, but this in itself was not the deciding factor. The Council's actions in general espoused a level of social change that threatened the corporate status quo.

Opposition to the Cost of Living Study and its principles also came from the local business community, long the backbone of the financial federations. The Board of Trade, the Property Owners Association, and others were opposed to the campaign of the Welfare Council to improve the provision of municipal relief primarily because it would increase the local rates. The success of the Council in influencing change in municipal affairs was in part due to a reform-minded administration at city hall. It is also probable that it succeeded because of anticipated improvements in senior government participation after the war, which shifted the focus of the antiwelfare lobby away from local government. While the opposition of local business organizations was serious, it was not as damaging to the Council's cause as that of the large national corporations.

This shift of responsibility for public welfare from municipal to senior levels of government accounts for the increasing involvement of large corporations in the Community Chest movement. The stakes in a welfare state were much higher than in a residual system where voluntary agencies carried the primary responsibility, backed by municipal relief when all else failed. The Depression experience and the plans for postwar reconstruction drove both the problem and the provision of services to the poor to higher levels of community. As the stakes grew larger, so did the involvement and concern of major stakeholders in the economic structure of society. This trend became critical in the fifties and is a theme in the chapter that follows. The conflict with the Community Chest over the circulation of the Red Book reopened the question of the structural relationship between the Chest and the Council. Over the next ten years this relationship was constantly under review. It was a decade of paralysing conflict that eventually ended in divorce.

CHAPTER SIX

Chest-Council Relations: A Decade of Conflict

Conflict over suppression of the Cost of Living Study and the Community Chest's opposition to the Toronto Welfare Council's social reform activities created an atmosphere of distrust between them. But as bad as the relationship may have seemed in 1948, it was destined to grow worse. Like a marriage that fails when two ill-matched partners grow in incompatible directions, the partnership between the Chest and Council, which had never been a happy one, began to unravel. Each party was essentially working for disparate and contradictory ends. This seems clear in hindsight, but as the Council entered the postwar period, its immediate thoughts were to smooth its relationship with the Chest and get on with the momentous task of helping build a humane and just social order.

Immediately after the departure of Bessie Touzel, the Council appointed Florence Philpott, an experienced social worker who came to Toronto from a position as executive director of the Winnipeg YWCA. Philpott had grown up in Toronto, graduated from the University of Toronto School of Social Work, and had worked briefly with the Toronto YWCA. Her position in Winnipeg brought her in contact with both the Community Chest and the Welfare Council in that city. Philpott was much more inclined to administrative work than Touzel and did not share her reputation as a reformer. But like Touzel, she was deeply committed to improving both the quality and effectiveness of social services.[1]

Philpott arrived in the midst of the Red Book crisis, and one of her first steps was to request a review of the relationship between the Chest and the Council. The Welfare Council board attached sufficient importance to the idea to agree to pay costs out of their own training funds, rather than risk having to negotiate with the Chest.[2] The review was conducted by C. William Chilman, executive secretary of the Syracuse Council of Social Agencies, who had a reputation for success in developing Council programs while maintaining good relations with the Community Chest. His report tied the Council's problems to a vagueness of the relationship between the Chest and Council and an underlying assumption, unsound in his opinion, that the Chest and the Council were in fact one unit with similar purpose, functions and policies. He suggested that this resulted in relegating the Council to a 'subservient, and poor relative status,' and a perception that the Council, like the Chest, was preoccupied with the funding of member agencies.[3]

Chilman recommended separation of the Chest and Council, which was consistent with practice elsewhere in the Community Chest movement, but only after a period of time in which the administrative practices of the Welfare Council could be strengthened. He was critical of the Council for pursuing a 'planless method of community organization, which appears to have followed the general theme of establishing a new committee whenever a new problem has arisen.' Rather than continuing the practice of using ad hoc committees, he recommended streamlining and strengthening the Council's division structure.

Like the early functional councils of the Federation for Community Service, the divisions were organized around fields of service. When the Toronto Welfare Council was formed, it moved away from this structure, adopting the position of the predecessor Child Welfare Council that ad hoc committees better served the issue-oriented approach of social reform. On the other hand, the Chest preferred the division structure, which favoured coordination of services, dividing the agencies into groups according to fields of service, and at least in theory, allowed the budgeting process to address problems of duplication and overlap.

While many of the structural recommendations of the Chilman report were implemented, a major exception was the one regarding clarification of the Council's relationship with the Community Chest.[4] But his recommendation that the Chest and Council ultimately be separated was important in that it legitimized the issue and provided a ready excuse for reopening the question as relations became increasingly strained and desire for independence grew.

These structural concerns, while important, were but symptomatic of much deeper problems of Chest-Council relations. A new round of controversy had emerged in the face of the chronic inability of the Community Chest to respond to agency requests for funds. The end of the Second World War released a flood of financial demands. Member agencies of the Chest, subject to fiscal restraint since the late twenties, sought funding not only for a backlog of pent up practical problems such as repair and replacement of aging buildings, but also for improved and expanded services. The pressure to expand was partly a result of rapidly increasing population, partly a rising cost of living, and partly a desire on the part of social work to improve salaries and to raise the level of professional involvement in service provision.

The response of the Community Chest to these requests was simply to hold the financial line to no more than modest annual increases. In 1947, the Chest approved a goal of $2 million for the following year; that was $400,000 less than the agencies had requested and $260,000 less than the approved budgets. Not only did the campaign goal fall short of needs of existing agencies, it provided nothing for six new agencies, most of them in the emerging suburbs, waiting to be admitted to Chest membership.[5]

In April of 1948, at the request of the Welfare Council, the Community Chest convened a meeting of agencies to discuss the serious gap between campaign revenues and agency requests. The concern of the agencies lay both in the failure of the campaign to meet their financial goals, and in the process of setting the goal itself. It brought to the fore a fundamental difference of opinion over whether the campaign goal should reflect the needs identified in the community by the Welfare Council and the member agencies, or whether it should reflect what the fund-raisers felt was possible. The campaign committee argued that their volunteers did not wish to be associated with a perceived failure. They took the position that the lack of funds was 'too bad and the agencies would just have to learn to tighten their belts.' Welfare Council volunteers, however, returned to a long-standing position that, given adequate publicity, the community would support a goal based on needs. Furthermore, they argued, it was impossible to explain service cutbacks to the public following a so-called 'successful' campaign. From the perspective of the agencies and the Council, a goal that could not meet agency needs was a failure before the campaign was even launched.[6]

The agency meeting failed to resolve this conflict and the Welfare Council passed a lengthy resolution that sought reconciliation between the two positions. Recognizing that 'it appears unlikely that the Chest will be able to raise, for 1949, sufficient money to cover the [agency] budgets,' the Council board called for efforts to reduce agency financial needs through transferring some services to the municipality, increasing provincial grants to child welfare, increased use of fees for service, coordination of agencies 'in the interest of greater efficiency and economy,' elimination of non-essential services, and limitations on admission of new agencies. While the resolution reflected some sympathy for the agencies, it generally leaned heavily on the side of the efficiency standards of the Chest. Perhaps realizing what it had done, a month later the Council passed another motion in support of the idea that the Chest establish a goal committee, which would include representatives from both the fund-raising and the planning side of the organization.[7]

Despite the participation of Council representatives in the goal-setting process after 1948, and the sustained pleas of the agencies, the Community Chest continued to fall far short of the financial needs of its members. The goal for 1951 was set at $2.495 million, almost $500,000 short of member agency requests. In the fall of 1951, with campaign revenues for 1952 projected at $800,000 below revised agency budgets of $3.4 million, only two of twenty-six programs recommended for additional funding by the Welfare Council's central planning committee were approved by the budget committee of the Chest. According to the economy-minded Chest volunteers, the amount of money raised would allow 'no funds for enlarging or special improvements in the ongoing programs.'[8]

What must have rankled almost as much as the increasing distance between Chest campaign goals and agency needs was the lack of participation of Chest-appointed volunteers on the panels that reviewed each agency's request. In 1950, Welfare Council volunteers were over twice as faithful in their attendance on the panels, appearing 80 per cent of the time compared to Chest volunteer attendance of only 33 per cent. The council had also willingly supplied scarce staff time to assist in the review process, hoping that it would give their staff both experience and an opportunity for 'interpretation.'[9]

The actions of Chest volunteers signalled an indifference to the budget review process and to the agency arguments for a needs-related campaign goal. The 'too bad' attitude towards campaigns that were successful in the eyes of canvassers but fell well below the needs of the agencies was also a measure of the indifference of the Chest organization to service goals. The ideals and objectives of the social workers and the needs of the social agencies and their clients were overpowered by the goals of economy and efficiency that governed the actions of the businessmen who controlled the Chest. Most of these men cared little for the services; their primary concern was the campaign and only the campaign.[10] Taking place as it did during a time of economic growth, this approach must have been doubly difficult for the social work community. It was a paradox of financial restraint in the midst of rising prosperity.

The demands on the Council's time for advising the Community Chest on the allocation of its funds became another major source of contention between the two partners. Council staff carried a heavy load, providing information on general trends and needs in the community, preparing reports on each agency, and providing consultation to the Chest's budget panels that reviewed each agency request in the various fields of service. The Council's central planning committee made detailed recommendations regarding admission of new agencies and requests for expansion of existing services. The Council's executive secretary acted as a consultant to the budget committee of the Chest as well as providing assistance to the central planning committee in carrying out its function. In addition, the Council conducted special agency reviews when requested by the Chest.[11]

These responsibilities were a substantial drain on the time and energies of the Council, especially during the time that agency budgets were being reviewed by the Chest. In 1950, it was estimated that Council staff spent 325 working hours related to budget committee proceedings, and another 100 hours to study proposals for 24 improved or expanded agency programs, only 2 or 3 of which were approved. This did not include the estimate of two months of the executive secretary's time and six weeks of time spent on allocations-related matters by the research department. This concentrated effort resulted in suspension of all other activity during budget review, making the Council 'friends with the Budget Department ... [and] somewhat unpopular in other quarters.'[12] It was a thankless task, alienating many of the Chest's member agencies whose requests were denied, as well as non-member agencies affiliated with the Council, who felt they were being ignored.

Severe financial restrictions meant that the process of allocating Chest funds was very painful. Lack of money also meant that the Chest was exceptionally persistent in its request that the Council develop a system of establishing priorities for funding. In the fall of 1951, when, as noted above, the $800,000 shortfall in campaign revenues appeared likely, the central planning committee was given only two weeks to prioritize new agency requests. Reluctantly, the Council suggested that priority be given to bringing present services up to standard and that its own capability for both short- and long-term planning be strengthened.[13] The urgency of the situation meant that the Council was placed in a position of ruling on agency requests without time for consultation, and in view of its own limited resources, put in the awkward position of arguing for preferential treatment over that given the member agencies. Both these factors placed great strain on the relationship between the Council and the agencies who were members of the Chest.

The Welfare Council responded to the dilemma by convening a conference of agencies. John Morgan, a faculty member from the University of Toronto School of Social Work and a member of the Council's board of directors, chaired the conference. Participants included representatives of the Catholic and Jewish agencies, professional associations for social work and nursing, agencies independent of any financial federation, as well as the Chest and Council. The belief of Morgan and the Council was that priorities should be established in the context of a comprehensive community study: 'Priorities must be based on a study of the total needs and resources of the community and must be determined through broad lay and professional citizen participation. It must also include wide participation and discussion between the agencies whose budgets are under consideration.'[14]

Morgan's approach combined ideas of central planning and decentralized citizen participation, ideas enhanced by the impending implementation of a two-tier metropolitan government for Toronto and the surrounding municipalities. A system of comprehensive, long-range planning for all social services in the metropolitan area was the ideal and the goal. Although the ideal included agency consultation, it emphasized planning based on identification of community needs through citizen organizations and neighbourhood or area councils rather than through the traditional method of drawing on the experience of existing agencies.[15]

Following the conference on priorities, which was held in the fall of 1953, the Welfare Council board approved the idea of developing a formal long-range plan. Once under way, other planning and research activities would be suspended until complete. Once done, it would provide the basis for ongoing review and updating. The board also stipulated that the cost must be over and above regular expenditures and that the study could not proceed until additional staff had been secured.[16]

From the perspective of the Chest budget committee, the Council's desire for rational, long-range, and comprehensive planning simply did not meet their needs. They wanted immediate answers, not more studies, and they certainly were not prepared to provide the funds for the increased professional staff to carry them out. Furthermore, the Council's practice of ranking requests without reference to available funds was an annoyance to the business-oriented Chest volunteers who could not understand how decisions could be made without consideration of cost.

For the Council, it was a classic double bind: the lack of funds meant a need for better planning; the need for better planning required funds for more social planning staff. In short, the two parts of the organization were poles apart in their approach to deciding on agency allocations.

A desire for long-range planning was not the only sore point between Chest and Council in the allocations process. Another major source of friction centred on the question of personnel policies and the amount of salary paid to social workers. The agencies were not only experiencing the need for more staff to meet the rising demand for services, they were also concerned with the level of salaries needed to attract skilled professionals. This was of primary concern to the Chest since the salary line on budgets submitted by the agencies was usually the largest, both in absolute amount and in relative increase.

It was the practice of the budget review panels to scrutinize individual salaries in the agencies' budgets. For this reason, the Chest made repeated requests for standardized information on salary and benefit levels for agency staff. Their motives were not so much related to consistency between agencies and certainly did not represent a concern for increasing salary levels to meet professional standards. Rather, the motive was to discourage the agencies from paying too much. The budget panels were made up of men, some of whom were 'aghast when they hear of a woman social worker being paid $5,000 a year.'[17] The idea of paying professional-level salaries to women, much less equal salaries to women and men, did not go down well in the male world of the Community Chest. Underlying the resistance was the patriarchal belief that social work was in essence simply caring for others, which was 'women's work,' and as such, not something for which one should be paid, much less given professional status.

By 1952, in its report for the Community Chest budget for the coming year, the central planning committee documented a growing crisis in the lack of trained staff in the agencies. In an effort to cope, the agencies had taken steps such as dropping staff positions in order to increase salaries, deferring expenditures on buildings and equipment, delaying filling vacancies, increasing staff loads, and shifting their priorities to programs with revenue-producing potential. The committee report recommended reapproval of twenty staff positions previously rejected by the Chest, approval of an additional fourteen full- and part-time positions, and reinstatement of nine staff positions lost in previous budget cuts. It was agreed to circulate the report to the agencies and to hold a special meeting in January to which the Chest and the press would be invited.[18]

While the absolute need for more staff was important, it was a growing emphasis on professional casework, seen as the particular strength of the voluntary sector, that was most at issue. According to current standards of social work, Toronto was considered to be lagging in the degree to which professionals were trained and employed: 'As one executive director said, "Modern social work came late to Toronto." There is some catching up to be done, but ... Toronto will profit by the experience of others and ... professional growth ... will not need to be as long and painful a process as it has been in comparable communities on the continent. The strengthening of all welfare services in Toronto is contingent upon the strengthening of family case work in the community.'[19] It was also argued that the refusal of the Fund to agree to increased salary budgets resulted in a drain of trained people, both from the city and from the voluntary sector. The profession considered non-government, personal social services far superior to state-run programs, but only if provided and supervised by trained social workers.

The Chest persisted in its refusal to consider these larger questions, requesting that the Council undertake a personnel classification study with a view to setting standards for both the agency boards and for the budget committee of the Chest. By 1954 the issue had escalated to the point where any survey to be done by the Council represented a 'formidable task.'[20]

Personnel issues cut to the heart of agency and professional concerns. The policy of Chest scrutiny of individual salaries was a violation of the autonomy of the agency as well as a challenge to the legitimacy of the profession. But the lengthy delays brought on by the seriousness of the issue only added to the annoyance of the budget committee volunteers who wanted immediate answers to their concern over salary expenditures. The Welfare Council was both subject to and party to Chest policy in its need for resources to carry out its own tasks and in its advisory role regarding standards of service delivery. An incomplete survey was eventually released to the agencies for comment in the fall of 1955. But the review of salaries, which was the central issue, was still outstanding, and the Council was seeking the services of an outside consultant for its completion.[21]

The deepening financial crisis, the desire for comprehensive, long-range planning that would draw on research rather than agency experience, and Chest intrusion into agency policy regarding salaries and benefits all posed a serious threat to the agencies and placed the Council in the middle of a three-way struggle. Where previously the Council and the agencies had stood together in face of unreasonable or unacceptable demands from a funding organization, they were now increasingly alienated. The Council could no longer count on agency support for strengthening its own position. The agencies were more and more seeing the Council's role as acting on behalf of the Community Chest. The Chest was constantly at loggerheads with the agencies and did not trust the Council.

The growing uneasiness of the agencies over their relationship with the Welfare Council was further heightened by the Council's changing policy on membership, which had broadened to include non-Chest agencies, both public and private, and a new emphasis on individual members who were valued for bringing a point of view different from that of the agencies. The ideal of a welfare council was shifting away from 'agency-mindedness' to a participatory process that started 'where the people are.' The division structure, long the stronghold of agency interests, was being unfavourably compared to a system of standing committees with individuals representing various interests rather than organizations.[22]

Despite these strained relations between the Council and the agencies, there was agreement on one overriding issue: the relationship with the Chest was not working, and the basic question of whether there should be one organization or two as recommended by the Chilman report was being evaded. In February of 1954 the Council established a special committee on Chest-Council relations, inviting the Chest to appoint four members to sit alongside four Council members, these eight to appoint an independent chair. The joint Chest-Council executive would establish the terms of reference subject to the approval of both boards, but the committee itself was ultimately to be accountable to the annual general meeting.[23]

The Chest, like the Council, was not happy with the current arrangement, but from its perspective the difficulty lay in the inadequate and inefficient response of the Council to budget committee requests for help. The Council's proposal to look at the 'whole health, welfare and recreation picture in Toronto' was not what Chest volunteers had in mind when charged with the immediate necessity of making financial decisions in the face of budget limitations and hostile member agencies. Nor was the Chest sympathetic to the estimated costs of such a comprehensive approach as noted above. The Chest response to the Council's invitation was to form their own review committee made up of past presidents of the Chest, signalling both the importance with which the matter was regarded and its intent to retain control over the process.[24]

In April of 1954, the Chest committee of past presidents brought in a damning indictment of the whole allocations process. In its considered opinion, there had been a lack of coordination, a lack of understanding of budget committee problems, a lack of guidance to the budget committee, and an ineffective use of Chest and Council staff and volunteers. It recommended that the board 'undertake forthwith to review the constitution and organization of the Community Chest of Greater Toronto.' It also recommended that until such a review was complete, the request from the Welfare Council to establish a joint but independent review would be held in abeyance.[25]

This evoked considerable debate on the part of the Council, with President Harold Clark resolving to move ahead with the Council's own review, and Chest Executive Director Bill Dewar counselling caution. Eventually the Council capitulated. But the whole affair created an atmosphere of distrust and hostility between the two parties which profoundly affected their relationship.

The increasing interest of social workers in comprehensive and long-range planning represented much more than a technique for identifying needs and establishing funding priorities. It was accompanied by an equally strong and related interest in models of decentralized planning that would involve citizens in determining the needs in their own local areas. Ideally, welfare councils were seen as central bodies at the hub of a group of district or area councils, providing staff and information to local planning. Central councils were also considered an important link between local citizen groups and decision-makers at higher levels in the urban hierarchy.

The interest in moving towards such a model in Toronto was stimulated by the profound physical, social, and political changes that were taking place in the metropolitan Toronto area. Indeed, this was one of the fastest growing urban areas in the Western world. Virtually all of this growth was taking place place in the suburban municipalities that surrounded the city of Toronto. The population of the 'Big Three,' Etobicoke, North York, and Scarborough, more than doubled from 196,000 to 413,000 between 1951 and 1956, and the city's share of the metropolitan population fell dramatically during the fifties.[26]

Not only was the Toronto area one of the fastest growing, it was also well on its way to harbouring the 'largest concentration of "ethnic" people in the country.' Immigration accounted for a significant part of the area's growth. Between 1951 and 1961, the foreign-born population of the city of Toronto went from 31 per cent to 42 per cent, and unlike previous generations of immigrants, who came predominantly from the British Isles these newcomers were primarily from Eastern and Southern European countries. Growth was accompanied by increasing concentrations of population in ethnic neighbourhoods. The most visible of these were the Italians, who numerically dominated the immigrant population, and the resident Jewish community, which migrated from the central part of the city to new neighbourhoods to the north and west. Immigration also included those who came to Toronto in search of work from other parts of Canada, chiefly the Atlantic provinces. It was a mosaic that affected the social fabric of the entire area, and one that led the Welfare Council into new, important work in the area of services for immigrants and migrants.[27]

Suburban development was in many respects also a feature of the change in Canadian ways of living, brought about by the availability of automobiles and the desire for new housing and the technological amenities of domesticity that came with a postwar market-driven economy. So, in addition to the pressures from immigration, there was a general migration to newly planned suburban communities that were highly differentiated and segregated along class and ethnic lines. But despite the planned nature of these suburban areas, the social and cultural amenities were virtually non-existent, especially for women and children, many of whom were stranded without adequate transportation. Social services were 'poorly handled, if handled at all,' causing those seeking service to turn to the established agencies in the city.[28]

Massive population growth, coupled with a general lack of services, led inevitably to demands for greatly increased services in the suburbs. The Toronto agencies were under pressure either to expand outward or to establish new agencies. The Community Chest in turn was under pressure, not only from agencies, but also from contributors, who were giving at work but living in the suburbs and expecting the same level of services as before. When this was not immediately forthcoming, citizen groups formed and petitioned the Welfare Council for assistance in identifying needs and advocating for services.

This lack of social services was a reflection of the serious inequities in tax-raising capabilities and distribution of services generally throughout the metropolitan area, inequities that were one of the chief sources of conflict that raged over how the area was to be planned and managed politically. The establishment of a two-tier metropolitan government in 1953, with its system of central and local levels of government, was largely a response to the need for rationalizing planning and a political solution to dilemmas of central control and local autonomy.[29] It reinforced the idea of organizing the social planning resources along both central and local lines.

There were major fiscal and political difficulties standing in the way of the Welfare Council assuming a role as a service centre for decentralized social planning. The cost of properly staffing citizen councils and of carrying out the related research was substantial. Furthermore, many in the business community did not understand, or if they did, were not sympathetic to the ideals of citizen participation and local autonomy.[30] Indeed, in some quarters the whole movement was regarded with suspicion as socialist-inspired. It is not surprising therefore that funding was also a major problem. Thus the issue of resources for working with citizen groups became another major conflict between the Welfare Council and the Community Chest.

During the Second World War, the city of Toronto was persuaded to lend support to the development of all manner of neighbourhood and citizen organizations. In part this was reflective of a general trend towards the use of neighbourhoods as the basis for collecting data for social planning purposes. The city's Civic Advisory Council, which had been established to advise on postwar civic development, and whose mandate included social welfare, urged the establishment of citizen councils to 'provide a means by which the people can participate and co-operate more effectively in the work of public and private agencies, and make a fuller contribution to their city.' By September 1947 there were thirty-three groups identified by the advisory council, including neighbourhood councils and associations, community centres, home and school associations, and tenants associations. The advisory council established the Community Council Coordinating Committee and city council authorized the hiring of a community counsellor to provide consultation and generally to assist in group development.[31]

Toronto's involvement with neighbourhood organizations owed much to the influence of faculty members from the University of Toronto School of Social Work. The school's director, Harry Cassidy, was vice-chairman of the Civic Advisory Council. Charles E. Hendry and Murray Ross, two of North America's leading experts on community organization at the time, served on the Community Council Coordinating Committee. Albert Rose, who had joined the school's full-time faculty after leaving the Welfare Council's employ, was the advisory council's research director. The approach of these men was guided by social work values of community self-determination and citizen participation. They were eager to experiment with new approaches in community organization, and drew on students from the school to work with the coordinating committee's community counsellor.[32]

The city sponsorship of the community counsellor had never been intended to be ongoing. Rather it was seen as an 'exploratory project,' originally for one year only, during which its relationship to the city and the Toronto Welfare Council was to be examined. When the year was over, the Civic Advisory Council surveyed the community councils and not surprisingly declared the project a success. Arguing that this kind of activity properly belonged in the voluntary sector, it urged that the project be assumed by the Welfare Council. Probably anticipating difficulty, the advisory council passed a strongly worded formal resolution that placed an obligation on the community to 'guarantee' provision of a service of such 'urgency and importance,' a service 'so basic' that 'if need be, adjustments in the present organization, personnel and budget of the Welfare Council might well be undertaken to attain this end.'[33]

The policy committee of the Welfare Council, in endorsing the request of the Civic Advisory Council for recommendation to the Chest board, observed that such a project was not simply a project to be assumed by the Welfare Council's recreation division, but that it cut across all divisions and introduced the 'whole question of a decentralized Council program.' The policy Committee affirmed the social work belief that effective community work must originate in neighbourhoods and citizen groups, and suggested that a decentralized operation was the logical next step in the welfare Council's development. At the same time, the Council was concerned that its staff was overburdened, and there were strong feelings that unless it could do the job properly, the Council should not raise expectations or make commitments that could not be met.[34]

The response of the Chest was a flat refusal to fund. The Community Chest by this time was besieged with requests for expansion of staff, and the Welfare Council's request may have been seen as simply one more new service that could not be met with existing revenues. The Chest suggested that because of budget and administration difficulties, the community councils should affiliate with the Welfare Council through the existing divisions.[35] The suggestion that the agency-based and service-specific division structure be used to coordinate citizen groups reflected a lack of understanding of the nature of the work. Also, the prospect of adding a new dimension through the community councils did indeed raise some fundamental questions about the whole structure and function of the Council. The Chest was not interested in encouraging the

Council to turn away from its responsibilities for allocative planning, and as noted above, the division structure best served this process. It was the first time, but by no means the last, that the Chest would argue that support for citizen councils could be absorbed by the existing resources of the Council.

Although the financial and structural concerns were important, the Chest had other reasons for refusing to support the Welfare Council's involvement with the community councils. The business community was decidedly suspicious of the Welfare Council's approach to community work. In 1944 the Board of Trade had provided money to the Community Chest to establish a department of youth services. The board's objective was coordination of neighbourhood projects intended to prevent 'juvenile delinquency' that were operated by both the Welfare Council and the city's Department of Public Welfare. A condition of the Board of Trade funding was placement of the new department on the Chest side of the organization, which in view of the general purpose of the Council, was a clear vote of non-confidence in the Council.[36]

Perhaps more important, the city's community council project, like the Cost of Living Study, was being subjected to the anticommunist hysteria that prevailed at the time. The community counsellor, Hugo Wolter, was given to rather lavish rhetoric on the subject of democracy and local autonomy. He envisioned the project as ultimately a joining together of labour, youth, and ethnic groups in support of their rights. These three groups were regarded in some circles as the seed-beds of communism and Wolter's vision was predictably branded a 'communist plot' by conservatives in the community. As with the Red Book crisis, support for community councils held the potential for controversy seen as damaging to the Chest campaign for funds.[37] Thus on several counts – fiscal, structural, and political – the Council's participation in the development of community councils met with the disapproval of the Community Chest.

The question of local community councils and their relationship to welfare councils inevitably resurrected the debate over whether or not the district associations of the Neighbourhood Workers Association (NWA) should be attached to the Welfare Council. A special meeting was held in 1947 to evaluate the function of the NWA central council, which coordinated the district associations. But Frank Stapleford, now in his thirtieth year as NWA general secretary, remained unyielding to any suggestion that part of his agency be transferred to the Welfare Council. While he acknowledged that much of the community work of the NWA had been turned over to the Toronto Welfare Council when it was founded in 1937, other functions continued, essentially the educational and fellowship function that the central council and district associations provided for workers and volunteers.[38]

Three years later, the Survey of Family and Children's Services, chaired by Barbara Cody and billed as an update to the Carstens survey of 1925, once again recommended that the district associations of the NWA be turned over to the Welfare Council; once again it was resisted by Stapleford and the NWA. Unlike the earlier report, however, the rationale reflected what was now conventional wisdom within social work – the separation of community work and casework. The resistance was the last hurrah of an old guard and would soon collapse. The recommendation of the new survey was also consistent with the growing interest in stimulating and supporting citizen (rather than agency) participation in planning through the development of local area councils. It reflected a growing emphasis within social work on community development and was gaining popularity among activists in the community as a means for fostering democratic participation. The Welfare Council placed 'urgent priority' on the establishment of area councils, but was unable to proceed because of lack of funding.[39]

Nonetheless the idea had been reintroduced and, as citizen groups became an established part of the way in which Toronto conducted its affairs, would not go away. By the mid-fifties, many in the community were questioning the effectiveness of the NWA's district associations and were seeking to replace them with more broadly representative and activist councils. Newly formed neighbourhood associations and citizen groups were bypassing the associations and going directly to the Welfare Council for assistance. Stapleford's death late in 1952 released the NWA to make the inevitable change. The stumbling block was no longer the NWA, it was the financial and philosophical barriers erected by the Community Chest.[40]

In 1955 the Welfare Council tried once again to convince the Chest to fund staff services for citizen groups in local areas. It proposed a pilot study of needs and resources in suburban North York and Weston, both of which had active citizen groups seeking the Council's help. The Council had a properly designed study in mind, requiring five staff and assistance from the staff of other agencies at a cost of $25,000. While the Council was intensely interested in developing its work with citizens' groups, it was committed to doing a professional job and this required trained staff, not volunteers as some had suggested.[41]

When the Chest once again refused, Executive Director Bill Dewar was frank in his appraisal of the reason. There had been a 'feeling on the part of some that this was the ongoing work of the Council and that it should be done without any additions to staff.' According to Dewar, the question that had been raised was 'why Council could not lay aside their on-going work and concentrate on this type of broad planning.' He indicated that what the Chest wanted was direct and specific answers, not 'tentative recommendations.'[42]

The suggestion that the Council lay aside its 'ongoing work' was a clear challenge to the autonomy of the Welfare Council to establish its own priorities. The Chest, not illogically, was equating the carrying-out of needs and resources studies with its concern for allocations, and therefore part of the expected role of the Council. But it is safe to assume that the Chest volunteers cared little for the finer points of community organization and citizen participation in identifying those needs, especially in light of the scepticism and disapproval of previous attempts to involve the Council with citizen groups. This was especially true when work with citizen groups was to cost money over and above the regular budget of the Council. Furthermore, work with the suburban groups held out the potential for increasing demands for agency services and funding. On several counts, the appeal by the Council for funding for area planning was a futile exercise.

The other serious implication of the Chest's view of where the Council's priorities should lie was for the service-specific planning that still consumed much of the Council's time and attention. The Welfare Council was deeply involved in activity with respect to immigrants and their needs, studies and briefs on the needs of older people, people with disabilities, housing, single mothers and adoptions, and standards and problems in health care. Council staff was turning out an impressive list of research and other reports, including a massive recreation survey providing detailed information on needs and resources in this field throughout the metropolitan area.[43]

Perhaps the most time-consuming was the perennial fight over unemployment assistance that had been a primary concern of social workers since the twenties. The late forties and fifties brought a rising crisis in unemployment in urban centres, and a public policy that denied any assistance whatsoever to the nearly one-half of the working population not covered by unemployment insurance. As it had in the thirties, this placed an intolerable burden on the private agencies, and also as in the thirties, the matter was subject to stonewalling and jurisdictional in-fighting on the part of all three levels of government.[44]

As a major urban centre and a magnet for both immigration and the unemployed, Toronto was particularly vulnerable. By 1954 estimates of the numbers of unemployed in Toronto were running as high as 35,000 and 7 per cent of the workforce, and the city of Toronto was drawing heavily on the Welfare Council for assistance in its campaign to convince both the provincial and federal governments to assume responsibility. The Council was also drafting persons of prominence to write letters and petitions to members of the provincial and national parliaments, and its staff was issuing press reports, speaking at public meetings and conferences, and supplying facts and figures gleaned from the agencies to local officials and concerned organizations. Although it was regarded as a national problem and the campaign was led by the Canadian Welfare Council, the Toronto Welfare Council was playing a major role.[45]

The suggestion from the Chest that the Council forgo all of this effort in favour of 'broad planning' in the suburbs was ludicrous. It was obvious that the Chest neither understood nor cared about some of the central issues and problems of social planning. It was single-mindedly concerned with priorities for funding its own member agencies. The social action activities of the Council were at best an unnecessary activity, at worst another example of an unacceptable left-wing stance. In sum, the Chest regarded the Council as a planning arm whose primary, and perhaps only task was to advise on allocations to its member agencies.

By the mid-fifties, the conflict between the Chest, its member agencies, and the Welfare Council had escalated to intolerable levels. Both the Chest and the Council were calling for a review of their relationship but, as previously discussed, were in substantial disagreement over the form that this review should take. The Council was holding out for an independent review in which both organizations would participate equally under the guidance of a neutral chair. The Chest was resolved to take matters into its own hands, following the recommendations of its ad hoc committee of past presidents. A new committee to study the organization's structure was struck, but rather than the equal partnership advocated by the Council, only two of the six committee members were from the Council, reflecting the proportion of Council representation on the Chest board of directors. Bowing to necessity, Arthur Pigott, the new president of the Welfare Council withdrew an earlier Council motion to proceed unilaterally, stating that the Council wished to fully cooperate.[46]

Pigott was the personification of efforts to bridge the differences

between the Chest and the Council. He was a teacher turned small businessman who had the confidence of both the agencies and the Chest. He
had served as chairman of the Council's central planning committee, and
while president of the Council also served as campaign chairman for the
Chest. Pigott came to Toronto from Winnipeg to join his brother in an
automobile dealership, a vocation that established his credentials as a
small businessman. His social service credentials lay in his previous job as
assistant superintendent of schools, and volunteer service with the Children's Aid Society as well as both the Chest and the Council in Winnipeg.
It was in Winnipeg that he had first worked with Philpott, and she was
instrumental in introducing him to the Toronto Council. Pigott had a
flamboyant personality and a ready wit that, despite sometimes landing
him in trouble, enhanced his popularity.[47]

The decision to carry out a review of Chest-Council relations in Toronto was not an isolated event. It was part of a general reconsideration of
the Community Chest movement in North America. Tension between
Chests and Councils had universally deteriorated after the war, to the
point where three-quarters of the executive directors of Chests and Councils in over fifty cities surveyed by the U.S. National Social Welfare Assem-
bly in 1949 expressed dissatisfaction with Chest-Council relations. The
issues elsewhere were similar to those in Toronto: conflicting goals, mis-
understanding, undue influence in agency management, acute financial
pressures, expansionary pressure, inclusion of public services in planning
and 'frozen patterns of service' that stifled innovation and fell short of
needs in the community.[48]

Once the review was under way in mid-1955, John Yerger, the Chest's
recently appointed associate executive director,[49] and Philpott were asked
to identify the current problems and to present the advantages and disadvantages of separation. According to their report, the advantages of a
united organization lay in the efficiency that would result from integration of planning and funding; its disadvantages lay in awkward membership arrangements and the probable bias in favour of financial rather
than social concerns. The advantages of independent organizations lay in
broader agency and volunteer participation overall, and the probability
that the Council would be less likely to embarrass the campaign with its
activities; its disadvantage lay in isolation and lack of communication
between planning and funding. The financial as well as the professional
fears of the Council were not expressed directly in the report, but were
implicit in the view that with separation, 'the Chest may end up by setting
up a planning committee for Chest agencies, thus duplicating the work

that should and could be done as part of the total health and welfare program.'[50]

Meanwhile, the desire for a separate Chest and Council was growing. The Council's central planning committee was considering requests from the agencies for seventy additional professional staff and total new budget expenditures of $346,096. This not only represented pent-up demand and a high level of dissatisfaction and anxiety among the agencies, it also meant that Council staff was burdened with allocations work. The pressure was reflected in the resignation of Margaret Kirkpatrick, who was the Council's associate executive secretary and an advocate for separation of Chest and Council. She left protesting, as had Touzel before her, that the relationship with the Chest did not allow her to make the best use of her knowledge and experience.[51] Nevertheless, separation was still regarded with the historic ambivalence that stemmed from a twin fear: that separation of planning and funding would result in loss of social work influence over all-important money decisions, and that the Council itself would suffer from the lack of a reliable source of funds.

In April of 1956, approximately one year after the review was established, the board of the Community Chest abruptly voted to seek establishment of a United Community Fund (UCF) within which there would be a social planning council. The Welfare Council was formally asked to propose appropriate by-laws for such an arrangement.[52]

The idea of a united community fund began in Detroit around 1950. It was promoted by the chief executive officers of some of the largest corporations in the United States. The UCF movement was motivated by the wish to avoid the annoyance of multiple appeals and by resistance on the part of agencies, especially large, national organizations such as the American Heart Foundation and the Cancer Institute, to coming under the umbrella of a Community Chest. The cause of the agency resistance, in the opinion of the UCF's corporate promoters, was 'the aggressive pressure of those representing the social worker viewpoint [which] did not permit the establishment of ... a "giver's philosophy."' The solution lay in replacing the Community Chest, which was seen as being under the control of 'second-string businessmen' and social workers, with a UCF, defined as 'any community-wide, federated fund raising effort that includes one or more of the six big national agencies.' The key to success was seen as 'active participation and direction by top business and labor leadership,' and 'control by big givers rather than by professional social workers.'[53]

Thus the UCF movement had three essential ingredients: first, it was a restructuring of private charity with the express intent of placing it under the control of the corporate and business community at the highest possible level; second, it was intended to move towards drawing into one comprehensive organization, the various fund-raising appeals that had proliferated since the earlier movement towards financial federation before and during the First World War; and third, it rejected involvement by social workers. In all respects, it resembled the endorsement movement that had begun in the business sector in the previous century – concerned with efficiency, with containing rising expenditures, and closing ranks to anyone 'directly or indirectly interested in the charitable institutions.'[54]

The Council's executive committee, meeting the day after the decision was made to establish a UCF, resolved to consider the establishment of a separate organization rather than the combined model proposed by the Chest. In light of the events that followed, it appears they were not aware of, or simply did not choose to believe, the hostility towards social workers on the part of the proponents of a UCF. The chief concerns expressed by the Council's executive were the badly deteriorated relations with the agencies and the burden of allocative planning:

There seemed to be a general opinion abroad that the Council exercised too much authority and the independent agencies did not wish to have their programs reviewed by the Council. The committee discussed this matter in great detail, and it was agreed that many of the criticisms were valid in the light of the duties and responsibilities which had been undertaken by the Council because they were part of the Chest. It was further agreed that in any re-organization, the Council should divest itself of those aspects of program which were appropriately the responsibility of the fund raising organization and should concentrate on broad community planning and cooperative efforts between agencies.

It was agreed that the whole idea of reorganization must start 'with a completely fresh outlook,' and the Council turned its attention to recruiting a committee that would set it on a course towards becoming an independent organization.[55]

The following month, the Council's executive approached Wallace McCutcheon to chair their committee on reorganization. McCutcheon was one of the most powerful businessmen in Canada. Formerly deputy chairman of the Wartime Prices and Trade Board, he was now vice-president and managing director of Argus Corporation, chairman of the board of National Life Assurance Company, and a director of about twenty other companies.[56]

In view of the strained relations between the social work and business communities, one wonders why the Council chose to approach someone in McCutcheon's position. Most likely the Council was seeking an ally with sufficient legitimacy with the funders to carry them through a separation. McCutcheon had served as president of the Community Chest and had clear credibility with its financial backers. He also had a background of charitable and social service, including with the Canadian Welfare Council, that gave him some credibility in the eyes of the Council. It is also probable that McCutcheon's wife Eva was an influence. She was a public health nurse and active in the Welfare Council, serving as a volunteer in the health division.[57]

Plans for a social planning council moved steadily ahead from the summer of 1956 when a small steering committee was formed. McCutcheon assumed the committee chair in the autumn, and by early 1957 an operational plan was completed. The Welfare Council membership was widely consulted regarding the proposed planning council and there was considerable agreement over the purpose and structure. But the sensitivity of the question of future relationship with the United Community Fund required that this part of the plan be handled with considerable discretion. Discussion was confined to the steering committee, which had been broadened to include area councils now functioning in suburban municipalities, and other fund-raising organizations. Those who were consulted agreed that the question of an independent council was the most important of all, and the consent of the new UCF, established in March of 1957, was sought before the full proposal was taken publicly to the membership.[58]

The steering committee proposed a separate, yet together kind of relationship between the UCF and a new social planning council: 'While the media for Fund Raising and for Social Planning are different and require different organization, they must be closely related. Planning must take into account financing; financing in order to be economical and efficient must give regard to planning.'[59] Gone was the cavalier attitude that it was the Council's job to propose needed service and the Fund's job to worry about how the money was to be found. In its place was commitment to the importance of planning for the purpose of efficiency and the necessity for a close relationship between planning and funding. It was not a surprising stance given the makeup of the steering committee and the lack of broad consultation with agencies.

The steering committee's report provided a long list of planning services that it suggested might be of help to the Fund. In effect, they were a restatement of the allocations planning functions that the Welfare Council was longing to avoid, including the staffing of UCF budget committees, carrying out of agency reviews, and cooperation with the Fund's public relations committee. The major exception was the proviso that the Council would undertake agency reviews only if agreed to by the agency concerned.

The proposed relationship between Council and Fund also acknowledged the vast changes in public funding of social services that had taken place over the previous two decades. A desire to involve public departments as well as agencies outside the boundaries of the Federation for Community Service had been one of the primary reasons for establishing a separate organization when the Toronto Welfare Council was founded in 1937. Thus the ideals of comprehensiveness were not new. But the growth of an interventionist state since the Second World War and the entrance of senior governments directly into the arena of human service expanded the sphere of social planning to matters well beyond the traditional concerns of non-government agencies. 'The Social Planning Council ... would be concerned not only with the programs of Fund supported organizations but with all organizations offering services in the fields of health, welfare and recreation. Developments in the public departments, at all three levels of government, have a direct bearing on the programs and budget needs of voluntary community service.'[60] The new Council was conceived as a comprehensive planning organization, useful to funders generally rather than to the UCF specifically. At the same time, the emphasis remained on the voluntary sector within which the UCF was a principal source of funds.

In some respects, the proposal for a social planning organization reveals the persistence of ideals of the nineteenth-century cooperative movement out of which the early councils of social agencies had grown. The plans made explicit a cooperative democratic philosophy that 'change takes place through discussion and reaching a consensus.' The board of directors was envisioned as a coordinator and mediator between participating individuals and organizations, all of whom would be free to interact in a democratic manner. Also as in the early councils, the gathering and disseminating of facts would be a central function, and 'membership sections' not unlike the original 'functional councils' would bring agencies and individuals together around fields of service.[61]

In other respects, the structure of the new Council reflected the fundamental changes in social work thinking that had taken place over the previous four decades. Membership was no longer agency-specific, and a system of local citizen planning councils throughout the metropolitan area was envisioned. Although research had been a priority from the beginning, it too had changed substantially, with the growing sophistication sought in comprehensive community needs and resources studies. Notable for its omission was all reference in the plan to social action. The closest suggestion was for 'carefully-selected small study groups' for special projects such as housing and immigrants.[62]

In short, the new Social Planning Council was designed to combine technical skills and central information resources with a democratic, participatory planning process. The object was to strengthen the community's ability to identify unmet needs and to convey this information to the appropriate funding body, where decisions could then presumably be made on a rational and informed basis. The 1957 proposal bore a remarkable resemblance to the initial plans for the Welfare Council in 1937. The only real difference was the substitution of citizen control for agency control.

On 7 May 1957, 350 members and friends of the Toronto Welfare Council gathered for dinner at Simpsons' Arcadian Court to approve the establishment of the Social Planning Council of Metropolitan Toronto. Arthur Pigott was elected the first chairman, Wallace McCutcheon the first vice-chairman. Lyman S. Ford of the Community Funds and Councils of America spoke on the topic 'What the Community expects of the Planning Council.'

Three days after the annual meeting at which the Social Planning Council was formally approved, Wallace McCutcheon and William Anderson called a special meeting of the executive committee. The first order of business was to elect Anderson, a newly elected board member, as chairman of the executive. The other item was consideration of a proposal put forward by McCutcheon that Art Pigott be hired as a staff person of the Council to provide 'extra assistance at the top administrative level.' He gave assurance that the UCF was in agreement with his proposal along with 'other key leaders.' As chair of the executive, Anderson was authorized to appoint a sub-committee to approach Pigott and to steer the necessary changes in by-laws through the board.[63]

The first meeting of the new Social Planning Council was chaired by Art Pigott, at least until regular business was dispatched, whereupon both he and Philpott retired. The board then proceeded to amend the corporation by-laws, appointing Pigott as vice-president and assistant to the president, Philpott as vice-president and executive director. Wallace

McCutcheon was appointed chairman and president of the board. Pigott was given a new and sumptuously furnished office and subsequently 'loaned' to the UCF to work with their campaign. During all of this, Philpott was not consulted.[64]

This astonishing turn of events echoed the strategy of the corporate elites within the UCF movement. The links between the Toronto UCF and the Three Cs of America ensured that the principles of the UCF movement were known. McCutcheon had much in common with the men who founded the UCF, and was probably familiar with their objective to remove control of charity from social work and from small businessmen, of whom Pigott was an example. McCutcheon had been a president of the Community Chest, as well as president of the Canadian Cancer Institute, one of the targets of the UCF drive for inclusiveness. He later admitted that he had indeed engineered his own appointment as president in order to bring the new organization under control.[65]

If control of charity was the object, a combined UCF and social planning council was most desirable. Indeed this was the recommendation of the Three Cs, despite the fact that most large urban centres in the United States had separate Funds and Councils. The combined organization in Toronto was the exception, not the rule, and years of escalating conflict had made it clearly unworkable. It is probable that public relations, a long-standing source of irritation between the Chest and Council, was the deciding factor. A planning council had the potential for damaging a campaign or stirring the political pot, whether it was part of the Fund or on its own. Opposing independence for the Social Planning Council could have driven the conflict into the open and generated too much unfavourable publicity. Nevertheless, an alternative was needed if business was to retain control. The assumption of board and executive positions by the chief executive officers of major Canadian corporations provided that alternative.

Thus the move by McCutcheon to seize control of the new Social Planning Council was significant, not because it was unusual, but because it conformed to a pattern of ensuring that the drive for autonomy on the part of the social service community would not go too far. The events in Toronto were perfectly consistent with what was happening generally as Community Chests were restructured by the UCF movement. The primary motivation for social workers in establishing an independent council was the belief that freedom from the coercive actions of the Chest would allow development of decentralized, participatory, and comprehensive social planning. But these ideals conflicted with the dominant values of the business community. Local autonomy, citizen participation, and democratic process are the antithesis of elite control. McCutcheon's take-over of the planning council demonstrated that autonomous, democratically controlled social planning was an illusion.

Violet Sieder was among those social workers who counselled caution in allowing a corporate elite to assume control. Sieder did considerable consulting in Toronto and wrote not too long after these events took place:

In at least one recent development, a closed association of 'top citizen leaders' has become a self-perpetuating body of guardians of the welfare interests of the community ... In such a situation, what recourse have agencies, citizen organizations, or the people served for selecting or removing the guardians of their welfare? ... As long as agencies continue to exist as autonomous bodies and are held responsible by society for provision and adaptation of services to meet recognized needs, it is hard to see how as entities they can be eliminated from a direct voice in the planning process.

Sieder blamed social workers for going too far in removing agency influence from welfare planning. She suggested that the technocratic approach to planning was responsible for encouraging some social workers to embrace planning models that sanctioned an elite leadership and substituted efficiency for the democratic principles of community organization. In this, she included the participation of agencies and their volunteer boards.[66]

This was precisely what happened in Toronto. The new Social Planning Council invited the powerful to sit on its board. The willingness to continue to provide advice to the Fund, despite the experiences of the past, rested on a technocratic model of social planning. The whole emphasis on needs and resources studies depended on a view of the social planner as the technician behind a rational decision-maker. It was not a coincidence that Wallace McCutcheon became enthusiastic about carrying out such studies. It was an approach to planning that fitted well with the efficiency goals and hierarchical structure of the male-dominated business community.

It is also significant that both Anderson and McCutcheon held prominent positions in the insurance industry. Anderson was vice-president and managing director of the North American Life Assurance Company; McCutcheon was chairman of the board of the National Life Assurance Company. Five other top-level insurance executives sat on the Social Planning Council board, all of them newly elected. Private insurance had grown rapidly and significantly during the early fifties and the Canadian Health Insurance Association had mounted a vigorous lobby against 'state medicine.' Anderson was one of its most knowledgeable and prominent spokespersons. His address to the annual meeting of the insurance company he headed reveals the extreme views that he and others held toward the prospect of national health insurance: 'I fear and distrust those who bring the "gift" of compulsory health insurance not only because it is compulsory but because it is not at all what it appears to be on the surface ... its purpose being the easy achievement of a system of state medicine as a major step towards complete socialism.'[67] The insurance industry joined with the Canadian Medical Association to advocate that government be confined to a residual role, subsidizing only those who could not afford to participate in the various commercial and voluntary insurance schemes available at the time.

It is difficult to believe that the presence of Anderson, McCutcheon, and five other insurance executives on the Council Board was benign. Along with its provincial and national counterparts, the Toronto Welfare Council had been vigorous in its promotion of ideals of the welfare state. A system of universal, publicly administered health insurance was considered by social workers and liberal reformers to be one of the most important components of a welfare state still to be achieved. The willingness of men like McCutcheon and Anderson to serve in positions of authority on the boards of social planning organizations reveals a strategy to contain further advances in state health insurance and ultimately the welfare state.[68] McCutcheon was later appointed by Prime Minister John Diefenbaker to the Royal Commission on Health Services. Malcolm Taylor speculates, in his history of the evolution of health insurance in Canada, that had McCutcheon not resigned from the commission when he was appointed to the Senate in 1962, Canada's health insurance program might have conformed to the alternative proposed by the medical-insurance industry lobby.[69]

McCutcheon played an active role in the Toronto Social Planning Council until his move to the Senate. According to Philpott, he became enthusiastic about social planning as a process of identifying needs and resources, but he never really changed his basic concepts about how social services ought to be organized and delivered. The Council had finally severed its ties with the Fund, but it had not escaped the control of a business community whose values and priorities were fundamentally at odds with some of the primary values of social work.

Social planning in Toronto had come a long way from a vehicle for agency cooperation and coordination to a broadly focused, citizens' planning organization. It had also moved from a female-dominated, reform-minded, and democratic organization to a male-dominated, technically oriented, and hierarchical one. Women were noticeably absent from positions of leadership, a situation that differed greatly from that of the previous three decades. Philpott was an obvious exception, but she was just that – an exception. This trend had commenced in the forties, but it was the following decade, with its emphasis on social planning, that brought the influence of women to an end.

The period after the Second World War was generally dominated and shaped by the corporate business world and the ethos of power and control that accompanied it. The world of business was a community of men, and women were excluded. It is no wonder then that women held little influence in welfare councils that existed in an arena dominated by business, at a time when the ranks of business were closed to women, and in a context of economy, efficiency, and containment of welfare values.

But the profession was not blameless. Women were excluded from community work by social work's acceptance of rational and technical planning as its major approach to social reform. Women were relegated to the sidelines not because they are incapable of such activity, nor because they rejected the technocratic approach. The reasons lie in the fact that planning itself became respectable and desirable as a professional pursuit in the burgeoning postwar urban economy. As such, it became attractive to men. This attractiveness applied to social planning as well as urban planning, all the more because of the growing desire to link with and emulate the urban planners.[70] Furthermore, given the relationship between social planning, coordination of services, and allocation of funds, this aspect of social work practice was regarded as the domain of men, necessary if the profession was to meet with the business community on a more equal footing.

Thus while social work remained largely a woman's profession, women were confined to roles as caseworkers and family counsellors, and subject to the control of their male colleagues and that of the men who held economic power. This is not to deny the importance of work with families and children, which is what made up the bulk of social casework practice in the fifties. On the contrary, it was and remains at the heart of social work practice, and to deny its importance is to deny the importance of the domestic sphere generally. But the nature of casework had changed as it moved away from community action. It now reflected only the marginalized and powerless nature of 'women's work' in a patriarchal Canadian society. It was yet another means of separating the personal and political.

Even the financial constraints imposed on the agencies was a product of gender bias of a somewhat more subtle but damaging variety. The resistance of the businessmen of the Community Chest to paying women a professional salary reflected not only the assumption that women should not be paid as much as men, but also a belief that women should not be paid at all. If women were not paid for caring in the home, why then should they be paid to do the same thing outside the home? If women volunteers had campaigned for social reform for years, why not continue? The suggestion by the Chest that the work of supporting citizens' groups and community councils could be carried out by volunteers was a reflection of this perceived relationship between social work, women, and volunteering. In the end, male pursuit of social planning notwithstanding, the perception of social work as women's work marginalized the profession as a whole and justified the paradox of financial restraint for social agencies in a time of economic growth and unprecedented prosperity.

CHAPTER SEVEN

Conclusions

Social work has always been at the interface between politics and everyday life, between the state and private lives of ordinary people. The very nature of the profession's social change goals forces its practitioners to act on a political plane. The early reformers knew this instinctively, and acted consciously and explicitly to change the economic and social order. We may not agree with the underlying assumptions they carried into their work, which resulted in the imposition of a dominant paradigm of efficiency, science, and traditional views of family and community on everyone alike. But early social workers did challenge the existing order, and because there were no easy or right answers, they also challenged each other. What grew out of these early practices was a complex profession, divided within along lines of political persuasion and gender, yet together in its resistance to social injustice, and in agreement on the necessity of opposing the coerciveness of capital. The point I wish to make is that in its origins social work was a political practice that combined broad goals of change with the smaller acts of individual charity.

The hegemony of corporate power that grew steadily as the twentieth century 'progressed' found a ready instrument to address the challenge of social work in the Community Chest and its successor organizations. The key lay in the concentration of financial resources that narrowed, and sometimes eliminated, the alternatives for charitable organizations seeking funds. In a modern, capitalist economy, money is the ultimate power over institutional social services. The money required for systematic relief of poverty and for financing the social agencies that provided assistance, once concentrated, could be used to control the 'philanthropic enterprise' through manipulation of an allocations process. The requirement that the Toronto Welfare Council primarily address questions of fund allocation was perfectly consistent with this agenda for control. In this process it was possible to contain funding and direct money to only those services considered acceptable. The coordination and efficiency goals of allocations planning were also very effective in crowding social action and advocacy from a welfare council's agenda. Partly this was a result of the time-draining aspects of allocations work that left no time to pursue social reform activities. Equally important is the fact that the intrinsic nature of coordination and efficiency goals meant that their achievement could do no more than fine-tune the status quo. They could not foster fundamental change.

The postwar welfare state was in part a progression of the concentration of financial power that began in the early financial federations. As noted in Chapter 5, businessmen supported the entry of the state into matters of welfare, and were well aware of the opportunity for control that it offered. The United Community Fund and the welfare state, as instruments of corporate power, worked in tandem in the fifties to ensure that social welfare did not pose too large a threat to the existing social and economic order. Mandatory, state-controlled health insurance challenged the limits of corporate tolerance. The participation of powerful men such as Wallace McCutcheon on the board of the Toronto Social Planning Council (and the Canadian Welfare Council) was a deliberate exercise of that control. McCutcheon's later move to the ranks of the governing party at the federal level was both symbolic and real in its illustration of the ease with which corporate power moved between state and private welfare institutions.

The limits placed on welfare also challenged notions of the democratic involvement of people in social planning and policy advocacy. The Community Chest, and later the United Community Fund, absolutely refused to recognize and fund citizen-controlled local councils, the support of which became, for many social workers, the *raison d'être* of the social planning councils. The resistance to funding social planning as a democratic and participatory practice is still evident today. As I write, the news is full of cutbacks that target non-government and citizen-based planning and advocacy organizations. Public funding has been withdrawn from programs that foster popular access to the policy development apparatus of the state. The United Ways are withdrawing funds from social planning councils or requiring them to assume responsibility for allocations work, to the detriment of research or policy advocacy activity. Social planning as a reform-oriented and participatory practice, already badly weakened, is being systematically eliminated.[1]

The manipulation of agency-controlled welfare councils cut at the heart of the profession's voice in the development of social welfare in Canada. These councils were the collective voice of social workers for a significant period of time. Much derision was eventually aimed at the early councils. They were seen as the 'vested interest' of the profession and the agencies, and ignored on the grounds of presumed self-interest. This has a ring of truth, but it is also a very convenient argument. Once these interests are considered alongside the early partnerships that the councils forged between social workers and the volunteers who governed the agencies, and alongside efforts to make research such as the Toronto Cost of Living Study an instrument of broad involvement in policy issues, and alongside the attempts in the postwar period to involve citizens through local area councils, I question whose vested interest was really at stake. An attack on the agency councils was an attack on the front lines of social workers' involvement in democratic reform. Marginalizing the agency councils contributed to the marginalization of the profession.

Social work as a profession was particularly vulnerable by virtue of its locus as an agency-based and salaried practice. As soon as social work shifted from a voluntary activity to one that depended on the willingness of the philanthropic community to pay a living wage, the problems began. For all of its weaknesses, the early volunteer base of social work had much greater power to work for social reform. But the early charities and agencies were necessary for a profession that neither practically nor in principle could depend on fees for providing services that sought to assist poverty-stricken families and reform the conditions of community life. Once social workers became salaried, the profession depended for it survival on the finances of the agencies within which they worked. It also inevitably meant the end to any form of radical practice, however restrained.

Social work was perceived, with considerable justification, as a woman's profession, creating a further source of vulnerability for the profession as a whole. For women entering social work, the shift from church to agency, from voluntary community work to professional practice, did not bring the hoped-for legitimacy and influence. Rather, it introduced a new form of dependency that was similar to the dependency of a 'ladies aid' on a male-dominated church hierarchy. The woman in social work became dependent on her male supervisor, on a male-dominated financial federation for her livelihood, and on male colleagues for her access to the power structures of society. For a time, she maintained an alliance with other women, people such as Barbara Cody and Lois Fraser, who were volunteers and who had access to power through their position in society. But eventually, as professionalism deepened, this too was closed off.

The separation of casework from community practice that began in the thirties simply reinforced and completed the task of relegating women to the 'domestic' and more or less invisible sphere of social work practice. Separating these previously integral forms of practice opened the door for some critical changes in the postwar period, changes that mark and, I would suggest, mar the professional practice of social work today. Separation made it possible for casework to go in a 'treatment' direction, taking on all the trappings of psychotherapy as it did in the fifties. Casework lost its community perspective and focused on the traditional family as it was constructed by the patriarchal assumptions and practices of corporate and state power. Women in casework practice became the agents of this construction and in the process unknowing agents of their own oppression.

Community work, on the other hand, absorbed the utilitarian attributes of planning, scientism, and state control of welfare. It connected well with an evolving public policy and hierarchical control of the institutions of a welfare state. Community practitioners, almost all of them men by the postwar period, conversed comfortably in a language that communicates in jargon and illustrates in statistics. It fell in with a convenient scientific paradigm that assumed the efficacy of objective knowledge and eschewed political activity in spite of the evidence of the politics of corporate power.[2] Community work in the fifties placed men in social work in roles as gatekeepers and power brokers, and women in the private closets of the profession, working as counsellors, care givers, and stewards of traditional forms of family life.

I do not wish to imply that women in social work struggled against these changes. Social workers, both women and men, participated fully in the shift away from a previously activist practice that challenged the existing order. Professionalism, with its reliance on science and expertise, and community work, with its newfound reliance on strengthening the institutions of the welfare state were enthusiastically embraced by the majority. It is difficult to ascertain how much of this was the temper of the times and how much a process of socialization to professional practice that was explicitly part of the goals of social work education. Certainly, the schools were dominated by men, and the male construction of community work as a scientific and technical method undoubtedly helped shape women's understanding of the socially acceptable limits of practice. Even today, the definitions, as well as the history of community practice, are articulated by men who invariable cite the beginnings of social work involvement in community as dating from the utilitarian approach of the 1939 Lane report.[3]

It is too easy to criticize social workers for accepting the political and economic status quo of the postwar period. The fifties were years of virulent repression of any departure from society's norms. The McCarthy inquisition in the United States had its subtle counterparts in Canada. Many radical social workers in the United States lost their jobs and the spectre of a similar fate must have loomed large for many Canadian social workers as well.[4] The constant necessity in the late forties and fifties of having to defend the profession against accusations of communism and disloyalty to the prevailing order underlined the already precarious existence of the profession. Moreover, the paradoxical financial restraints placed on service agencies in the midst of a generally expanding economy left social workers fighting a rearguard battle in which any expression of fundamental change goals pushed the cause yet further behind. And finally, the widespread postwar propaganda that relegated women to domestic roles affected both the participation of women in the profession and the social theories that informed their practice.

When social work developed as a profession, it provided a means for independent women to gain an economic self-sufficiency that would free them to work for social change. The vision of these early reformers may have been limited, and may have reinforced what by today's standards seems conservative and oppressive. There is no question that they carried into their work the views of their class, religion, and cultural heritage, and imposed it on others. But they did have vision and they were not afraid to act on it. There is also no question this vision became clouded by overemphasis on science and rationality. But I am not convinced it was as clouded as some may think. The oppressive tactics of the forties and fifties accounted for much of the retreat into neutrality and psychotherapy that took place after the Second World War. So too did the male-dominated schools of social work, which gave their women students no latitude for feminist concerns.

The possibility that a feminist core remained within social work must be entertained. At the very least, I would argue that a feminist vision lay dormant and unorganized, waiting to be gathered together and made visible in more recent times. Social work is still a woman's profession, and is still dedicated to social change, albeit in varying political hues. Both attributes have power to attract women committed to any one of several causes, which includes justice for women and goes beyond, to the search for justice in global terms. I see shadows of 'militant mothering' in the socialist feminist cause today, and it is one of the perspectives that draws some radical women to social work. It remains a profession whereby women can act on their beliefs while earning a livelihood, in much the same way early reformers turned to the profession as an avenue to public life.

But social work is still also a profession in the grip of utilitarian values, emphasizing a scientific and efficiency-oriented approach to its tasks that relies on assumptions of expertise and objectivity and delivery of the greatest good for the greatest number. As long as this is so, social work will remain subject to the concentrated power of the state and other funding organizations such as the United Way, both of which are instruments of patriarchy. As such, it is a dilemma for women who seek a radical practice.

It appears that there are two contradictory realities that women in social work who seek change must face. The story of the Toronto Welfare Council and its predecessor, the Child Welfare Council, suggests that in order to escape the overwhelming grip of patriarchy and state power, women in social work must forgo the relatively secure bases of agency and state employment. Solidarity with the women's movement and with the rapidly emerging consciousness of racism, ageism, and heterosexism, which is spawning important companion social movements on a global scale, also indicates the necessity for rethinking the locus of our practice. It suggests the necessity of labouring in the cause without being paid.

The other reality for most women is the necessity of putting bread on our tables, caring for children who depend on us, and making a life with partners whom we love – the daily round of life that does not leave us free. Early feminists consciously gave up marriage and children in order to pursue their careers.[5] Most women today are not prepared to do this. What we are left with is the necessity of learning to live with contradiction and, for many, continuing to struggle from within against the forces of state, agency, and other forms of concentrated economic and social power. There is no longer a marriage between business and social work. But there may be a dependency 'because of the children' and we will have to learn to make the best of it.

One very effective way of pushing our vision back into the closet is to suggest that social work is simply what can be done by a good volunteer, that salaries are simply paying someone to carry out good deeds that ought to be done without regard for reward. Social workers deal with some of the most intractable and complex problems of society. The view that it is primarily a purview for dedicated volunteers suggests that social work can be done without regard for training and education, or that somehow professionally trained people (meaning primarily women in this case) should pursue its ends in their 'spare' time. This is no different from the men of the Community Chest in Toronto who were 'aghast at the thought of paying women social workers' a decent salary. Today one wonders if the critical analysis that late twentieth-century social work education can provide is not also being suppressed, along with the usual conflation of social work as women's work and therefore of no economic value. To marginalize the profession by insisting it return to the era of kindly volunteers is not only atavistic, it is a way of controlling and containing a force for social change.

To be consistent, my suggestion that radical practice can only be done from outside the financially dependent structures of social agencies may be seen as part of a move to unhook social work from its fiscal life-source. But my suggestion is fundamentally different from the view that social work is simply a caring job, a view that parallels an understanding of social work as only a modern variation of social casework devoid of commitment to community change. While I believe non-institutional radical practice is desirable, it is simply not a viable choice for most women, and it is on this ground that I reject it as an ideal. What we can do is rethink the role of small non-government agencies and coalitions. Social agencies can be useful instruments of collective social action, especially if banded together in alliance with each other, with citizens, and with professionals. It is an approach not unlike the early councils of social agencies, and is quite alive in Canada today, in such various forms as community centres, shelters for women and men, and day-care advocacy coalitions.

The idea of relying on small-scale organization has potential for recovery of political practice. Although agencies can become bureaucratic and rigid, and subject to manipulation by funders, they are also creations of women and men. If not allowed to become too large or too easily subject to external control, they can be very malleable and adaptable to diverse and changing human conditions. A diversified funding base is imperative, together with new ways of assembling resources using innate citizen power in alliance with professional skills. Ultimately it means a paradigm shift away from the historic models of professionalism and bureaucratic welfare. Such agencies are everything corporate and state power sought to crush.

While social work in Canada is still firmly rooted in its white, middle-class, primarily British origins, fortunately a radical critique of social work and social welfare has begun. Both the profession and its agencies are being shaken up and out by women and minorities who heretofore have usually been the unwilling objects of social work. It is the small and open-ended agencies that can best encompass new ways of addressing the problems of poverty and injustice raised by their critics. In coalition with each other, in partnership with social movements and with the covert support of those professionals who remain within the bureaucracies of the state, they offer hope.

Federation for Community Service, 1919

Organizations in the Federation, 1919

The Aged Men's Home
The Aged Women's Home
Big Brother Movement
Big Sister Association
Bureau of Municipal
  Research
Business Girls' Club
Carmelite Sisters
  Orphanage
Catholic Big Brothers
Catholic Big Sisters
Catholic Charities
Child Welfare Council
Church of England
The Creche
Deaconess House Social
  Service Work
Church Home for the Aged
Danforth Day Nursery
Down Town Church Workers'
  Association
East End Day Nursery
Girls' Club
Girls' Friendly Society
  Lodge

Good Shepherd Female
  Refuge
GWVA – Toronto
  District Command
The Haven and Prison Gate Mission
House of Providence
Humewood House
Industrial Refuge
The Infants' Home and
  Infirmary
The Kings Daughters' Rest
  and Lunch Room for
  Business Girls
Ladies Social Service
  Auxiliary
Moorelands Summer Home
Neighborhood Workers'
  Association
North Toronto Women's
  Patriotic League
Personal Service Club
Preventorium (IODE)
Queen St. East Day
  Nursery
Sacred Heart Orphanage

St. Elizabeth's Visiting
Nurses Association
St. Faith's House
St. John's Hospital
St. Mary's Infants Home
St. Mary's Maternity
Hospital
St. Michael's Hospital
St. Vincent de Paul
Children's Aid Society
Samaritan Club
The Social Service
Council of Ontario

Spadina Lodge
Toronto Daily Vacation
Bible Schools Association
Toronto Free Hospital for
Consumptives
Toronto General Hospital
Toronto Humane Society
Toronto Vacant Lots Cultivation
Association
University Settlement
Victorian Order of Nurses
Women's College Hospital
Women's Patriotic League

Source: 'Outline of the Work Done by the Organizations in the Federation for
Community Service,' CTA SC/40/114/5

Toronto Welfare Council, 1938

Member Agencies of the Council, 1938

Big Brother Movement, Incorporated
Big Sister Association
Boys Home
Catholic Children's Aid Society, St.
  Vincent de Paul
Catholic Junior League
Catholic Welfare Bureau
Catholic Women's League, Ava Maria
  Division
Catholic Women's League, City Sub-
  division
Camp B'Nai B'Rith
Canadian National Institute for the
  Blind
Central YWCA
Children's Aid Society
Children's Aid Society, York County
Church Home for the Aged
Community Gardens Association
Community Vacation Church Schools
Corporation of Forest Hill Village
Council of Jewish Women
Cradleship Creche, York Township
Downtown Church Workers

Earlscourt Children's Home
East End Day Nursery
Federation of Catholic Charities
Federation for Community Service
Federation of Jewish Philanthropies
Glen Mawr Old Girls
Good Neighbors
Heather Club, IODE
Hebrew Maternity Aid Society
Hebrew National Association
Home Service Association
Humewood House Association
Infants' Home and Infirmary
IODE Preventorium
Jewish Child Welfare Association
Jewish Community Centre Association
Jewish Family Welfare Bureau
Jewish Girls Camp
Junior League of Toronto
Kiwanis Club
Mildmay Institute
Mothers and Babes Rest Home
Neighborhood Workers Association
Parent Education Council

Particular Council of St Vincent
   de Paul
Protestant Children's Home
Queen Street East Day Nursery
Rotary Club of Toronto
St Faiths Lodge
St John's Industrial School
St Christopher House
Salvation Army
St Simon's Church Nursery School
Social Service Index
Samaritan Club of Toronto
Social Service Association, Toronto
   General Hospital
The Haven
Toronto Hebrew Free Loan
Toronto Men's Hostel
Toronto Traveller Aid Association
Toronto YMCA

University Settlement
United Jewish Welfare Fund
Victorian Order of Nurses, Toronto
Victorian Order of Nurses, York
   Township
Victoria Creche
Visiting Homemakers
West End Creche
Wimodausis Club
Women's Patriotic League

Special Memberships

Department of Public Welfare
Department of Public Health

Source: 'Memorandum,' 1938, CTA
   SC40/31/10

Committees of the Council, 1938–9

Membership
Public-Private Relations
Interpretation
Research
Leisure Time
Community Health
Day Nursery and Creche
Child Placement
Illegitimacy
Cost of Living
Study of the Feebleminded

Study of the Second Mile Club
Rowell Commission Brief
Study of the Unemployed Single Man
Conferences on Poliomyelitis
Family Court Jurisdiction
Study of Problems of Child Protection
Committee On Mothers' Allowances
Maternity, Boarding Home and Private
   Hospitals

Source: CTA, SC40/31/6

Notes

CHAPTER 1 Introduction

1 Robert H. Wiebe, *The Search for Order, 1877–1920* (New York: Hill and Wang 1967).

2 See, for example, Mariana Valverde, *The Age of Light, Soap, and Water: Moral Reform in English Canada, 1885–1925* (Toronto: McClelland and Stewart 1991). While Valverde makes an important contribution to our understanding of moral reform and of the influence of the social purity movement in particular on social work, she conflates moral reform and social reform. She thereby conveys the notion that this reflects the whole of social work at this time.

3 For both historical and modern perspectives on these values in community work see Marie Weil, "women, community, and organizing," in Nan Van Den Bergh and Lynn B. Cooper, eds., *feminist visions for social work* ([New York]: National Association of Social Workers 1986).

4 The other early centre was Montreal and the school at McGill University. The pages of the reformist periodical *Social Welfare*, which became the official organ of the profession, reflect the leadership of social workers from these two cities.

5 Roy Lubove, *The Professional Altruist: The Emergence of Social Work as a Career, 1880–1930* (Cambridge, MA: Harvard University Press 1965), 159.

6 See for example, Walter I. Trattner, *From Poor Law to Welfare State: A History of Social Welfare in America*, 2d ed. (New York: Free Press 1979), 217.

7 The history of social work in Quebec is bound up with the dominance of the Roman Catholic Church and the role of Catholic vocations and institutions in social welfare in that province. This includes ultramontanism, which imposed

the idea of supremacy of church over state and presented a much different perspective on the role of a welfare state.

8 This assumption is not on very firm ground and usually rests on the notion that the existence of a socialist stream in Canada's political economy fostered greater radicalism here. The weight of evidence that I found during this study points to a heavy reliance by Canadian social workers on professional developments in the United States.

CHAPTER 2 The Roots of Social Work in English Canada

1 James M. Pitsula, "The Relief of Poverty in Toronto, 1880–1930" (PhD thesis, York University 1979).

2 My use of the word "disadvantaged" illustrates one of the dilemmas of trying to fit the whole of social work into a single mould. It carries with it deeply political connotations consistent with liberal ideology. An alternative is to use the word "oppressed," which has equally deep ideological connotations and is preferred by some for these very reasons. The reader may choose which word is preferable.

3 Kathleen Woodroofe, *From Charity to Social Work in England and the United States* (Toronto: University of Toronto Press 1962).

4 My description of the COS is primarily drawn from Lubove, *The Professional Altruist*, 1–54.

5 Mary E. Richmond, *Social Diagnosis* (New York: Russell Sage Foundation 1917), 25.

6 Woodroofe, *From Charity to Social Work*, 69.

7 Allen F. Davis, *Spearheads for Reform: The Social Settlements and the Progressive Movement, 1890–1914* (New York: Oxford University Press 1967). A systematic study of the influence of settlements on Canadian social work has not been done, but I was struck when examining the records by how many of the caseworkers also had settlement experience.

8 In Toronto the president of the university, Sir Robert Falconer, was persuaded to change his previous opposition to establishing the school through his involvement with the University Settlement, Lorna F. Hurl, "*Building a Profession: The Origin and Development of the Department of Social Service in the University of Toronto, 1914–1928*," Working Papers on Social Welfare in Canada, no. 11 (Toronto: University of Toronto, Faculty of Social Work 1982), 2.

9 For a discussion of the evolution of social work education from an agency-based apprenticeship to a graduate degree program, see Lubove, *The Professional Altruist*, 140–56. The tension between practical technique and theoreti-

cal knowledge that accompanied this shift remains a major divisive factor in social work education.

10 Ramsay Cook, *The Regenerators: Social Criticism in Late Victorian English Canada* (Toronto: University of Toronto Press 1985).

11 Richard Allen, "The Background of the Social Gospel in Canada," in *The Social Gospel in Canada*, National Museum of Man, History Division, Paper no. 9 (Ottawa 1975) 4.

12 Salem Bland, *The New Christianity: Or the Religion of the New Age* (1920; reprint, Toronto: University of Toronto Press 1973, 9; the differences between the radical and progressive wings of the social gospel grew following the First World War, see Richard Allan, *The Social Passion: Religion and Social Reform in Canada 1914–1928* (Toronto: University of Toronto Press 1971), chap. 4.

13 Allen, *The Social Passion*, 18–34; I discuss this relationship in "Values of Community Practice: Legacy of the Radical Social Gospel," *Canadian Social Work Review* 9/1 (winter 1992), 28–40.

14 Allen, *The Social Passion*, 289.

15 It is more accurate to characterize social work practice as arising out of Judeo-Christian practice. While I am not aware of any empirical studies in this regard, it has been my observation both from experience and from my research that there is an important Jewish consitituency in social work that can be attributed to religious practice in that community and culture.

16 Valverde, *The Age of Light, Soap, and Water.*

17 Charles Frankel, "The Moral Framework of the Idea of Welfare," in John S. Morgan, ed., *Welfare and Wisdom* (Toronto: University of Toronto Press 1966), 147–164.

18 Technology as the central moral value in society is well described in Jacques Ellul, *The Technological Society*, trans. John Wilkinson (New York: Alfred A. Knopf 1965).

19 I am indebted to Marlene Shore's study for the information about the McGill school included here, *The Science of Social Redemption: McGill, the Chicago School and the Origins of Social Research in Canada* (Toronto: University of Toronto Press 1987).

20 Dale later became the head of the school at Toronto and influential in the social work community there; see Hurl, *Building a Profession*, 24–36.

21 Shore, *The Science of Social Redemption*, especially chap. 2.

22 Neil Betten and Michael J. Austin, *The Roots of Community Organizing 1917–1939* (Philadelphia: Temple University Press 1990). See especially the summary of the work of Charles Lindeman and Jesse Steiner found in chap. 2.

23 Robert P. Lane, "The Field of Community Organization," *Proceedings of the*

National Conference of Social Work, (New York: Columbia University Press 1939), 495–511.

24 In an introductory essay to a reprint of his own 1943 *Report on Social Security for Canada* (Toronto: University of Toronto Press 1975), Leonard Marsh cites Beveridge's "pioneer work on the analysis of unemployment and the labour market" as the foundation of the work both men did on the postwar welfare state, xxi. See also Maurice Bruce, *The Coming of the Welfare State*, rev. ed., (New York: Schocken Books 1966) for a detailed account of the work and influence of Beveridge on employment policies in Britain between 1908 and 1942.

25 Shore, *The Science of Social Redemption*, 208.

26 Allan Irving, "A Canadian Fabian: The Life and Work of Harry Cassidy" (PhD thesis, University of Toronto 1982); Marsh and other Fabian scholars in Canada were instrumental in founding the League for Social Reconstruction, the intellectual wing of the CCF, Michiel Horn, *The League for Social Reconstruction: Intellectual Origins of the Democratic Left in Canada 1930–1942* (Toronto: University of Toronto Press 1980).

27 Elie Halévy's comprehensive treatment of nineteenth-century utilitarianism, originally published in 1923, remains relevant, *The Growth of Philosophic Radicalism* (1923; London: Faber & Faber 1942).

28 David Roberts, *Victorian Origins of the British Welfare State* (New Haven: Yale University Press 1960).

29 Gale Bauman [Wills], *Efficiency and Social Planning: A Means-End Confusion*, Working Papers on Social Welfare in Canada, no. 19 (University of Toronto, Faculty of Social Work 1986), 13–14 29.2.

30 Thomas Bender, *Toward an Urban Vision: Ideas and Institutions in Nineteenth-Century America* (Lexington, KY: University Press of Kentucky 1975), 15.

31 Samuel Haber, *Efficiency and Uplift: Scientific Management in the Progressive Era 1890–1920* (Chicago: University of Chicago Press 1964).

32 Gale Wills, "The Gospel of Efficiency: Social Work's Bridge from Cause to Function," paper presented to the Canadian Conference of Schools of Social Work, June 1987.

33 Carol Baines, "The Professions and an Ethic of Care," in Baines, Patricia Evans, and Sheila Neysmith, eds., *Women's Caring: Feminist Perspectives on Social Welfare* (Toronto: McClelland and Stewart 1991).

34 The Poor Laws in England, dating from the codification of various laws to regulate both labour and begging in 1601, set out a role for the state, as different from that of parish or church. The reforms of 1834 greatly tightened the control to be exercised over able-bodied unemployed people, utilizing principles of the "work house test" and of holding benefits to levels that would not exceed the purchasing power of the lowest-paid worker. These principles

transferred to the colonies, with or without statutory enforcement. Karl de Schweinitz provides an excellent comprehensive discussion of British Poor Laws, *England's Road to Social Security* (1943; reprint New York: A.S. Barnes, Perpetua Edition 1961). The actual enactment of Poor Laws in Canada only took place in the Maritime provinces, possibly because of the fiscal resistance of local governments. For a discussion of Ontario's refusal to enact such a law, see Richard B. Splane, *Social Welfare in Ontario 1791–1893* (Toronto: University of Toronto Press 1965).

35 There are more similarities than differences in urban development between the United States and Eastern Canada. M.J. Heale explores the blurring of civic roles in mercantile New York in "From City Fathers to Social Critics: Humanitarianism and Government in New York, 1790–1860," *Journal of American History* 63/1 (June 1976).

36 Wendy Mitchinson, "Early Women's Organizations and Social Reform: Prelude to the Welfare State," in Allan Moscovitch and Jim Albert, eds., *The 'Benevolent' State: the Growth of Welfare in Canada* (Toronto: Garamond Press 1987).

37 See Baines, "The Professions and an Ethic of Care," 44–5; women in the Roman Catholic orders who ran hospitals and orphanages also provide a good example of management skills, Teresa Lukawiecki, "Class, Gender and Charity: The Experiences of Older Women in Three Ottawa Charitable Institutions, 1865–1890" (MSW thesis, Carleton University 1993).

38 "Maternal feminism" is the term used by Canadian historians to describe this belief. See Wayne Roberts, "'Rocking the Cradle for the World': The New Woman and Maternal Feminism, Toronto 1877–1914," in Linda Kealey, ed., *A Not Unreasonable Claim: Women and Reform in Canada, 1880s–1920s* (Toronto: Women's Educational Press 1979). I prefer the term "maternalism" which has the advantage of not necessarily associating these ideas with feminism.

39 The role of social workers in promoting nutrition education is taken up in detail in Chapter 5.

40 Child Welfare Council (CWC), Annual Meeting Report, 28 May 1930, CTA, SC40/87/10.

41 Joe Salzberg, a prominent Canadian communist in the 1930s, described a group of women in social work who were allied with or sympathetic to socialist ideals. Joe's late wife, Dora Wilensky, was the executive director of the Jewish Family Services in Toronto and a friend of a number of the women who were active in the Toronto Child Welfare Council. Interview with author, 13 Jan. 1987.

42 See, for example, Valverde, *Age of Light, Soap, and Water;* Franca Iacovetta and Mariana Valverde, eds., *Gender Conflicts: New Essays in Women's History* (Toronto: University of Toronto Press 1992); and Carol Lee Bacchi, *Liberation Deferred?*

The Ideas of the English-Canadian Suffragists, 1877–1918 (Toronto: University of Toronto Press 1983).

43 Lori D. Ginzberg, *Women and the Work of Benevolence: Morality, Politics, and Class in the Nineteenth-Century United States* (New Haven: Yale University Press 1990).

44 Seth Koven and Sonya Michel, eds., *Mothers of a New World: Maternalist Politics and the Origins of Welfare States* (New York: Routledge 1993), 4.

45 Barbara Taylor, *Eve and the New Jerusalem* (London: Virago Press 1983), 286–7; see also Eileen Yeo, "Robert Owen and Radical Culture," in Sidney Pollard and John Salt, eds., *Robert Owen: Prophet of the Poor* (Lewisburg: Bucknell University Press 1971).

46 Joan Sangster, *Dreams of Equality: Women on the Canadian Left 1920–1950* (Toronto: McClelland and Stewart 1989). See especially chap. 4.

47 Ibid., 93. In a somewhat different context, Thomas Socknat has also suggested a radicalization of women, arguing that after the First World War committed pacifist women moved away from "liberal pacifism," developed a radical critique of capitalism, and aligned themselves with the political left, *Witness against War: Pacifism in Canada, 1900–1945* (Toronto: University of Toronto Press 1987), 56–9 and 132–4.

48 For example, Margaret Gould and Dorothy Livesay.

49 Susan Prentice, "Workers, Mothers, Reds: Toronto's Postwar Daycare Fight," in M. Patricia Connelly and Pat Armstrong, eds., *Feminism in Action: Studies in Political Economy* (Toronto: Scholars' Press 1992).

50 For a history of the Rank and File movement, see Jacob Fisher, *The Response of Social Work to the Depression* (Cambridge, MA: Schenkman 1980). Canadian social workers were well aware of this movement. In Toronto, the Social Work Publicity Council invited Mary Van Kleeck, perhaps the most prominent among the Rank and File to speak, Federation for Community Services (FCS) Minutes, 20 May 1935, CTA SC40/115/2. I also found a complete set of *Social Work Today*, the journal published by the Rank and File movement, on the shelves in the University of Toronto School of Social Work reading room.

51 Paradoxically, women in social work accepted the administrative role of men in order to enhance the prestige of the profession, James Struthers, "'Lord Give Us Men': Women and Social Work in English Canada, 1918 to 1953," in Moscovitch and Albert, eds., *The 'Benevolent' State.*

52 Ruth Roach Pierson, *"They're Still Women After All:" The Second World War and Canadian Womanhood* (Toronto: McClelland and Stewart 1986).

53 Two very influential papers presented at the National Conference of Social Welfare set out a stern warning that social workers ought not to engage in partisanship: Wilber Newstetter, "The Social Intergroup Work Process," and Kenneth L.M. Pray, "When Is Community Organization Social Work Practice?"

Proceedings of the National Conference of Social Work, 1947, (New York: Columbia University Press 1947), 194–217.

54 The importance of urban and social planning for social work practice is discussed in Chapter 6.

55 See John Friedmann's critique of sociologist Saul Alinsky, who was considered to be one of the leaders of radical community practice, in *Planning in the Public Domain: From Knowledge to Action* (Princeton: Princeton University Press 1987), 284–6.

CHAPTER 3 The Organization of Charity in Toronto

1 Growth in Toronto between 1881, when the population stood at 86,415, and 1911 was 335.7%, growth since 1901, 80.9%, *Census of Canada*, cited in J.M.S. Careless *Toronto to 1918: An Illustrated History* (Toronto: Lorimer 1984), 201.

2 Toronto, "Report of the Charities Commission 1911–12," CTA/RG Reports/2.

3 Mary Joplin Clarke, "Report of the Standing Committee on Neighbourhood Work," Canadian Conference of Charities and Corrections, Sept. 1917, in Paul Rutherford, ed., *Saving the Canadian City: The First Phase 1880–1920* (Toronto: University of Toronto Press 1974), 189.

4 de Schweinitz, *England's Road to Social Security*, 147–8; Lubove, *The Professional Altruist*, 1–21. Both de Schweinitz and Lubove stress the importance of the COS's coordination goals.

5 The idea of a central registry appeared in the minutes of the Toronto Welfare Council in the fifties. In my own experience, it was proposed as a function of the social planning council for which I worked in the seventies. I have found no evidence that it ever worked in practice.

6 Pitsula, "The Relief of Poverty in Toronto," 127.

7 Ibid., 133.

8 Bernard W. Lappin, "Stages in the Development of Community Organization Work as a Social Work Method" (PhD thesis, University of Toronto 1965), 190–9.

9 Lubove, *The Professional Altruist*, 9–10.

10 de Schweinitz, *England's Road to Social Security*, 184–98.

11 Elizabeth Bloomfield, "Boards of Trade and Canadian Urban Development," *Urban History Review* 12/2 (1983). The business community in Canadian cities drew heavily on American experience when it came to matters of local government. See John C. Weaver, "Municipal Reform: The Corporate Ideal and New Structures of Government," in *Shaping the Canadian City: Essays on Urban Politics and Policy, 1890–1920* (Toronto: The Institute of Public Administration of Canada 1977).

12 Frank J. Bruno, *Trends in Social Work, 1874–1956*, 2d ed. (New York: Columbia University Press 1957), 199–200; William J. Norton, *The Cooperative Movement In Social Work* (New York: Macmillan 1927), 24–9.
13 Howard Strong, "The Business Man – Charities and Social Welfare," *Proceedings of the Canadian Conference of Charities and Corrections, 1913*, 67–9.
14 Norton, *The Cooperative Movement*, 29–34.
15 Ibid., 31.
16 G.A. Stanford, *To Serve the Community: The Story of Toronto's Board of Trade* (Toronto: Board of Trade 1974), 120–1.
17 Toronto, "Report of the Charities Commission, 1911–12," 8, CTA/RG Reports/2.
18 Bureau of Municipal Research, *Toronto Gives* (Toronto 1917), 4.
19 Bruno, *Trends in Social Work*, 200; Monna Heath and Arthur Dunham, *Trends in Community Organization: A Study of the Papers on Community Organization Published by the National Conference on Social Welfare, 1874–1960* (Chicago: University of Chicago, School of Social Service Administration 1963), 23.
20 In a classic essay, Martin Rein deals with the evolution of the concept of coordination from the COS to modern times, "Coordination of Social Services," in *Social Policy: Issues of Choice and Change* (New York: Random House 1970).
21 Norton, *The Cooperative Movement*, 14–22; Bruno, *Trends in Social Work*, 199–201.
22 The relationship between scientific management and social reform in the United States is well illustrated by Haber, *Efficiency and Uplift*.
23 Ibid., 110–16; John C. Weaver, "The Modern City Realized: Toronto Civic Affairs, 1880–1915," in Alan F. Artibise and Gilbert A. Stelter, eds., *The Usable Urban Past: Planning and Politics in the Modern Canadian City* (Toronto: Macmillan 1979).
24 Haber, *Efficiency and Uplift*, 111.
25 Bureau of Municipal Research, *Toronto Gives*, 6.
26 The New York Bureau of Municipal Research ran a training school for public service in an effort to make public service a profession "equal to law and medicine." It eventually became the National Institute of Public Administration in the United States. Brittain was probably a graduate of this program, Haber, *Efficiency and Uplift*, 112.
27 *Canadian Who's Who, 1955–57*; Brittain chaired a committee of the Canadian Conference of Charities and Corrections in 1917, Report of 16th Annual Meeting, Ottawa, 1917; see also Hurl, *Building a Profession*, 20.
28 Bureau of Municipal Research, *Toronto Gives*.
29 Charles Hastings' role as Toronto's medical officer of health is a central theme in Paul A. Bator, "'The Struggle to Raise the Lower Classes': Public Health Reform and the Problem of Poverty in Toronto, 1910 to 1921," *Journal of Canadian Studies* 14/1 (1979).

30 Toronto, Council Minutes, 30 May 1921, and "Report of the Special Committee Re: Social Service," Appendix A, 372–4 and 734.

31 A copy of the original constitution was not found. Information regarding the structure at the founding of the Federation has been gleaned from various minutes and reports. See FCS, Annual Report 1921, "Secretary's Report," CTA, SC40/114/5 and FCS, Minutes 1924, CTA, SC40/114/2.

32 FCS, Minutes, Joint Committee Meetings, Central Council and Budget Committee 1919, 1920, 1922, CTA, SC40/114/2.

33 Norton, *The Cooperative Movement*, 127–8.

34 Bruno, *Trends in Social Work*, 203.

35 Ibid., 204.

36 Norton, *The Cooperative Movement*, 39.

37 Ibid., 45–6.

38 Bruno, *Trends in Social Work*, 195–6.

39 Toronto, Council Minutes, 3 Nov. 1914, and "Problem of Outdoor Relief," Board of Control Report No. 41, Appendix A, 1849–50; Frank N. Stapleford, *After Twenty Years: A Short History of the Neighbourhood Workers Association* ([Toronto]: Neighbourhood Workers Association [ca. 1938]), 8.

40 The collaboration is described by Stapleford in *After Twenty Years*.

41 The House of Industry continued as a thorn in the side of Toronto social workers until its demise in 1934.

42 Information about Frank Stapleford is scattered throughout the documents of his time. The Family Service Association of Metropolitan Toronto Archives (FSA Archives) is a valuable source. See, for example, "F.N. Stapleford – a Profile" [1968]. Information was also obtained by the author from conversation with John Stapleford, and an interview with Bessie Touzel, 18 Mar. 1986.

43 FCS, Minutes, Central Council, 20 Mar. 1922, CTA SC40/114/6; FCS, Annual Meeting Reports, 1922, 1923, and 1924, CTA SC40/114/5.

44 C.C. Carstens, "Recommendations on Survey Reports of Organizations in Federation," (prepared for the Federation of Community Services, 1925), 45–7, FSA Archives.

45 Ibid., 46.

46 FCS, Minutes, Policy Committee, 30 Mar. 1925 and 9 Jan. 1926, CTA, SC40/114/2; "Outline of Report of Committee on Pros and Cons of a Council of Social Agencies," 27 Apr. 1925, CTA, SC40/88/9.

47 FCS, Minutes, Committee for the Revision of the Constitution, Special Public Meeting, 14 Apr. 1927, CTA, SC40/114/1; Norton, *The Cooperative Movement*, 39–41; see also Lubove, *The Professional Altruist*, 182.

48 Francis H. McLean, "Survey of Family Social Work Field of Toronto, Canada" (prepared for the Federation for Community Services, 1927), 21 FSA Archives.

49 Ibid., 28–39.
50 Ibid., 73–5.
51 Pitsula, "The Relief of Poverty in Toronto," 238–9.
52 FCS, Minutes, Special Public Meeting, 14 Apr. 1927, CTA SC40/114/1; Child Welfare Council, Minutes, 9 May 1927, CTA SC40/32/6.
53 FCS, Minutes, Annual Meeting, 16 Apr. 1922, CTA SC40/114/5; FCS, Minutes, Policy Committee, 5 May 1924, CTA SC40/114/2.
54 FCS, Minutes, Policy Committee, 22 Mar., 28 Apr., 5 May 1924, CTA SC40/114/2; FCS, Minutes, Central Council, 15 July, 24 Sept. 1924, CTA SC40/114/6. The agencies in question were the Catholic Big Brothers, Catholic Big Sisters, St Vincent de Paul Childrens' Aid Society, the St Elizabeth's Visiting Nurses.
55 FCS, Minutes, Policy Committee, 22 Apr. 1925, CTA SC40/114/2. The comments are attributed to Stapleford as author of a special report attached to the minutes that used the first person throughout.
56 FCS, Minutes, Joint meeting Central Council and Budget Committee, 17 May 1927, CTA SC40\114\2.
57 FCS, Minutes, Joint meeting Central Council and Budget Committee, 17 May to 22 July 1927; Minutes, Annual Meeting 18 Jan. 1928, CTA SC40/114/2 & 5.

CHAPTER 4 Direct Action versus Slow Interpretation

1 Saul Alinsky, "The Basis in the Social Sciences for the Social Treatment of the Adult Offender," *Proceedings of the National Conference of Social Work, 1938* (New York: Columbia University Press 1938), 714–24. The annual proceedings of the National Conference of Social Work (later Social Welfare) are an excellent source for examining debates among social workers.
2 While the Federation of Settlements appears on all the membership lists, there is no evidence that it was active. The relationship appears to have been strained and the reasons pose an interesting question that merits separate examination.
3 The weight of child welfare activities is seen in the Federation for Community Service membership. Twenty-three of the fifty member organizations were classified as child-caring, absorbing over 41% of the budget, FCS, Minutes, Central Council, 20 Mar. 1922, CTA SC40/114/6.
4 Child Welfare Council, Minutes, 3 Sept. 1918, CTA SC40/32/6; "Outline of Work Done by the Organizations in the Federation for Community Service," [1919], CTA, SC40/114/5.
5 Child Welfare Council, Minutes, 17 Jan. 1923, and 11 May 1923, CTA, SC40/

32/6; reference to Robert Mills's background is in Lappin, "Stages In the Development of Community Organization Work," 228.

6 Child Welfare Council, Minutes, 3 Sept. and 29 Nov. 1918, CTA, SC40/32/6; Child Welfare Council, Minutes, 29 Mar. and 2 May 1928, 23 Apr. 1930, CTA, SC40/32/6. Veronica Strong-Boag suggests that socially prominent women such as Huestis, who was the adopted daughter of Henry Gooderham, used their power to legitimize the organizations they worked with and to calm fears of "feminine radicalism," *The Parliament of Women: The National Council of Women of Canada 1893–1929* National Museum of Man Mercury Series, History Division, Paper no. 18 (Ottawa 1976), 142.

7 Touzel, interview; Suzann Buckley, "Ladies or Midwives? Efforts to Reduce Infant and Maternal Mortality," in Kealey, ed., *A Not Unreasonable Claim*, Ibid., 131–49; *National Encyclopedia of Canadian Biography, 1935*.

8 Touzel, interview.

9 Thomas Fisher Rare Books, J.S. Woodsworth Memorial Collection, League for Social Reconstruction Papers, Membership Book, Toronto Branch.

10 Interview with Joe Salzberg, 13 Jan. 1987.

11 Profiles of Fraser and Parker may be found in OA, Ontario Welfare Council collection, series 12, box 70, "Miscellaneous Biographical Data"; MacGregor's position at the University is in Lorna F. Hurl, *Building a Profession*, 21; other information is taken from minutes and letterheads in CTA, Social Planning Council collection.

12 Child Welfare Council, Minutes, Annual Meeting, 14 May 1924, CTA SC40/32/6.

13 Whitton's relationship with the Child Welfare Council was peripheral in the early years. Her views were decidedly contrary to those held by the women in the Child Welfare Council in later years. Whitton's career is described in P.T. Rooke and R.L. Schnell, *No Bleeding Heart: Charlotte Whitton, A Feminist on the Right* (Vancouver, University of British Columbia Press 1987).

14 Clifford J. Williams, *Decades of Service: A History of the Ontario Ministry of Community and Social Services: 1930–1980* (Toronto: Ontario Ministry of Community and Social Services 1984), 1–4; Williams attributes the idea for the new department to Premier Howard Ferguson, but the evidence in Child Welfare Council records of agency input into the Ross Commission proceedings does not support this conclusion. The council was given equal representation with the Association of Children's Aid Societies and with the Social Service Council itself; Ontario Welfare Council, Child Welfare Committee, Minutes, January 1926 to January 1930, OA, Ontario Welfare Council collection, series 3, box 14.

15 See Veronica Strong-Boag, "'Wages for Housework': Mothers' Allowances and

the Beginnings of Social Security in Canada," *Journal of Canadian Studies*, 14/1 1979, 24–34.

16 CWC, Minutes, Annual Meeting, 28 May 1930, SC40/87/10. The report of the executive secretary, Margaret Gould, is a useful overview of Council activities from 1918 to 1930.

17 Board lists may be found in Annual Reports, CTA SC40/115/2; business connections are taken from *Toronto City Directory, 1930*.

18 I have used the name Department (or School) of Social Work throughout to avoid confusion, although the correct name at this time was Department of Social Science. The originial name was Department of Social Service until it was changed in 1925. It was changed again to Department of Social Work in 1941. Urwick arrived in Canada in 1924 having held a similar position at the London School of Economics and began teaching at the University of Toronto the following year. In 1927 he was appointed both head of the Department of Political Economy and acting director of the School of Social Science. He remained in the latter position until he retired in 1937. See Irving, "A Canadian Fabian: The Life and Work of Harry Cassidy," 61.

19 Caseworkers in Toronto's City Division of Social Welfare studied first-time applicants in the summer of 1928, concluding that casework services were needed in every case. They proposed a pilot project to refer people in "temporary difficulties" to private agencies for help, *Social Welfare*, 11/8 (May 1929), 188.

20 Charlotte Whitton was a classic example of the exception, advocating a conservative approach to relief on the grounds that casework services would significantly reduce caseloads. She was bitterly opposed by many social workers. See James Struthers, *No Fault of Their Own: Unemployment and the Canadian Welfare State 1914–1941* (Toronto: University of Toronto Press 1983).

21 FCS, Minutes, Annual Meeting, 27 Jan. 1931, CTA SC40/114/5; FCS, Minutes, Federation Council, 23 Feb. 1931, Joint Meeting Board of Directors and Social Policy Committee, 4 June 1931, CTA SC40/115/3.

22 FCS, Minutes, Social Policy Committee, 16 Feb. 1931, CTA SC40/115/3; see also "Plan For A Council of Social Agencies in the City of Toronto," [1930], CTA SC40/88/9.

23 FCS, Minutes, Social Policy Committee, 25 Feb. 1931, CTA SC40/115/3.

24 Ibid.

25 FCS, Minutes, Federation Council, 28 Nov. 1932, Social Policy Committee, 9 Nov. and 8 Dec. 1932, CTA SC40/211/1.

26 FCS, Minutes, Federation Council, 23 June 1936, Social Policy Committee, 3 Nov. 1936, CTA SC40/115/2.

27 Correspondence, R.E. Mills to Martin Cohn, 4 May 1932, CTA SC40/32/5; for reference to the undesirability of superimposing a model of a council of social

agencies on "unique" Toronto, see FCS, Minutes, Social Policy Committee, 3 Feb. 1931, CTA SC40/115/3.

28 FCS, Minutes, Social Policy Committee, 26 Nov. and 10 Dec. 1931, CTA SC40/115/3; FCS, Minutes, Sub-committee Re a Council of Social Agencies, 1 Dec. 1931, CTA SC40/88/2.

29 F.N. Stapleford, "Policies and Trends," 15 Oct. 1937, FSA Archives.

30 Margaret E. Rich to F.N. Stapleford, 29 Nov. 1937, FSA Archives; Stapleford's opposition to women in leadership positions was also confirmed by Bessie Touzel, interview.

31 F.N. Stapleford to A.D. Hardie, 2 Dec. 1936, CTA SC40/32/5.

32 FCS, Minutes, Social Policy Committee, 12 Jan. 1933, CTA SC40/211/1.

33 FCS, Minutes, Social Policy Committee, 9 Mar. 1933, CTA SC40/211/1.

34 Reports attached to the minutes of a joint meeting of the Federation board of directors and the Social Policy Committee, 14 Nov. 1933, provide a vivid picture of the catastrophe of the Depression and campaign shortfalls on the agencies and their clients, CTA SC40/211/1.

35 "Report of Sub-committee to the Council of Social Agencies Group," 6 Jan. 1937, CTA SC40/88/2.

36 James Lemon, *Toronto since 1918: An Illustrated History* (Toronto: James Lorimer 1985), 35–6.

37 FCS, Minutes, Social Policy Committee, "Report of the sub-committee on Township Relief," 7 Oct. 1930, CTA SC40/115/3; "Children's Aid Inquiry Asked for Township," Toronto *Evening Telegram.* 5 Feb. 1934, 3.

38 Correspondence, Margaret Gould, Secretary, Child Welfare Council of Toronto, to Hon. Lieutenant-Colonel W.H. Price, K.C., LL.B., Attorney General of Ontario, 12 Feb. 1934, OA, RG4, Attorney General's Dept., 1934, no. 811, Central Files.

39 See, for example, "Premier Denies Any Politics in Children's Aid Charges," Toronto *Mail and Empire,* 3 Feb. 1934, 4.

40 Memo to Attorney-General from I.A. Humphries, Deputy Attorney-General, 28 Feb. and 15 Mar. 1934, OA RG4 1934, no. 811, Dept. of Attorney-General Central Files; Editorial, Toronto *Star,* 3 Mar. 1934 and 12 Mar. 1934, 2; newspaper clippings, Scrapbooks, Superintendent of Neglected and Dependent Children (J.J. Kelso), Vol. 7, pp. 10, 36, and 48–9, OA RG29.

41 The records of the Parker inquiry were not found. Information on the findings is taken from press reports found in Kelso's Scrapbooks, vol 7, pp. 72–88, OA RG29.

42 "Steno Notes of Meeting, Feb. 11, 1937," CTA SC40/88/2.

43 There were a number of potential candidates for the job that would open up if the Child Welfare Council dissolved and factions began to line up behind

these candidates depending on their particular style and approach to community work. Touzel, interview.

44 CWC, Minutes, Special Meeting of Council, 31 May 1937, CTA SC40/87/10.

45 FCS, Minutes, Federation Council, 23 June 1936, CTA SC40/115/2; CWC Minutes, 14 June 1934; "Relationship of Child Welfare Council to the Council of Social Agencies," 4 Apr. 1934, CTA SC40/88/9.

46 Correspondence, [A.D. Hardie] to [Martin] Cohn, 28 and 30 Mar. 1935, CTA SC40/32/5.

47 CWC Minutes, 16 and 17 Apr. 1935, CTA SC40/88/9.

48 FCS, Social Policy Committee, "Report to Committee Studying the Establishment of a Council of Social Agencies," 3 Nov. 1936, CTA SC40/88/9.

49 CWC Minutes, General Meeting, 4 Nov. 1936, CTA SC40/88/2; a different version of these minutes may be found in SC40/87/10. The second version contains a fuller account of Hoppers's remarks and appears to be the one circulated to agencies. The distinction between the "business world and our own" is in CWC, Annual Meeting Report, 28 May 1930, CTA, SC40/87/10; The suicide comment appears on untitled and unsigned notes, 14 Dec. 1936, CTA SC40/88/9.

50 CWC "Notes Regarding a Council of Social Agencies," 3 Dec. 1936.

51 "Resolution," Executive Committee Child Welfare Council, 15 Dec. 1936, CTA SC40/88/9.

52 "Reason for Presenting Outline to Present Group," 1936; see also untitled notes dated 14 Dec. 1936, CTA SC40/88/9.

53 CWC, "Notes Regarding a Council of Social Agencies," 3 Dec. 1936, "Executive Committee Resolution," 15 December 1936, CTA SC40/88/9; CWC, Minutes, Special Meeting, 10 [11] Dec. 1936 and 8 Jan. 1937, CTA SC40/87/10.

54 FCS, Minutes, General Meeting to Discuss Forming a Council of Social Agencies in Toronto, 11 Feb. 1937; "Steno Notes of Meeting, Feb. 11, 1937," CTA SC40/88/2.

55 FCS, Minutes, Planning Committee on a Council of Social Agencies, 17 May 1937, CTA SC40/88/2.

56 FCS, Minutes, Meeting Re a Council of Social Agencies for Toronto, 14 June 1937; see also Urwick's comments in "Steno Notes of Meeting, 11 Feb. 1937," CTA SC40/88/2.

57 I have reviewed the profession's approaches to community work in the thirties in Gale Bauman [Wills], *Efficiency and Social Planning*, 19.

58 Robert P. Lane, "Report of Groups Studying the Community Organization Process," *Proceedings of the National Conference on Social Work 1940* (New York: Columbia University Press 1940), 456–73; see also Lappin, "Stages in the Development of Community Organization Work;" while community work was

recognized as a distinct method by the National Conference of Social Work in 1939, formal approval by the professional association in the United States (which included Canadians) did not take place until 1962.

59 CWC Minutes, Special Meeting of Council, 31 May 1937, CTA SC40/87/10.

60 The resistance of the women in the Child Welfare Council to handing over control of their affairs suggests that not all women in social work shared responsibility for the gender inequality that resulted from beliefs in the superior abilities of men as administrators as suggested by Struthers, "Lord Give Us Men," 126–43.

CHAPTER 5 A Measured Minimum

1 Allan Irving, "Canadian Fabians: The Work and Thought of Harry Cassidy and Leonard Marsh, 1930–1945," *Canadian Journal of Social Work Education* 7/1.

2 Alvin Finkel, *Business and Social Reform in the Thirties* (Toronto: Lorimer 1979).

3 Toronto Welfare Council (TWC), Minutes, Provisional Board of Directors, 22 June and 5 July 1937, CTA SC40/87/9; "Invitation to a Public Meeting," 15 Dec. [1937], CTA SC40/31/10; TWC, "Memorandum," [winter, 1939], CTA SC40/31/10.

4 TWC, Minutes, Provisional Board of Directors, 21 July 1937, CTA SC40/87/9; "Memorandum," [1938], CTA SC40/31/10.

5 TWC, Minutes, Provisional Board of Directors, 21 July 1937, CTA SC40/87/9; "Memorandum," [1938], CTA SC40/31/10.

6 TWC, Minutes, 17 Nov., 17 Dec. 1937, 25 Feb. 1938, CTA SC40/87/9; "An Outline of Welfare Council Activities 1938," CTA SC40/31/10.

7 TWC, Minutes, 14 Jan., 11 Mar., 22 Apr., 5 May, 5 June, 7 July, 4 Aug. 1938, CTA SC40/87/9.

8 TWC, Minutes, Provisional Board, 21 July 1937, Board of Directors, 19 May 1938, CTA SC40/87/9.

9 TWC, Minutes, Board of Directors, 21 Dec. 1939, CTA SC40/88/1; Executive Secretary [K. Gorrie] to Dr H.M. Cassidy, 7 June 1938, CTA SC40/80/13.

10 TWC, Minutes, Board of Directors, 14 Sept., 16 Nov., and 21 Dec. 1939, CTA SC40/88/1.

11 Struthers, *No Fault of Their Own*, 149–50.

12 Touzel, interview with author; Linda Patton-Cowie, "'Change With Progress': Bessie Touzel, 1904–1948," (paper, University of Toronto, Faculty of Social Work 1986).

13 TWC, Minutes, Board of Directors, 16 Apr. 1942, CTA SC40/168/1.

14 TWC, Minutes, Housing Committee, 24 Sept. 1942, CTA SC40/86/10; TWC, "The Cost of Living," revised 1944, 2–3, Metropolitan Toronto Reference

Library. The strength of the opposition to public housing is reflected in a
statement attributed to Prime Minister Louis St Laurent: "No government of
which I am a part will ever pass legislation for subsidized housing," *Housing
Digest* (1 Nov. 1947), CTA SC40/86/10.

15 TWC, Minutes, Board of Directors, 20 June 1946, 20 Nov. 1947, CTA SC40/
    168/2; see also Prentice, "Workers, Mothers, Reds."
16 City of Toronto, Board of Control Correspondence, #510, 11 Feb. 1942.
17 See especially material in CTA RG7A1/11/20.8.2 and 20.8.A and 20.8.B.
18 TWC, Minutes, Board of Directors, 18 July 1940, CTA SC40/168/1.
19 Stanford, *To Serve the Community*, 205.
20 TWC, Minutes, Board of Directors, 19 June 1941, CTA SC40/168/1; see, for
    example, Arlien Johnson, "The Obstacle of Limited Participation in Local
    Social Planning," *Proceedings of the National Conference of Social Work, 1940*, 425–
    35; (New York: Columbia University Press 1940), Touzel, interview.
21 B.W. Lappin, "Joint Fund-Raising in Toronto: The Role of the Jewish Commu-
    nity" (MSW thesis, University of Toronto 1947), 34–40; TWC, Minutes, 19 June
    1941, CTA SC40/168/1; FCS, Minutes, Social Policy Committee, 15 June 1936,
    CTA SC40/115/2.
22 See letterhead correspondence, CTA RG7A1/11/20.8.1, and biographical
    mayors' files, #47; For association with FCS leaders see Community Welfare
    Council of Ontario, Minutes, Board of Directors, 2 May 1932, OA OWC Collec-
    tion, series 1/1.
23 TWC, Minutes, Board of Directors, 20 May 1943, CTA SC40/168/1.
24 TWC, Minutes, Board of Directors, 20 May and 26 July 1943, CTA SC40/168/
    1; Executive Committee, 30 June 1943, CTA SC40/205/1.
25 J.S. Duncan to Bessie Touzel, Nov. 1943, cited in Lappin, "Joint Fund-Raising
    in Toronto," 43–4.
26 TWC, Minutes, Board of Directors, 18 Nov. 1943, CTA SC40/168/1; TWC,
    Minutes, Board of Directors, Jan. to Apr. 1944, CTA SC40/168/1.
27 TWC, Minutes, Board of Directors, 25 May 1944, CTA SC40/168/1.
28 FCS, Minutes, Social Policy Committee, 1937, CTA SC40/115/1.
29 TWC, Minutes, Jan. 28, 1938, CTA SC40/87/9.
30 H.L. Brittain to Flora E. Hurst, 20 June 1938; TWC, Minutes, 7 July 1938, CTA
    SC40/87/9; *Canadian Who's Who, 1955–57*.
31 TWC, "Copy of Notes, Public-Private Relations," [6 May 1938], CTA SC40/89/
    10.
32 Dr G.P. Jackson to Mayor W.D. Robbins, 10 August 1937, CTA RG7/A1/16/
    21.1.A.
33 TWC, Minutes, Board of Directors Special Meeting, 13 July 1938, CTA SC40/
    81/9; "Copy of Notes, Public-Private Relations," [1938], CTA SC40/89/10.

Cross also noted that the policy of keeping relief below minimum wages was the policy of the Dominion Government set out in an agreement with the provinces.

34 TWC, Minutes, Board of Directors, 18 May 1939, CTA SC40/168/1, Executive Committee, 4 May 1939, CTA SC40/88/1; Welfare Council of Toronto and District, *The Cost of Living: A Study of the Cost of a Standard of Living in Toronto which Should Maintain Health and Self-Respect* (Toronto: 1939).

35 J.W. MacMillan, "The Doctrine of Minimums," *Social Welfare* (1 Oct. 1918), 7–8.

36 Marjorie MacMurchy, "A Survey of Women's Work, 1919," in Ramsay Cook and Wendy Mitchinson, eds., *The Proper Sphere: Woman's Place in Canadian Society* (Toronto: Oxford University Press 1976), 197.

37 Harry Cassidy, *Unemployment and Relief in Ontario 1929–1932* (Toronto: J.M. Dent 1932,), 186.

38 Correspondence, Marjorie Bradford, Secretary, Montreal Council of Social Agencies to A.D. Hardie, Executive Secretary, Toronto Federation for Community Services, 19 Dec. 1930, CTA SC40/32/5; Leonard C. Marsh, head of the McGill Social Science Research Project drew on these studies in his book, *Health and Unemployment* (Toronto: Oxford University Press 1938), 162–3.

39 TWC, "Committees – Description and Members," [1938–9], CTA SC40/31/6; FCS, Minutes, Federation Council, 30 Jan. 1933, CTA SC40/211/1; Ontario Medical Association, "Relief Diets," *Bulletin* (December 1933), OA RG29-01/42/1704.

40 FCS, Minutes, Social Policy Committee, 11 Nov., 26 Nov. 1936, and 4 Jan. 1937, CTA SC40/115/1 & 2.

41 E.W. McHenry, "Nutrition in Toronto," Lecture to the Royal Canadian Institute, 17 Dec. 1938, "Nutrition – General 1942–69," OA, RG29-01/42/1705.

42 TWC, *The Cost of Living*; McHenry, "Nutrition in Toronto."

43 TWC, *The Cost of Living*, 1–2.

44 TWC, "Council Comments," Nov. 1939, CTA SC40/143/22.

45 Toronto, "Report on Study of Relief Food Allowances and Costs," Nov. 1941, CTA RG7A1/17/21.3.

46 TWC, Minutes, 19 March 1942, CTA SC40/168/1; see also TWC, Minutes, Executive Committee, 8 May 1942, CTA SC40/205/1.

47 TWC, "Some Observations on Welfare Council 'Cost of Living' analysis," 4. A copy of this report was given to me by Albert Rose, the council's research director at the time.

48 Toronto, Council Minutes, 1942, Committee on Public Welfare, Report #13, Appendix A, 1047–50.

49 Property Owners' Association of Toronto to Mayor Conboy, 19 Jan. 1943, CTA RG7A1/17/21.3.
50 Ontario Nutrition Committee, Minutes, 30 Jan. 1942, OA RG29-01/42/1706.
51 The *Report on Provincial Policy on Administrative Methods in the Matter of Direct Relief in Ontario* (Campbell Report) is discussed in Clifford J. Williams, *Decades of Service*, 17–18.
52 "Province Will Boost Relief Food Schedule," *Toronto Globe and Mail*, 22 Sept. 1944, OA RG29-01/42/1704.
53 TWC, "Provincial Food Standards Not Yet Accepted," in "Council Comments," Dec. 1944; OA RG29-01, temp. box 124, file "Unemployment Relief – General, 1943–1945."
54 E.W. McHenry to J.S. Band, 25 Sept. 1946, OA RG29-01/42/1704.
55 E.W. McHenry, *Report on Food Allowances for Relief Recipients in the Province of Ontario* (Toronto: Ontario Department of Public Welfare 1945), 13.
56 Toronto, City Clerk to Council Members, 28 May 1943, CTA RG7A1/17/21.3; B.W. Heise, Deputy Minister of Public Welfare, to A.W. Laver, Toronto Commissioner of Public Welfare, 3 Nov. 1944, OA RG29-01, temp. box 125, "Unemployment Relief – Toronto Correspondence 1944–50." The draft of the Heise letter contains a note from the minister explicitly rejecting the TWB standard.
57 Ontario Nutrition Committee, Minutes, 22 Oct. 1942, OA RG2901/42/1706; the McHenry report strongly emphasized the importance of public education.
58 Interdepartmental Committee on Nutrition Material, Minutes, OA RG29-01/42/1707.
59 TWC, Minutes, Executive Committee, 19 July 1948, CTA SC40/205/2. One article, "Criticism of NWA," *Canadian Motorist*, Mar. – Apr. 1947 (FSA Archives), suggested that 90% of Toronto social workers were communist or had communist sympathies. I have also confirmed the seriousness of these accusations in personal conversations with social workers active in Toronto at the time.
60 TWC, *The Cost of Living* (Toronto: 1944 revision). Only a schedule from the 1947 revision was found.
61 TWC, Minutes, Board of Directors, 6 July and 14 Sept. 1944, CTA SC40/168/1; TWC, "Some Observations on Welfare Council 'Cost of Living' Analysis"; Touzel, interview.
62 TWC, Minutes, 16 Oct. 1947, CTA SC40/168/2.
63 TWC, Minutes, Board of Directors, 16 and 30 Oct. 1947, SC40/168/2; TWC, "Some Observations on Welfare Council 'Cost of Living' Analysis."
64 TWC, Minutes, Special Meeting, 30 Oct. 1947, CTA SC40/168/2.
65 Touzel, interview.
66 TWC, Minutes, Board of Directors, 25 July 1941, 21 Jan 1943, 14 Sept. 1944,

CTA SC40/168/1; interview Touzel; Linda Patton-Cowie, "'Change With Progress.'" Use of the Toronto studies as a "chief argument for family allowances" may be found in a memo from B.W. Heise, deputy minister of public welfare to R.P. Vivian, Ontario minister of public welfare, 5 Oct. 1944, OA RG29-01/41/1665.

67 Touzel, interview.

68 TWC, Minutes, 3 June 1948, CTA SC40/168/2.

69 TWC, Minutes, 23 Sept. 1948, CTA SC40/168/2.

CHAPTER 6 Chest-Council Relations

1 TWC, Minutes, Board of Directors, 11 Dec. 1947, CTA SC40/168/2; "Miscellaneous Biographical Data," OA, Ontario Welfare Council collection, series 12, box 70; Florence Philpott, interview with author, 10 Apr. 1986.

2 TWC, Minutes, Board of Directors, 18 Nov. and 16 Dec. 1948, CTA SC40/168/2.

3 Chilman Report, 17 Jan. 1949, CTA SC40/26/10.

4 TWC, Minutes, 24 Mar., 4 Apr., 23 June 1949, CTA SC40/168/2; "Report of Findings Committee," [June 1949], CTA SC40/26/10.

5 TWC, Minutes, 11 Sept., 30 Dec. 1947, CTA SC40/205/2; TWC, Minutes, 22 Apr. 1948, CTA SC40/168/2.

6 TWC, Minutes, 11 Sept. 1947, CTA SC40/205/2; Florence Philpott, interview. This debate was still vigorous in the United Way in the early 1980s, leading to incorporation of social planning information in goal-setting committees and a strategy called "campaign to potential."

7 TWC, Minutes, 22 Apr., 27 May 1948, CTA SC40/168/2.

8 TWC, Minutes, Board of Directors, 29 June and 14 14, 1950, 8 Nov. 1951, CTA SC40/168/3. "Revised" agency budgets meant that agency requests had already been pared to a level considered appropriate by budget committee volunteers. The campaign results are later projected before the beginning of the year for which they are intended, and if necessary, further cuts approved.

9 TWC, Minutes, Board of Directors, 19 Oct. 1950, CTA SC40/168/3; "Analysis of Budget Committee Attendance, fiscal year 1950," 28 Mar. 1951, CTA SC40/26/5.

10 This single-minded concern for the campaign, as well as the control exerted by the men at the top of the corporate hierarchy, were principal findings in a study of the Montreal Community Chest conducted by Aileen D. Ross in the fifties. See Ross, "Organized Philanthropy in an Urban Community," *Canadian Journal of Economics and Political Science*, 18/4 (Nov. 1952), 474–86; and Ross,

"The Social Control of Philanthropy," *American Journal of Sociology*, 58 (Mar. 1953), 451–60.

11 Kate G. Macdonnell, "The Community Chest Budgetting Process," (MSW thesis, University of Toronto 1955), 1–6.

12 TWC, Annual Report, 1950, 7 Feb. 1951, CTA SC40/168/3.

13 TWC, Minutes, Board of Directors, 8 Nov. 1951, CTA SC40/168/3.

14 TWC, Minutes, Board of Directors, 15 Oct. 1953, CTA SC40/168/5.

15 TWC, Minutes, Board of Directors, 15 Oct. and 12 Nov. 1953, CTA SC40/168/5.

16 TWC, Minutes, Board of Directors, 10 Dec. 1953, CTA SC40/168/5.

17 Macdonnell, "The Community Chest Budgetting Process," 65–6.

18 TWC, Minutes, Board of Directors, 9 Oct. and 13 Nov. 1952, CTA SC40/168/4.

19 "The Survey of Family & Children's Services," 3 Jan 1950, 24, FSA Archives.

20 Macdonnell, "The Community Chest Budgetting Process," 71; TWC, Minutes, Board of Directors, 10 June 1954, CTA SC40/168/6.

21 TWC, Minutes, Board of Directors, 21 Sept. 1955, CTA SC40/168/7.

22 TWC, Minutes, Board of Directors, 12 Feb. 1953; "Notes on Council Reorganization," Nov. 1953; "Use of Divisions in Welfare Councils," 18 Aug. 1953; "Notes on Membership and By-laws Report," 18 Jan. 1954; CTA SC40/36/5 and 3.

23 TWC, Minutes, Board of Directors, 20 Jan. and 11 Feb. 1954, CTA SC40/168/6.

24 TWC, Minutes, Board of Directors, 13 May 1954, CTA SC40/168/6.

25 TWC, Minutes, Board of Directors, 13 May 1954; "Report to Board of Directors of Community Chest ... re Problems Relating to Co-ordination of Planning and Budgeting," 28 Apr. 1954, CTA SC40/168/6.

26 TWC, *The Inner Nine* (Dec. 1957), CTA SC40/197/35; Lemon, *Toronto since 1918*, 113.

27 Ibid., 113–15.

28 Ibid., 108; see also Strong-Boag, "Home Dreams."

29 Timothy J. Colton, *Big Daddy: Frederick G. Gardiner and the Building of Metropolitan Toronto* (Toronto: University of Toronto Press 1980), 66–73; for a good overview of the context see Ontario, *Report of the Royal Commission on Metropolitan Toronto*, (Robarts Commission), vol. 1 (Toronto: Queen's Printer 1977), 11–24.

30 The Robarts' report contains a very revealing observation: "The demand for a direct voice in local decision-making ... challenged Canada's tradition of representative government and left many elected representatives bewildered and angry." Ibid., 23.

31 Civic Advisory Committee of Toronto, *Report of the Community Council Committee*

18 Sept. 1947 – 31 Mar. 1948, CTA RG149, RG Reports/144; Lemon, *Toronto since 1918*, 106.

32 Civic Advisory Committee, *Report of the Community Council Committee.*

33 Civic Advisory Committee, Annual Report, 1949, CTA RG249, RG Reports/144.

34 TWC, Minutes, Board of Directors, 10 Nov. 1949, CTA SC40/168/2.

35 TWC, Minutes, Board of Directors, 9 Mar. and 13 Apr. 1950, CTA SC40/168/3.

36 TWC, Minutes, Board of Directors, 20 Apr., 25 May, 23 Nov., and 21 Dec. 1944, CTA SC40/168/1; Executive Committee, 9 Nov. and 7 Dec. 1944, CTA SC40/205/2; G.A. Stanford, *To Serve the Community*, 205.

37 Toronto, "Report of the Community Counsellor to the Community Council Committee," Sept. 1949, CTA RG249/15/7.

38 Neighbourhood Workers Association (NWA), Minutes, Central Council, Oct. 1947, FSA Archives.

39 "Survey of Family and Children's Services," 20; NWA, Minutes, Central Council, 5 Dec. 1950, FSA Archives. See also Gwen Davenport, "District Association to Area Council – A Study in Change," (MSW thesis, University of Toronto 1962).

40 Ibid., 33–9; NWA, Minutes, Committee on District Development, 5 Nov. 1954, 17 Jan. 1955, FSA Archives; TWC, Minutes, 17 Sept. 1956, CTA SC40/168/8.

41 TWC, Minutes, Executive Committee, 15 Mar. 1955, Board of Directors, 20 Apr. 1955, CTA SC40/205/2 and 168/7.

42 TWC, Minutes, Board of Directors, 13 Jan., 1 Feb. and 9 Mar. 1955, CTA SC40/168/7.

43 TWC, *The Recreation Survey of Metropolitan Toronto: An Inventory of Facilities and Programs in Relation to Population Data* (Dec. 1956).

44 James Struthers, "Shadows from the Thirties: The Federal Government and Unemployment Assistance, 1941–1956," in Jacqueline S. Ismael, ed., *The Canadian Welfare State: Evolution and Transition* (Edmonton: University of Alberta Press 1987).

45 TWC, Minutes, Board of Directors, 11 Feb. and 10 June 1954, CTA SC40/168/6. The issue of unemployment assistance is a major theme running through the minutes from 1948–57. The importance of the Toronto position and the role of the Toronto Welfare Council is described in J.D. Wismer, "Public Assistance in Ontario, 1950–61" (MSW thesis, University of Toronto 1964).

46 TWC, Minutes, Board of Directors, 11 Nov. 1954; CTA SC40/168/6; Memo, W.H. Dewar to Committee regarding study of structure and organization of the Community Chest, 29 Mar. 1955, CTA SC40/36/4.

47 Information on Arthur Pigott is scattered throughout the minutes of the time; information was also given by Florence Philpott, interview. See also, Obituary, *Toronto Star*, 19 Feb. 1987.

48 Ray Johns, "Critical Issues of Council-Agency Relationships," *Proceedings of the National Conference of Social Work, 1951* (New York: Columbia University Press 1951), 323–34.

49 John Yerger's appointment was part of a move by the Chest to replace Dewar with an executive director more closely associated with the funding side of the organization. Dewar had been with the Toronto YMCA prior to his appointment and was popular with the agencies who saw him as an ally in their struggle to maintain their influence with the Chest. Dewar's forthcoming retirement, to take place in 1957, was announced, and while he retained the title of executive director, he was no longer the executive in charge. TWC, Minutes, 13 Jan. 1955, CTA SC40/168/7; "Miscellaneous Biographical Data," OA, Ontario Welfare Council Collection, Series 12/70; Philpott, interview.

50 "Some Problems Involved in the Present Structure," 9 June 1955, CTA SC40/36/4; see also recommendation that the Chest have more women on its board, TWC, Minutes, Board of Directors, 18 Jan. 1956, CTA SC40/168/8.

51 TWC, Minutes, Board of Directors, 1 Feb., 9 Mar., 15 June 1955, CTA SC40/168/7.

52 TWC, Minutes, Executive Committee, 26 Apr. 1956, CTA SC40/205/2.

53 Don S. Connery, "Business and Charity: The Pittsburgh Skirmish," *Fortune* (Apr. 1957), 145.

54 Ibid., 144–5 and 250–4; the quote is in reference to the limitations set out for the Toronto Social Service Commission in 1911, see p. 38.

55 TWC, Minutes, Executive Committee, 26 Apr. 1956, CTA SC40/205/2.

56 OA, Ontario Welfare Council Collection, "Miscellaneous – Biographical Data," series 12, box 70.

57 Ibid.

58 "Report to the Executive Committee of the United Community Fund," 8 Mar. 1957, CTA SC40/36/1.

59 "Manual of Proposed Organization and Procedures for a Social Planning Council of Metropolitan Toronto," [Mar. 1957], CTA SC40/36/3.

60 Ibid.

61 Ibid.

62 "Report to the Executive Committee of the United Community Fund," 8 Mar. 1957, CTA SC40/36/1.

63 Social Planning Council, Minutes, Executive Committee, 10 May 1957, CTA SC40/205/3.

64 Social Planning Council, Minutes, Board of Directors, 12 June 1957, CTA SC40/168/9; Philpott, interview.

65 Philpott, interview.

66 Violet M. Sieder, "The New Look in Community Planning," *Social Work*, 5/2 (Apr. 1960).

67 Cited in Malcolm G. Taylor, *Health Insurance and Canadian Public Policy: The Seven Decisions that Created the Canadian Health Insurance System* (Montreal: McGill-Queen's University Press 1978), 194.

68 McCutcheon also served on the Canadian Welfare Council and the Ontario Welfare Council.

69 Ibid., 418. Although Taylor based his speculation on statements made by McCutcheon to the press, he had himself served as research consultant to the royal commission and would have been familiar with McCutcheon's views, see 342.

70 The Community Planning Association of Canada was an attempt to join social planning and urban planning. It met for the first time in 1947, presided over by R.E.G. Davis, executive director of the Canadian Welfare Council, *Housing Digest* (Nov. 1 1947), CTA SC40/86/10.

CHAPTER 7 Conclusions

1 For example, the Ottawa Social Planning Council has been required to assume responsibility for managing a project that is attempting to coordinate the planning and funding of all social and health services on a community-wide basis. It is essentially an allocations-related task and is considered to be a requirement of continuation of its existing funding base; the province of Manitoba has cut all grants to organizations that it does not consider to be providing "direct service."

2 Toronto social workers were well aware of and ignored Floyd Hunter's study of the small group of men who exercised power in "Regional City," and his conclusions regarding the second-class status of community councils, *Community Power Structure: A Study of Decision Makers* (Chapel Hill: University of North Carolina Press 1953).

3 Lane, "The Field of Community Organization," 495–511; see for example, Brian Wharf, *Communities and Social Policy in Canada* (Toronto: McClelland and Stewart 1992), 27.

4 See Fisher, *The Response of Social Work to the Depression*. Fisher was one of those whose job was lost and who was unable to gain regular employment for many years.

5 Rooke and Schnell, *No Bleeding Heart*, 38.

Bibliography

Primary Sources

I ARCHIVES AND SPECIAL COLLECTIONS

City of Toronto Archives (CTA)
Social Planning Council Collection (SC40)
  This collection, the largest in the Toronto Archives, was the primary source of information. Citations from this source are recorded by using a slash (/) to separate the collection number, box number and file number, in that order. For example: SC40/115/1 may be found in file no. 1, in box no. 115, in collection no. SC40.
Minutes of Council, City of Toronto
Minutes of the Board of Control, City of Toronto
Board of Control correspondence files
Mayors' correspondence files (RG7)
Public Welfare Committee files (RG23)
Civic Advisory Committee files (RG249)
  Citations from the RG files are recorded in the same manner as the SC collection noted above.

Ontario Archives (OA)
Ministry of Community and Social Services
  Deputy Minister's files (RG29, series 01)
  Scrapbooks of J.J. Kelso (RG29, vol. 7)
Ministry of the Attorney-General (RG4)
  Central files
Ontario Welfare Council Collection

Family Service Association (FSA) Archives
The records of the Neighbourhood Workers Association are held in the offices of the Family Service Association of Metropolitan Toronto. Except for a list of files, they are not systematically organized.

Thomas Fisher Rare Books Library, University of Toronto

Metropolitan Toronto Reference Library
This was the sole location for some of the early publications of the Toronto Welfare Council.

II INTERVIEWS

Florence Philpott, 10 April 1986
J.B. (Joe) Salzberg, 13 January 1987
Bessie Touzel, 18 March 1986

III NEWSPAPERS (TORONTO)

Evening Telegram, Globe and Mail, Mail and Empire, Star

Secondary Sources

I BOOKS AND MONOGRAPHS

Allen, R. *The Social Passion: Religion and Social Reform in Canada 1914–28.* Toronto: University of Toronto Press 1971
Bacchi, C. L. *Liberation Deferred? The Ideas of the English-Canadian Suffragists, 1877–1918.* Toronto: University of Toronto Press 1983
Bauman [Wills], G. *Efficiency and Social Planning: A Means-End Confusion.* Working Papers on Social Welfare, no. 19. Toronto: University of Toronto, Faculty of Social Work 1986.
Bender, T. *Toward an Urban Vision: Ideas and Institutions in Nineteenth Century America.* Lexington, KY: University Press of Kentucky 1975
Betten, N., and M.J. Austin. *The Roots of Community Organizing 19171939.* Philadelphia: Temple University Press 1990
Bland, S.G. *The New Christianity: Or the Religion of the New Age.* 1920. Reprint. Toronto: University of Toronto Press 1973
Bruce, M. *The Coming of the Welfare State,* rev. ed. New York: Schocken Books 1966

Bruno, F.J. *Trends in Social Work, 1874–1956*, 2nd ed. New York: Columbia University Press 1957

Bureau of Municipal Research. *Toronto Gives: Can a Community Plan Its Giving for Community Purposes – A Discussion of Haphazard versus Planned Philanthropy*. Toronto: June 1917

Careless, J.M.S. *Toronto to 1918: An Illustrated History*. Toronto: Lorimer 1984

Cassidy, H. *Unemployment and Relief in Ontario 1929–1932*. Toronto: J.M. Dent 1932

Colton, T.J. *Big Daddy: Frederick G. Gardiner and the Building of Metropolitan Toronto*. Toronto: University of Toronto Press 1980

Cook, R. *The Regenerators: Social Criticism in Late Victorian English Canada*. Toronto: University of Toronto Press 1985

Davis, A.F. *Spearheads for Reform: The Social Settlements and the Progressive Movement, 1890–1914*. New York: Oxford University Press 1967

de Schweinitz, K. *England's Road to Social Security*. 1943. Reprint. New York: A. S. Barnes, Perpetua Edition 1961 edition

Ellul, J. *The Technological Society*, trans. John Wilkinson. New York: Alfred A. Knopf 1965

Finkel, A. *Business and Social Reform in the Thirties*. Toronto: Lorimer 1979

Fisher, J. *The Response of Social Work to the Depression*. Cambridge, MA: Schenkman Publishing 1980

Friedmann, J. *Planning in the Public Domain: From Knowledge to Action*. Princeton, NJ: Princeton University Press 1987

Ginzberg, L.D. *Women and the Work of Benevolence: Morality, Politics, and Class in the Nineteenth-Century United States*. New Haven: Yale University Press 1990

Haber, S. *Efficiency and Uplift: Scientific Management in the Progressive Era 1890–1920*. Chicago: University of Chicago Press 1964

Halévy, E. *The Growth of Philosophic Radicalism*. 1923. Reprint. London: Faber and Faber 1942

Heath, M., and A. Dunham. *Trends in Community Organization: A Study of the Papers on Community Organization published by the National Conference on Social Welfare, 1874–1960*. Chicago: University of Chicago, School of Social Service Administration 1963

Horn, Michiel. *The League for Social Reconstruction: Intellectual Origins of the Democratic Left in Canada 1930–1942*. Toronto: University of Toronto Press 1980

Hunter, Floyd. *Community Power Structure: A Study of Decision Makers*. Chapel Hill: University of North Carolina Press 1953

Hurl, Lorna F. *Building a Profession: The Origin and Development of the Department of Social Service in the University of Toronto 1914–1928*. Working Papers on Social Welfare, no. 11. Toronto: University of Toronto, Faculty of Social Work, 1983

Iacovetta, F., and M. Valverde, eds. *Gender Conflicts: New Essays in Women's History*. Toronto: University of Toronto Press 1992

Koven, S., and S. Michel, eds. *Mothers of a New World: Maternalist Politics and the Origins of Welfare States.* New York: Routledge 1993

Lemon, J. *Toronto since 1918: An Illustrated History.* Toronto: James Lorimer 1985

Lubove, R. *The Professional Altruist: The Emergence of Social Work as a Career, 1880–1930.* Cambridge, MA: Harvard University Press 1965

Marsh, L. 'Introduction.' In *Report on Social Security for Canada.* 1943. Reprint. Toronto. University of Toronto Press 1975

Marsh, L.C. (with A. Grant Fleming and C.F. Blackler). *Health and Unemployment.* Toronto: Oxford University Press 1938

Norton, W.J. *The Cooperative Movement in Social Work.* New York: Macmillan 1927

Pierson, R.R. *'They're Still Women After All': The Second World War and Canadian Womanhood.* Toronto: McClelland and Stewart 1986

Richmond, M.E. *Social Diagnosis.* New York: Russell Sage Foundation 1917

Roberts, D. *Victorian Origins of the British Welfare State.* New Haven: Yale University Press 1960

Rooke, P.T., and R.L. Schnell. *No Bleeding Heart: Charlotte Whitton, A Feminist on the Right.* Vancouver: University of British Columbia Press 1987

Sangster, J. *Dreams of Equality: Women on the Canadian Left 1920–1950.* Toronto: McClelland and Stewart 1989

Shore, M. *The Science of Social Redemption: McGill, the Chicago School, and the Origins of Social Research in Canada.* Toronto: University of Toronto Press 1987

Socknat, T.P. *Witness against War: Pacifism in Canada, 1900–1945.* Toronto: University of Toronto Press 1987

Splane, R.B. *Social Welfare in Ontario 1791–1893.* Toronto: University of Toronto Press 1965

Stanford, G.A. *To Serve the Community: The Story of Toronto's Board of Trade.* Toronto: Board of Trade 1974

Stapleford, F.N. *After Twenty Years: A Short History of the Neighbourhood Workers Association.* [Toronto]: Neighbourhood Workers Association [c. 1938]

Strong-Boag, V.J. *The Parliament of Women: The National Council of Women of Canada 1893–1929.* National Museum of Man, Mercury Series, History Division, Paper no. 18. Ottawa 1976

Struthers, J. *No Fault of Their Own: Unemployment and the Canadian Welfare State 1914–1941.* Toronto: University of Toronto Press 1983

Taylor, B. *Eve and The New Jerusalem.* London: Virago press 1983

Taylor, M.G. *Health Insurance and Canadian Public Policy: The Seven Decisions that Created the Canadian Health Insurance System.* Montreal: McGill-Queen's University Press 1978

Trattner, W.I. *From Poor Law to Welfare State: A History of Social Welfare in America,* 2d ed. New York: The Free Press 1979

Valverde, M. *The Age of Light, Soap, and Water: Moral Reform in English Canada, 1885–1925.* Toronto: McClelland and Stewart 1991

Wharf, B. *Communities and Social Policy in Canada.* Toronto: McClelland and Stewart 1992

Wiebe, R.H. *The Search for Order, 1877–1920.* New York: Hill and Wang 1967

Williams, C.J. *Decades of Service: A History of the Ontario Ministry of Community and Social Services: 1930–1980.* Toronto: Ontario Ministry of Community and Social Services 1984

Woodroofe, K. *From Charity to Social Work in England and the United States.* Toronto: University of Toronto Press 1962

II ARTICLES AND UNPUBLISHED PAPERS

Alinsky, S. 'The Basis in the Social Sciences for the Social Treatment of the Adult Offender.' National Conference of Social Work, *Proceedings* 1938, 714–24

Allen, R. 'The Background of the Social Gospel in Canada.' In *The Social Gospel in Canada,* 2–34. National Museum of Man, History Division, Paper no. 9. Ottawa 1975

Baines, C. 'The Professions and an Ethic of Care.' In Baines, P. Evans, and S. Neysmith, eds., *Women's Caring: Feminist Perspectives on Social Welfare,* 36–72. Toronto: McClelland and Stewart 1991

Bator, P.A. '"The Struggle to Raise the Lower Classes": Public Health Reform and the Problem of Poverty in Toronto, 1910 to 1921.' *Journal of Canadian Studies,* 14/1 (1979), 43–9

Bloomfield, E. 'Boards of Trade and Canadian Urban Development.' *Urban History Review,* 12/2 (1983), 77–99

Buckley, S. 'Ladies or Midwives? Efforts to Reduce Infant and Maternal Mortality.' In L. Kealey, ed., *A Not Unreasonable Claim: Women and Reform in Canada 1880s–1920s,* 131–49. Toronto: Women's Educational Press 1979

Clarke, M.J. 'Report of the Standing Committee on Neighbourhood Work,' Canadian Conference of Charities and Corrections, Sept. 1917. Reprinted in P. Rutherford, ed., *Saving the Canadian City: The First Phase 1880–1920,* 172–93. Toronto: University of Toronto Press 1974

Connery, D.S. 'Business and Charity: The Pittsburgh Skirmish.' *Fortune,* Apr. 1957, 144–5 and 250–4

Frankel, C. 'The Moral Framework of the Idea of Welfare.' In J.S. Morgan, ed., *Welfare and Wisdom,* 147–64. Toronto: University of Toronto Press 1966

Heale, M.J. 'From City Fathers to Social Critics: Humanitarianism and Government in New York, 1790–1860.' *Journal of American History,* 63/1 (June 1976), 21–41

Irving, A. 'Canadian Fabians: The Work and Thought of Harry Cassidy and Leonard Marsh, 1930–1945.' *Canadian Journal of Social Work Education*, 7/1, 7–27

Johns, R. 'Critical Issues of Council-Agency Relationships.' *Proceedings of the National Conference of Social Work, 1951*, 323–34. New York: Columbia University press

Johnson, A. 'The Obstacle of Limited Participation in Local Social Planning.' *Proceedings of the National Conference of Social Work, 1940*, 425–35. New York: Columbia University Press 1940

Lane, R.P. 'The Field of Community Organization.' *Proceedings of the National Conference of Social Work, 1939*, 495–511. New York: Columbia University Press 1939

– 'Report of Groups Studying the Community Organization Process.' *Proceedings of the National Conference of Social Work, 1940*, 456–73. New York: Columbia University Press 1940

MacMillan, J.W. 'The Doctrine of Minimums,' *Social Welfare*, 1/1 (1 Oct. 1918), 7–8

MacMurchy, M. 'A Survey of Woman's Work, 1919.' In R. Cook and W. Mitchinson, eds., *The Proper Sphere: Woman's Place in Canadian Society*, 195–7. Toronto: Oxford University Press 1976

Mitchinson, W. 'Early Women's Organizations and Social Reform: Prelude to the Welfare State.' In Allan Moscovitch and Jim Albert, eds., *The 'Benevolent' State: The Growth of Welfare in Canada*, 77–92. Toronto: Garamond Press 1987

Newstetter, Wilber. 'The Social Intergroup Work Process.' *Proceedings of the National Conference of Social Work, 1947*, 205–17. New York: Columbia University Press 1947

Patton-Cowie, L. '"Change with Progress": Bessie Touzel 1904–1948.' Paper, Faculty of Social Work, University of Toronto 1986

Pray, K.L.M. 'When Is Community Organization Social Work Practice?' *Proceedings of the National Conference of Social Work, 1947*, 194–204. New York: Columbia University Press 1947

Prentice, S. 'Workers, Mothers, Reds: Toronto's Postwar Daycare Fight.' In M.P. Connelly and P. Armstrong, eds., *Feminism in Action: Studies in Political Economy*, 175–200. Toronto: Scholars' Press 1992

Rein, M. 'Coordination of Social Services.' In *Social Policy: Issues of Choice and Change*, 103–37. New York: Random House 1970

Roberts, W. '"Rocking the Cradle for the World": The New Woman and Maternal Feminism, Toronto 1877–1914.' In L. Kealey, ed., *A Not Unreasonable Claim: Women and Reform in Canada, 1880s–1920s*, 15–45. Toronto: Women's Educational Press 1979

Ross, A.D. 'Organized Philanthrophy in an Urban Community.' *Canadian Journal of Economics and Political Science*, 18/4 (1952), 474–86

- 'The Social Control of Philanthropy.' *American Journal of Sociology*, 58 (1953), 451–60
Sieder, V.M. 'The New Look in Community Planning.' *Social Work*, 5/2 (1960), 105–8
Strong, H. 'The Business Man – Charities and Social Welfare.' *Proceedings of the Canadian Conference of Charities and Corrections, 1913*, 67–9
Strong-Boag, V. 'Home Dreams: Women and the Suburban Experiment in Canada, 1945–60.' *Canadian Historical Review*, 4 (1991), 471–504
- '"Wages for Housework": Mothers' Allowances and the Beginnings of Social Security in Canada,' *Journal of Canadian Studies*, 14/1 (1979), 24–34
Struthers, J. '"Lord Give Us Men": Women and Social Work in English Canada, 1918 to 1953.' In A. Moscovitch and J. Albert, eds., *The 'Benevolent' State: The Growth of Welfare in Canada*, 126–43. Toronto: Garamond Press 1987
- 'Shadows from the Thirties: The Federal Government and Unemployment Assistance, 1941–1956.' In J.S. Ismael, ed., *The Canadian Welfare State: Evolution and Transition*, 3–32. Edmonton: University of Alberta Press 1987
Weaver, John C. 'Municipal Reform: The Corporate Ideal and New Structures of Government.' In *Shaping the Canadian City: Essays on Urban Politics and Policy, 1890–1920*, 55–76. Toronto: The Institute of Public Administration of Canada 1977
- 'The Modern City Realized: Toronto Civic Affairs, 1880–1915.' In A.F.J. Artibise and G.A. Stelter, eds., *The Usable Urban Past: Planning and Politics in the Modern Canadian City*, 39–72. Toronto: Macmillan 1979
Weil, M. 'women, community, and organizing.' In N. Van Den Bergh and L.B. Cooper, eds., *feminist visions for social work*, 187–210. [New York]: National Association of Social Workers 1986
Wills, G. 'The Gospel of Efficiency: Social Work's Bridge from Cause to Function.' Paper presented to the Canadian Conference of Schools of Social Work, June 1987
- 'Values of Community Practice: Legacy of the Radical Social Gospel.' *Canadian Social Work Review*, 9/1 (Winter 1992), 28–40
Yeo, E. 'Robert Owen and Radical Culture.' In S. Pollard and J. Salt, eds., *Robert Owen: Prophet of the Poor*, 84–114. Lewisburg: Bucknell University Press 1971

IV DISSERTATIONS AND THESES

Davenport, G. 'District Association to Area Council – A Study in Change.' MSW thesis, University of Toronto 1962
Irving, A. 'A Canadian Fabian: The Life and Work of Harry Cassidy.' PhD thesis, University of Toronto 1982
Lappin, B.W. 'Joint Fund-Raising in Toronto: The Role of the Jewish Community.' MSW thesis, University of Toronto 1947

- 'Stages in the Development of Community Organization Work as a Social Work Method.' PhD thesis, University of Toronto 1965
Lukawiecki, T. 'Class, Gender and Charity: The Experiences of Older Women in Three Ottawa Charitable Institutions, 1865–1890.' MSW thesis, Carleton University 1993
Macdonnell, K.G. 'The Community Chest Budgetting Process.' MSW thesis, University of Toronto 1955
Pitsula, J.M. 'The Relief of Poverty in Toronto, 1880–1930.' PhD thesis, York University 1979
Wismer, J.D. 'Public Assistance in Ontario, 1950–61.' MSW thesis, University of Toronto 1964

VI REPORTS AND PROCEEDINGS

Canadian Conference on Charities and Corrections. *16th Annual Report* 1917
Carstens, C.C. 'Recommendations on Survey Reports of Organizations in Federation.' Prepared for the Federation for Community Service, 1925. FSA Archives
Chilman, C.W. 'Report.' Prepared for the Toronto Welfare Council, 1949. FSA Archives
McHenry, E.W. *Report on Food Allowances for Relief Recipients in the Province of Ontario.* Toronto: Ontario Department of Public Welfare 1945
McLean, F.H. 'Survey of Family Social Work Field of Toronto, Canada.' Prepared for the Federation for Community Service, 1927. FSA Archives
National Council of Social Work/Welfare. *Annual Proceedings.*
Ontario. 'Report of the Royal Commission on Metropolitan Toronto' (Robarts Commission). Vol. 1. Toronto: Queen's Printer 1977
'Survey of Family and Children's Services.' [Toronto: Community Chest] 1950
Toronto. 'Report of the Charities Commission.' 1911–12
Toronto Welfare Council. *The Recreation Survey of Metropolitan Toronto: An Inventory of Facilities and Programs in Relation to Population Data,* 1956
- *The Inner Nine,* 1957
- *The Cost of Living: A Study of the Cost of a Standard of Living in Toronto Which Should Maintain Health and Self-Respect.* 1939

V REFERENCE WORKS

Canadian Who's Who, 1955–57
National Encyclopedia of Canadian Biography, 1935
Toronto City Directory, 1930

Index

community councils 118–21

Community organization. *See* community work

Community Planning Association of Canada 169n. 70

community surveys 50; comprehensive 31, 112; of recreation services 122

community work: joined with casework 21, 48, 51, 68; male dominance in 5, 11, 31, 78, 133, 138–9; the NWA and 48, 68; as a practice method 21, 139, 160–1n. 58; radical 13, 153n. 55; separated from casework 10, 31, 78, 121, 133–4, 138; settlement house movement and 16; social science and 21; as a woman's practice 4–5, 26

Conboy, Fred 87, 96

Cook, Ramsay 17

cooperation, values of 17, 18, 26, 30–1, 45

cooperative movement, Owenite 28

coordination of services 14, 96, 108, 154n. 20; comprehensive 55, 65; efficiency and 33–4, 39, 67, 82, 89; emphasis on, over social reform 78; role of the NWA in 48, 57; school of social work as a centre for 20; separation of public-private roles in 42, 47. *See also* charitable organizations, regulation of

corporate influence: in the Community Chest 10, 105–6, 135, 165–6n. 10, 169n. 2; in the Federation for Community Service 63–4; in the UCF 125–6; on the welfare state 81, 105–6, 136

Cost of Living Study 9, 91–5, 98, 101–6

Council of Jewish Social Agencies 66

council of social agencies 9, 49; and coordination of services 65; independence of a 7, 50, 51–2, 57, 65, 70–1, 75 (*see also* Toronto Welfare Council, independence of the); plans for a 50–2, 56, 66–71, 74–7. *See also* Social Planning Council of Metropolitan Toronto

Council of Social Agencies, Montreal 92

councils of social agencies: dependence on financial federations 46; as precursors of social planning councils 128; purpose 45–6, 50; use of, by social workers 6–7, 137

Cross, Eric 91

Dale, James A. 20, 149n. 20

Darwinism 17, 21

Davis, R.E.G. 169n. 70

Dawson, Carl A. 20

democracy: direct 17, 45, 52, 128; efficiency versus 24, 30, 131; radical 18, 21

Dewar, Bill 116, 121–2, 168n. 49

Dewey, John 21

district: conferences 48; councils of the NWA 50–1, 66, 68, 120–1; organization of the COS 15, 34–5; secretaries of the NWA 48, 51

Division of Social Welfare (City of Toronto). *See* Public Health, Department of

Driscoll, Mrs J.S. 61

efficiency: the Bureau of Municipal Research and 41–2, 90; and coordination of services 39, 67, 88–9, 109; and democracy 24; gender and 30; as the motivation for federation 6, 33–4; social 23–4, 40; and social planning 127, 131; standards of, for

in community work 68–9, 120–1; on
professional practice 50–1, 54; role in
the Federation for Community Service 48–9, 57, 64; views on women 69
Stewart, Bryce 103
Stewart, William J. 65
Strong-Boag, Veronica 157n. 6

Taylor, Barbara 28
Taylor, Frederick W. 40
Taylor, Malcolm 132, 169n. 69
Tisdall, F.F. 93, 94, 95
Tisdall-Willard-Bell (TWB) report 95–
 7, 99
Toronto: and corporate power 81;
growth of 5, 33, 116–17, 153n. 1
Toronto Welfare Council: activities 29,
61–3, 85–6, 122–3, 167n. 45; campaign for adequate relief 89–91, 95–
7, 99; conflict with the Community
Chest 10, 101, 102–6, 111, 112–16;
founding of the 9, 77–8; funding of
the 83–4, 87–8, 125 (see also Community Chest, refusal to fund community work); social philosophy 81, 100;
independence of the 10, 82, 87, 103,
104, 108, 115, 122, 124–5, 126 (see also
council of social agencies, independence of a); influence on the welfare
state 80–1, 103, 123, 164–5n. 66; joins
the Community Chest 87, 89; purpose and structure 81–3, 108, 145;
relationship with City Council 87–8,
96, 98; service to community councils
119–21
Touzel, Bessie 84–5, 87, 103–4
Toynbee Hall 16
Trades and Labour Council 43, 105
United Community Fund (UCF) 10,
125–6, 130, 136

United Way 11, 136, 165n. 6
United Welfare Fund 86, 88. *See also*
Community Chest
urban planning and social planning 31,
133
urban reform 5, 31, 37
Urwick, Edward (E.J.) 64, 77, 84, 158n.
18
utilitarianism 22–4, 42; and social planning 78; and social work 8, 24

Valverde, Mariana 19
Van Kleeck, Mary 152n. 50
Vivian, R.P. 98

Welfare Council of Ontario 87, 169n.
68
welfare state: as a concentration of
financial power 136; Fabian socialist
origins 20; health insurance and the
132; and ideology 91; influence of
maternalism on the 28; influence of
the Toronto Welfare Council on the
80, 103, 123, 164–5n. 66; involvement
of the, in service provision 62, 87;
and the Marsh Report 22; and public
housing 85, 161–2n. 14; and a social
minimum 101; utilitarianism and the
23. *See also* municipal government,
role in social welfare; social welfare
welfare state (Britain) 22
Whitton, Charlotte 61, 157n. 13, 158n.
20
Wilensky, Dora 151n. 41 (26)
Willard, Alice 93, 95
Wolter, Hugo 120
Women: activists in the Child Welfare
Council 59–61; and agency management 25, 86, 151n. 37, 152n. 51, 161n.
60; charity work and 24–5; domestic